Postmodern(ized) Simmel

Working on multiple levels of analysis the authors present a reading of Simmel which shows how his writings can have a constituent role in current postmodernist discourses. By staging encounters between Simmel and such culture theorists and critics as Jacques Derrida, Michel Foucault, Claude Lévi-Strauss and Friedrich Nietzsche, the authors reveal the many ways in which modernists can make the transition to postmodernism or at least understand that process. *Postmodern(ized) Simmel* shows readers how they might postmodernize themselves.

The book addresses the uses of Simmel's writings as postmodern discourses in the areas of intellectual ethics, textual methodology, sociological theory, philosophy of history and cultural theory. It is the first sustained attempt to show the significance of Simmel's writings for postmodernism and it challenges the prevailing view that Simmel was a 'sociological impressionist.' It provides fresh ideas on postmodernity and a remarkable new interpretation of one of the major figures in the development of sociology.

Deena Weinstein is Professor of Sociology, DePaul University, Chicago, Illinois; **Michael A. Weinstein** is Professor of Political Science, Purdue University, West Lafayette, Indiana.

Postmodern(ized) Simmel

Deena Weinstein and
Michael A. Weinstein

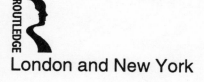

London and New York

First published 1993
by Routledge
11 New Fetter Lane, London EC4P 4EE

Simultaneously published in the USA and Canada
by Routledge
29 West 35th Street, New York, NY 10001

Typeset in Baskerville by
NWL Editorial Services, Langport, Somerset

Printed and bound in Great Britain by
T.J. Press (Padstow) Ltd, Padstow, Cornwall

British Library Cataloguing in Publication Data
A catalogue record for this book is available from the
British Library

Library of Congress Cataloging in Publication Data
Weinstein, Deena.   Postmodern(ized) Simmel/Deena and
Michael Weinstein
    p.   cm.
    Includes bibliographical references and index.
    1. Simmel, Georg, 1858–1918.   2. Sociology –
Germany – History.   3. Postmodernism – Social
aspects.   I. Weinstein, Michael A.   II. Title.
HM22.G3S525   1993   92–39589
301′.0943 – dc20   CIP

ISBN   0–415–08269–2
        0–415–08270–6 (pbk)

Contents

Acknowledgements

We thank our editor Chris Rojek for his aid in bringing this book to publication and for his sympathy with the project. We thank our desk editor Christina Tebbit for expertly steering the work into print.

We thank Barry Smart for his very careful and helpful reading of the manuscript. We thank Donald Levine for his encouragement and for his cogent and constructive criticism.

We acknowledge Helmut Loiskandl and Michael Kaern for the fine conversations that we have had with them about Simmel over the years.

We thank those who have made contributions to the Simmel literature. Simmel studies is a polycentric web of interpretive initiatives, adding new centres as new issues arise in human/culture studies: a congenial place for Postmodern(ized) Simmel.

A reader's guide to style

A. A reader's guide to style precedes the work to follow because that work is, in Derrida's sense, a heterogeneous text.

B. A 'reader's guide' to style precedes/introduces the work(s) to follow because that (those) work(s) is (are), in Derrida's sense, (a) *heterogeneous* text(s).

Much of the work to follow is written in the straight academic style of paragraph A. Other portions are written in the deconstructionist style of paragraph B, which is at the extreme of graphic density, as rough as it gets. The rest is in between, leaning toward A. The text is heterogeneous because it encapsulates our own process of postmodernization – from existential-phenomenology to post-structuralism (without giving up the former). Style marks the stations along the way. Reflexivity about style and its power is a mark of post-structuralism. The straight and deconstructive styles are read differently.

Straight expository style seeks to create a seamless flow of meaning. The reader assumes or is seduced into believing that the author is in control of the text, that the author knows what he or she is talking about and has been able to express it precisely. The reader moves along seeking to understand the author's meaning, which is assumed to be univocal, unless otherwise explicitly stated, in which case a new voice takes over for its duration. If the flow is broken and the reader fails to understand to his or her satisfaction he or she takes on the burden of proof and works to understand better (up to a point). Failure to achieve closure of meaning in the text is either a failure of the reader to understand or of the author to deliver on the always implicit and in academic writing almost always explicit promise of closure. Academic texts, indeed, are ordinarily structured according to the unilinear and regimented conventions of thesis-demonstration or hypothesis-test. Texts written under the conventions of straight academic writing are not purposely left open (except for the crack of 'problems for future research').

Deconstructive style opens existing texts and/or produces explicitly open texts, those with some indetermination of meaning or, as Derrida says, 'undecidability' designed into them. 'Deconstruction' is often understood to imply that all texts are vulnerable to undecidability and, therefore, that closure of meaning in a writing cannot be achieved. The proof of that claim is in deconstructive practices, not in *a priori* speculation, and the issue does not concern us here. When we use deconstructive style we are deconstructing (opening) a text or are producing a pre-deconstructed text. It is our aim, when we write in this way, to proliferate indetermination (undecidability), because we believe that that undecidability is – we have to say it – (genuine) ('genuine').

A pre-deconstructed text breaks up the flow of reading, purposefully creating obstacles and snares for the reader – points of doubt (indecision), incisions in the text. The reader is made to halt and entertain possibilities held in suspension. A decision may result or the reader may carry forward the in(de)cision. Pre-deconstructed texts are as accessible as straight texts as long as the reader does not expect them to offer a seamless flow of meaning, but is prepared to stop to entertain options that are not meant to be closed, but which the reader is free to close on his or her own account. The pre-deconstructed text yields, to the participative reader, at many points, a range of meanings rather than a single meaning, resulting in a heightened awareness of difference that has not yet become irrelevance.

Undecidability is displayed and produced with graphic marks. Let us return to paragraph B and see how they are used to deconstruct paragraph A. We will take paragraph B by chunks, creating a glossary as we proceed.

'A "reader's guide" to style . . . '

" " – Derrida (1985: 180) writes of a word 'rising up to quotation marks,' meant ironically (perhaps) in light of the cultural privilege of high over low. To raise to quotes is to lift out of the flow and single out as borrowed from somewhere else, as alien, or as just this specific item; sometimes as honored, sometimes as suspect, often both. It is the sign of the 'so-called,' a mark of (in)distinction. Watch for plays in which a word is raised to quotes and then lowered back into the flow, etc. Does a reader's guide defeat the purposes of deconstruction?

' . . . precedes/introduces . . . '

/ – By the slash two or more terms are simultaneously united and separated. Sometimes the separation is stressed, sometimes the unity is emphasized, and sometimes they are balanced. Derrida's (1985: 188-89) 'concept' of the 'hymen' is appropriate here. 'Hymen' comes down to us with two meanings in a play of opposition – as marital union and as the membrane over the vagina that must be broken to achieve the woman's first sexual union. Does this 'reader's guide' precede what follows or is it part of what follows? We are undecided, leaning toward both alternatives.

' . . . the work(s) to follow because that (those) work(s) is (are), . . .'

(s), etc. – The plural is made an option to throw unity into question. Parentheses are used here for supplementation, specifically to provide an alternative (they can also be used to provide a possible, though perhaps dubious, enhancement). Is this a single work or is it many texts between two covers? Is a *heterogeneous* text' a contradiction in terms?

' . . . ~~in Derrida's sense,~~'

– Derrida calls the strikeout 'holding under erasure.' It takes the line of suspicion possible in " " to its extremity. Should we even use such a phrase as 'in Derrida's sense' when we are aware of what deconstructive readings reveal/produce about texts? Erasure neither lets one give up the term it marks nor allows one to give that term credibility.

' . . . (a) *heterogeneous* text(s).'

Italics – Italics, small capitals, and capitals are used in the normal way to provide degrees of emphasis. We have chosen to privilege *heterogeneous* in paragraph B (it links us with the lexicon of 'deconstruction'). Watch for plays of stress and capitalization within the uses of a term and between terms. Such plays produce undecidability about importance.

Now let us proceed to the marks '(genuine) ("genuine")' that appear three paragraphs after paragraph B.

() () – The use of two or more parentheses in direct succession without any unprotected term to anchor the parenthetical terms indicates that none of the terms is necessary or privileged. The reader is encouraged to choose any, all, or none of them (even at the risk of having grammatically-based meaning break down). Is undecidability genuine or is it very doubtful that we can use (significantly) the term ('genuine') in this context at all? After all, even postmodernization has not made us surrender modern ways of (thinking) (writing).

Proceed to ('Postmodernized Simmel').

→

Permissions

Chapter 1

Introduction(s)

Postmodernizing Simmel means everything from connecting his writings to discourses and texts that are generally designated as 'postmodern(ist)' to describing a characteristically Simmelian postmodern. Both ends of that spectrum will be covered here along with many intermediate moves. But before postmodernizing Simmel it would be proper to provide some understanding of what we mean by 'postmodern(ism).'

Our postmodern is already (what we believe is) a characteristically Simmelian postmodern. That is, we self-consciously define 'postmodern(ism)' so that it will be as congenial as possible to Simmel, in the sense of his writings being able to make the most (fruitful) connections between discourses and texts that are generally designated as 'postmodern(ist).' Our procedure is not circular, but an attempt at rapprochement between Simmel's writings and postmodern(ist) texts, and between those writings and – dare we say it? – contemporary Life.

We are helped in defining 'postmodern(ism)' by Bryan Turner (1991: 1, 5) who provides such encouraging words as that the term is 'irredeemably contested' and that 'the very playfulness of postmodernism(s) precludes any premature foreclosure of its own meaning.' These words are encouraging because they give us a lot of latitude. Postmodern(ism) is a generous domain, not an exclusive coterie. Can it include *anything*? We won't let it because we want to demarcate this writing within the terms in which the term(s) 'postmodern(ism)(s)' are already irredeemably contested. We are not here to reform the contest, to declare a victor, or to reconcile the opponents, but to make a contribution to one side of the (struggle) (play), the side where we have decided that Simmel belongs.

As a convenience we will now orient the reader to what we consider to be conventionally postmodern – a partial canon of convenience. First and, of course, most important, the French 'post-structuralists,' namely, Jean Baudrillard, Jacques Derrida, and Jean-François Lyotard; then a couple of French structuralists or semi-structuralists, Michel Foucault and Claude Lévi-Strauss, taken in primarily because of the ways they de-center the 'subject'; then the Canadian 'viral critic' Arthur Kroker, whose *The Possessed Individual* is our favorite elucidation-of and contribution-to French theory; finally, American 'anti-foundationalists' such as Justus Buchler and Richard Rorty who have articulated a criticism of metaphysics and totalization that is parallel to that of the pluralist wing of French theory.

The above list does not come near to exhausting everything we would include under the rubric 'postmodern(ist).' It is meant to mark off some of the (what we consider to be) unproblematic elements of a 'postmodern(ist)' 'discursive formation' (the latter term used in a very generous sense). We will not, however, confine ourselves to ostensive definition. We follow Turner in believing that 'postmodern(ism)(s) are irredeemably contested,' but we will go a step farther and try to define, in sketch, what is at stake in the contest(s). That will allow us to arrive at the discursive site(s) for postmodernizing Simmel.

Barry Smart (1991: 26) has written of 'the "postmodern flip" inflicted upon the modern paradigm.' We find that image to be perfect for evoking how the postmodern(ism)(s) comes to be. The 'postmodern flip' is simply an inversion of the old ' "man"– culture' relation. The modern paradigm makes 'Man,' 'Society,' the 'Individual,' etc. into creators of culture: subjects. The postmodern ~~paradigm(s)~~ reverse the privilege by interpreting 'Man,' 'Society,' the 'Individual,' etc. as 'mere' signifiers, elements in discourses and texts, discursive operators, subject positions. Postmodernity is the triumph of Culture over Life as the 'Central Idea,' to express it in a Simmelian way. Postmodernity is the age of Cultural Hegemony, and the 'Culture' that we are talking about here has become (almost) – or fully – objectivized, a 'web' of objects ('contents') and operations ('forms') with no central unit of internal control, no central nervous system. It isn't Culture as pretender to the throne of Absolute Subject, but Culture as what Arthur Kroker (1986: 88) calls 'dead power,' a very dynamic death, though, an ever new ~~(ever same?)~~ mediascape, dynamized by Culture's minions, ourselves. The flip: we (very inclusively meant) once thought that culture served us, but now we know better. We are Culture's servants, even though we know that culture exists only through our 'praxis.'

Michel Maffesoli (1986: 109) presents a parallel reading of the postmodern in his study of Simmel and the 'aesthetic paradigm.' For Maffesoli we live in times in which 'the Word, and its counterpart the Image, prevail over Action.' He notes how the electronic media have 'capillarized themselves through the entire social body.' We add a reminder of how phrases like 'language speaks us' and 'there is nothing outside the text,' and terms like 'the simulacrum' and 'virtual reality' populate postmodernist texts. Some aspects of Simmel would feel at home in this postmodern, the ones that were responsive to 'the hypertrophy of objective culture.'

How far does Cultural Hegemony's writ run? Here we come upon Turner's irredeemable contest within the precincts of postmodern(ism)(s). One gets one's certification as a postmodern(ist) by making the flip, declaring C(c)ulture to be (King?) (privileged?). Therein lies the issue: is C(c)ulture Culture or *privileged* culture?

What does it mean for Word to prevail over Action? Exclusiv(ist) postmodernism, toward which Baudrillard and Kroker, and sometimes Derrida and Foucault tend, holds that the triumph of Culture means the effacement of all spontaneous initiative on the part(s) of anything other to Culture. That means that for exclusiv(ist) postmodernism Culture is *formative* and not *expressive* or even, primarily, *instrumental*: formative certainly of the 'subject(s)' and sometimes it seems of EVERYTHING. Exclusiv(ist) postmodernism is *post*modernist: it rejects the spontaneity and dynamism of the noncultural including the privileged Subject. In opposition, inclusiv(ist) postmodernism rejects only the privileged Subject and not the (possibility of) (some measure of) spontaneity in that which is other to culture. That other is severely problematic. It is not some nameable Subject like an Individual, Nation, Class, or Race. It is not God or any God-wish or God-substitute. It is not the Other. It is whatever is left after Culture has been allowed to function as protagonist, something that can beckon signifiers to clarify itself rather than something that is simply coded. It is the margin(s) at which society and individual still live in lower case and ask to be expressed and described. Lyotard and Rorty, and sometimes Derrida, Foucault, and Lévi-Strauss (his project of theorizing the 'superstructure' autonomously) tend to inclusiv(ist) postmodernism.

Postmodernized Simmel surely belongs among the inclusivists. His theory of the dominance of objective culture is surrounded by resistances and is counterpointed by a rebellion of 'Life' against objective culture. But those resistances and that rebellion never fix the noncultural, not even 'Life,' in a logos. That is, (Simmelian) inclusiv(ist) postmodernism is post*modernist*. It is continuous with modernism's rebellion against unities, but it no longer shares modernism's persistence in trying to privilege spontaneity over form. Carlo Mongardini (1986: 122, 123), assimilating Simmel to postmodern sociologies, notes that 'Simmel's sociology decomposes the idea of society' and 'destructures individuality.' Julien Freund (1986: 17) observes that Simmel irritates *les chevaliers de la totalité.*

The simultaneous rejection of totality and resistance to a reductionism of objective culture allows for the possibility of a postmodern(ist) sociology and even psychology, as well as a postmodern(ist) culture theory. That sociology and psychology describe the detotalized society and decentered individual that co-constitute that which is culture and that which is other than/to culture. That is, the sites for postmodernizing Simmel are the culturescape and the 'destructured society' ('objective culture' and 'the metropolis' in his terms).

Exclusiv(ist) and inclusiv(ist) postmodernisms are irredeemably stalemated. On the one hand, what status does a description of extreme Cultural Hegemony by an exclusiv(ist) have? Is there no distance between observer and observed implied, a distance that is contradicted by extrem(ist) ideas of Cultural Hegemony? On the other hand, the acceptance of the privileges of culture by inclusiv(ists) seems to make it difficult for them to keep their margins of spontaneity clear of prior inscription. From what point can distance, genuinely, be taken? We will not attempt to break the stalemate, but will simply take the side of the inclusiv(ists) because Simmel fits best with them, though the exclusiv(ists) should welcome his theory of objective culture. The inclusiv(ists) can welcome that theory and much more in 'his' writings.

The essential elements of postmodernized Simmel are his theory of objective culture, his descriptions of society and individual as detotalized, and his identification of responses, both playful and rebellious, to 'the scene.' None of these elements find favor with adherents of 'the modern paradigm.' Indeed, the Simmel literature has been dominated by a debate over Simmel's (intellectual) character, pitting moderns attacking Simmel against (post)modernists and modernists defending him. The play of attack and defense over the topics of character itself and character as evinced in Simmel's methodology, sociology, and culture theory provides the materials for a character sketch of a postmodernized Simmel who is already lurking in the literature about his writings. In the following review of the character issue we place our project within the extant literature and acknowledge our affinities with allies and our differences with opponents, never striving for victory but only, in Simmelian fashion, for a stalemate.

THE CHARACTER ISSUE

The character issue is a stumbling block in the way of postmodernized Simmel. As David Frisby (1981) amply shows in *Sociological Impressionism*, Simmel has been in trouble about his character from the beginning. He has had detractors on the right and left, and even in the center, some of them severe and some of them (once) devoted students. Indeed, Frisby's book, the major contemporary study of Simmel, is a criticism of his (intellectual) character, synthesizing what the detractors had said up to its publication. But Simmel has also had passionate defenders, also from the beginning, including students and his philosopher-lover Gertrud Kantorowicz. The fight over who the 'real' Simmel is wouldn't interest us at all if it didn't play the most important part in the Simmel literature and if the detractors didn't imply that the character flaw they find in Simmel infects and contaminates his work. Much of what we are calling 'postmodernized' Simmel is, for the detractors, evidence of neurosis. They are out to tarnish Simmel's image! As pro-Simmelites, although not *that* ardent, and with the help of Simmel's (post)modernist and mainly modernist defenders, we enter the fray briefly to parry the attack with a counter-image of Simmel, burnished for postmodernity.

We begin by cutting off all concern with determining anything about the character of the real Simmel. We are concerned only with his image in the literature, how he has been interpreted (through his 'character'). We will then add our bit to the defender's image, just as Frisby did to the detractor's, perpetuating the legend of the good Simmel, now in the form of postmodernized Simmel's character. That is, we are in the realm of mythology, at a second remove from any source events, playing within the texts. Character is dead. We are into images, bio-fictions. They are what rule the literature on the character issue anyway. Bio-fiction is also a postmodern(ized) Simmelian move. Patrick Watier (1986: 236–7) bases his theorization-of and commentary-on Simmel's concept of 'sociability' on the proposition that 'neither individuality nor sociability are simply realities, but are also types, elements constituting social reality, elements that are not only ideal in the Weberian sense, but also fictive stylizations of the given.' So, on to stylizing Simmel's image.

Simmel's detractors generally find that his work is un-systematic, impressionistic, undisciplined, not sustained, indecisive, and uncommitted. These intellectual 'vices' are then often implicated in a deeper or more comprehensive character flaw. Frisby, who has culled from the literature unfavorable comments on Simmel, provides the most pointed presentation of the charges in an attempt to hoist Simmel by his own petard. Seizing upon A. Koppel's description of Simmel as 'the intellectual neurasthenic,' Frisby (1981: 80) uses Simmel's own description of the neurasthenic as one who cannot touch reality 'with direct confidence but with fingertips that are immediately withdrawn' to imply that Simmel suffered from the very disease that he diagnosed.

Simmel the neurasthenic is afraid of the world and develops a strategy of keeping a distance from it in order to keep that fear under control. He is most of all afraid of commitment. Frisby (1981: 79) quotes Siegfried Kracauer's comment that 'Simmel is full of interest in the world but he holds all that he has interpreted at that distance which is expressed in the concept of interest understood in its widest sense, i.e., he never engages his soul and he forgoes ultimate decisions.' Simmel the neurasthenic, then, is someone who cannot give himself or devote himself to the other. He has, in Walter Kaufman's terms, 'decidophobia.' Alfred E. Laurence (1975: 40, 42–3) surmises that Simmel 'was possibly unable to participate in traditional personal relations because of personality problems' and then accuses Simmel of committing Julien Benda's 'treason of the intellectuals' by his rabid support for the German cause in World War I: 'There is, in the eyes of this former inmate of Dachau, no justification in and for Simmel's irresponsible elitism and irrationalism while flowers bloom and children laugh anywhere on this beautiful earth.' Laurence brings up Simmel's failure to help fellow Jews, his adultery, and his failure to acknowledge his illegitimate daughter to paint a picture of a weak, unfeeling, and deeply selfish man.

Laurence's portrait is consistent with Frisby's. Together they make Simmel into a pathetic and disreputable character. Under the glitter of his 'interesting' genius we find someone who protects himself from his weakness by backing off from engagement, becoming callous to others, and retreating into selfishness. A scared Jew, perhaps. So scared, maybe, that he identified with those who despised him. He could get just close enough to others to play over the appearances of their relations, but he could never get deeply involved. He used the idea of 'tragedy' to opt out of commitment. He was, as Frisby implies, Robert Musil's 'man without qualities.'

What were Simmel vices to his detractors become virtues for his defenders, under a new interpretation. Countering Ernest Bloch's (Maus 1959: 195) version of the case against Simmel, that he is 'a man born without a hard core,' 'a psychologist who forever winds himself into everything and out again,' Heinz Maus (1959: 195) rejoins:

> Perhaps all this is true. But if it is true, it may be because Simmel represented a social reality which is not yet a matter of the past . . . Today, however, that sensitivity, that capacity for listening and contemplating, that ability to tend to the singular and specific because it might illuminate the general and the broadly significant – all of that which, around the turn of the century, was condemned as decadent, un-German, and without basis – has become even more rare.

For Maus, Simmel is not a neurasthenic, but someone who appreciates, who takes things seriously, who uses his sensitivity as an opportunity to listen and contemplate.

Arthur Salz (1959: 236), a student of Simmel, reinforces Maus's image of the strong Simmel, the super-sane, indeed, the wise Simmel: 'Tolerant of the most diverse views and malicious toward none, he freely admitted that life is a medley of material, banal and spiritual, sublime elements; however, he was not a relativist who wavered and talked with tongue in cheek.' For Salz Simmel had a 'serenity of mind,' from which 'morbid "tragicism" ' was absent, and believed that 'life is a daring adventure, and that in its periods of trial, we must take up the cudgels with vigor and audacity.' Far from being uncommitted Simmel (Maus 1959: 195) 'distrusted the great collectivities and insisted on the individual's right to follow his own thoughts, even if they were as playful and inconspicuous as the fleeting strokes of a pencil sketch.' Maus and Salz do not go far to counteract Laurence's Simmel (one can surmise that Simmel, who did not draw boundaries to his scope of sympathy, did draw them sharply in his overt relations), but they show some basis for reports that Simmel was beloved of women (including his wife and his lover) and of foreign students. Simmel the appreciator was far from afraid of the world. Indeed, he welcomed and embraced the other *as* other; he did not leave his writing unresolved because he was afraid of commitment but because he had a keen awareness of the intelligibility of difference. The 'same' characteristics, then, have a different 'inner' sense for Simmel's detractors than they have for his defenders.

Postmodernized Simmel is Simmel the appreciator who (Salz 1959: 236) 'knew how to make the polarity of phenomena both plausible and bearable,' not by approaching them 'with fingertips that are immediately withdrawn,' but by participating in them with the full powers of his observation, imagination, and sympathy. M. Kenneth Brody (1982: 80), commenting on Simmel's essay 'The Metropolis and Mental Life,' observes that '*ambivalence*, rather than indecision or inconsistency, is the key to understanding Simmel's delicate intermixture of positive and negative assessments concerning metropolitan culture': 'His posture is clearly not one of resolute neutrality, for he is alternately praising and censorious about features of the metropolis and the ways in which its inhabitants are found to cope. Instead, Simmel seems figuratively to feel "both ways" about his topic, but nonetheless certain of his appraisals.' Postmodernized Simmel is Brody's Simmel who acknowledges differences out of his *hold on them*. He is also Mongardini's (1986: 130) Simmel who believes that the world is to be met by an 'ethic of contradiction' rather than by a Weberian 'ethic of choice.'

It is the contrast between the ethic of choice urged by Simmel's detractors and the ethic of contradiction urged by his defenders that demarcates the character of postmodernized Simmel. The 'good Simmel' practices the ethic of contradiction. As Gertrud Kantorowicz (1959: 8) remarks, Simmel teaches that we should accept what is given to us and 'exhaust it to its limits.' In our bio-fiction of Simmel we are concerned to stress Simmel the appreciator of difference (who therefore refuses to reduce it to some form of monotony) as over against Simmel the neurasthenic (who refuses to commit himself). The former is postmodernized. The latter is what suspicious moderns understand when they encounter the postmodern(ized).

METHOD/STYLE

Simmel as appreciator has an intellectual style (a method?) that suits his character. Indeed, that style/method is an *expression* of his character (remember, this is, still, bio-fiction), the way it is evinced intellectually. Postmodernized Simmel is an intellectual, not an artist and certainly not an aesthete. Nor is he a moralist, though his writing is informed by the ethic of contradiction, the will to KEEP ONE'S GRIP on life's differences. He seeks to understand; that is why he writes. He does not write out of nervous habit or neurotic compensation or compromise formation, but out of the desire to clarify and to celebrate life-experience by making its forms conspicuous. That desire is deeper than any conclusions that he reaches in his writings, including the metaphysical doctrines of evolution, universal interaction, and tragic conflict that he (the modern Simmel) added as dogma to the play of differences across polarities. Postmodernized Simmel is a trickster of the mind, bringing forth in his texts the structure of diversity.

Of course, the above account of the good Simmel is disputed by Simmel's detractors who see the project of mapping multiple detotalized orders as disorder. The character issue cuts most deeply here because the credibility of Simmel's intellectual practice is directly in question. Indeed, among the most severe detractors are the other two (so-called) FOUNDERS of modern (modernist?) sociology, Émile Durkheim and Max Weber.

The case against Simmel's style of work is made in the most extreme and devastating form by Durkheim (1979: 328) who wrote in reference to Simmel's *Philosophy of Money*,

Imagination, personal feelings are thus given free reign here, and rigorous demonstrations have no relevance. For my own part, I confess to not attaching a very high price to this type of hybrid-illegitimate speculation [*spéculation bâtard*] where reality is expressed in necessarily subjective terms, as in art, but also abstractly, as in science.

Within this short passage are almost all of the features of the bad Simmel. He is unsystematic, egotistic, anti-scientific, and abstract. That is, Simmel throws together a bunch of arbitrary 'insights,' which are united only in his imagination and according to his whim. Here is the 'elitist' and 'irrationalist' Simmel of Laurence at his worst, a punk imposing his sacred ego on the academic community and calling it philosophy or sociology. Let no one say that Simmel's reputation was tarnished only by anti-Semites.

Max Weber echoes Durkheim, though with an entirely different rhetoric. Weber (1972: 158) is impressed by the brilliance and fruitfulness of Simmel's insights, but asserts that 'crucial aspects of his methodology are unacceptable.' In particular, Weber questions Simmel's reliance on analogical construction as the style/method of his work, noting (Weber 1972: 160) how specialists who are concerned with the 'intrinsic nature' or 'specific context' of some set of phenomena will judge the ' "analogous" aspect' of those phenomena to be 'something "external." ' They will regard the phenomenon viewed through analogy as 'conceived entirely "obliquely" in its "essence," and misunderstood with respect to its causal components.' Again, just as for Durkheim, Simmel in Weber's hands is a scientist, or a positivist *manqué*. He is neither logically systematic nor rigorously empirical.

The most influential of the critics of Simmel's methodology/style has been Georg Lukács, whose reading of Simmel's intellectual character has been taken up by Frisby and even appears as the title of the latter's book, *Sociological Impressionism*. Fixing in a positive term Durkheim's notion that Simmel is both subjective and abstract, Lukács (1991: 146, 147) argues that Simmel is 'the genuine philosopher of Impressionism.' As impressionist, Simmel has a 'pluralistic-unsystematic tendency' which is mixed with a disposition to hold firm 'to the absoluteness of every single positing.' For Lukács impressionism is a transitional phenomenon, 'preparing for a new classicism which renders eternal the fullness of life.' Simmel becomes for Lukács in 1918 'a Monet of philosophy who has not yet been followed by a Cézanne.' (Did we ever get a Cézanne of philosophy?) Frisby (1981: ix) picks up on Lukács's suggestion to characterize Simmel as an aesthete, the human twin of the fictional Ulrich ('the man without qualities' of Robert Musil), both of whom share 'an interest in phenomena without a commitment to them, a conscious essayism, a rootlessness, and aestheticization of reality, a perspectivism.' In Frisby's hands Simmel's exile from the (academic?) (intellectual?) (scientific?) ~~community~~ becomes complete: he is an 'aesthetic' ~~thinker~~. Durkheim's 'bastard speculation' of subjectivism and abstraction is a form of neurotic art, not an intellectual method/style at all.

The debate over Simmel's method mirrors the controversy over his character. The detractors detect merely a lack of integrity, which allows for a profusion of 'fragments.' They grasp a surface effect which they then attribute to a personal flaw or, in Lukács's case, to a fruitful limitation. The defenders, in contrast, find a method in the apparent madness.

The most effective and profound of Simmel's defenders in the *methodenstreit* is F. H. Tenbruck, who meets directly the charge that Simmel is guilty of a bad abstractionism. Addressing the field of sociology, Tenbruck argues, along with traditional commentary, that Simmel was concerned with describing forms of sociation. But he cautions that the concept of form does not, in Simmel, refer to abstract generality. Forms are not arbitrary containers for isolated fragments, bastard offspring of subjectivity and abstraction; but are patterns of order within concrete life-experience. Simmelian abstraction (Tenbruck 1959: 75) 'is not – it could not be – abstraction from content-*phenomena* [as Durkheim, Weber, Lukács, and Frisby all understand it], in which the forms inhere and through which alone they can be set forth, but abstraction from a content-*perspective*.' That is, 'the forms are by no means generalizations which retain only the most common characteristics of all contents.' Rather, ' "abstracting" must be understood in the radical sense of extracting or extricating from reality something which is not a directly observable and common element in it.' First and foremost in Simmel's sociology, as Tenbruck points out, is the radical abstraction of interaction as reciprocal orientations from the motives for specific social relations.

Surface abstraction is the vice of the neurasthenic Simmel, whereas radical abstraction is the first move of the appreciative Simmel's method/style. That radical abstraction, as Tenbruck (1959: 76) notes, can never extricate a form of forms: 'For Simmel no true theory of form seemed feasible.' Thus, 'lacking such a theory, he could set forth the general meaning of form only by analogy.' That is, each pattern, whether in individual experience, sociation, culture, or the relations among them, that Simmel elucidates could only be an aspect which begged to be supplemented by others. A form, such as 'domination,' is an aspect of social life, which can be displayed analogically across a field containing every institution and motivational complex. Indeed, the form becomes apparent as an object of knowledge by being exemplified. Yet despite its wide scope, 'domination' is not a Dominant form. It is supplemented, for example, by 'sociability.' Radical abstraction, detotalization, analogical elucidation, and the appreciation of forms of *detotalized* order are the prime elements of Simmel's intellectual method/style. Used together they yield a cartography of the scene, a set of specialized maps tracing common elements that are not directly observable, like the patterns on a weather map. This is a highly intellectual practice, which employs analogy to highlight patterns. One might say that Simmel's practice is a (playful) *discipline* of pattern recognition. Far from being 'bastard speculation' or 'impressionism,' Simmel's mix of specific example with abstraction is the discipline of what we call 'aspectival totalization.'

More than others, North American defenders of Simmel have understood the distinctiveness of his nonpositivistic (not 'irrationalist') method/style. For example, Erving Goffman (1959: xii), writing about his own work, states: 'The justification for this approach (as I take to be the justification for Simmel's also) is that the illustrations fit into a coherent framework that ties together bits of experience the reader has already had and provides the student with a guide worth testing in case studies of institutional social life.' Murray Davis (1973: 153), using the metaphors of art and aesthetics in a different way than Lukács and Frisby do, characterizes Simmel's method as one of 'aesthetic compre-hension,' which works by the procedure of 'universalization through particularization': 'Unlike inductive logic which ascends from the individual to the universal slowly through intermediate steps, aesthetic comprehension bridges this gap immediately by a sudden leap.' That is, 'universalization through particularization' is the way in which the forms grasped through radical abstraction are effectively displayed. Leaps among particulars generate analogies. The reader must then see the form through the illustrations and connect the dots between them by imagining, remembering, or observing new examples.

For the defenders of Simmel's method/style what appears to the detractors as fragmentation is an elucidation of detotalized forms. They are detotalized in two and often in three senses: first, detotalized in the sense that none of them is the master form of all other forms; second, detotalized in the sense that they cannot be organized coherently into a logical system of forms; third, detotalized because the form itself often contains opposition within its own description. Postmodernized Simmel is the exponent of intellectual understanding under the conditions of detotalization. Neurasthenia is to appreciation as bastard speculation is to aspectival (de-)totalization. In his method/style more than perhaps anywhere else (the good) Simmel *is* *postmodern(ist)*.

POLITICAL-INTELLECTUAL
COMMITMENT/CHARACTER

We have brought forth postmodernized Simmel as an appreciator of detotalized life-experience who has an appreciative method based on radical abstraction and elucidating analogies, issuing in aspectival totalizations. How does this play in the world? That is, what consequences does Simmel's practice as an intellectual writing on human affairs have on 'one's' commitment to those affairs? What is Simmel's political-intellectual commitment/ character?

The character issue leads to the question of commitment. Would anyone care if Simmel suffered from decidophobia if they were not concerned with urging commitment? The root of the attack on Simmel, as Frisby has shaped it, is that he fails as a public intellectual. He did not tell us what the good fight was and how to fight it. Indeed, he did the opposite. He showed us how to escape from commitment by issuing seductive invitations to play or to wallow in tragedy, or both.

Does any of this matter? It does to what is broadly designated in contemporary (human) (Culture) studies as 'critical theory,' in the Frankfurt sense. That is the precinct from which today's assault on Simmel is mounted. His image is a proverbial political football in a skirmish between critical theorists and an assorted group of (more-or-less) Simmel enthusiasts, including modernists, postmodernists, and many shades between. None of the latter group, including us, would be involved in the fight if the other side had not started it. Simmel scholars do not tend to study him because of his direct political significance but because of his clarification of life-experience, his diagnoses and descriptions, not his (mostly absent) therapies and prescriptions. They do not tend to attach overriding significance to his abstinence from public political commitment. Other concerns take priority on their intellectual agendas. But, for critical theorists, whose aim is to evaluate and also to be true to social reality, writers on human (cultural) affairs should be judged on their commitments, which are their ultimate tests as intellectuals. Do they, that is, affirm and support a 'rational' society?

Thus, in the final act of the character drama the defenders of Simmel are fighting on alien ground in a battle they did not choose. It would be easy to say that critical theorists have probably done little to change political conditions through their writings, but we will leave that (irony) aside and said. We will, instead, present the case of Simmel's detractors and then supplement their image with an image of a 'political' (at least (post)modernized) Simmel drawn from the literature.

Klaus Lichtblau (1989–90: 109), referring to Jurgen Habermas and Walter Benjamin, and borrowing Frisby's characterization of Simmel's writings as 'sociological impressionism,' presents the case against Simmel the (un)public intellectual succinctly. Working within the understanding of Simmel's method as one of surface abstraction, Lichtblau states that Simmel 'emphasizes the distinctiveness of the esthetic-expressive sphere as against the institutional core of modern society.' Having 'crossed . . . the bridge to cultural modernism,' which exalts 'the transitory, the fugitive and the contingent,' Simmel offers not only an 'abstract opposition to history' (Habermas) but also the basis for a 'gay polytheism,' which expresses itself in 'the change of fashion and the multitude of styles.' In the process Simmel's cultural modernism 'immobilizes history proper.'

Simmel the gay polytheist joins Simmel the neurasthenic and Simmel the bastard speculator. The problem is not merely that he is not committed but that he takes our field of action away from us by diverting his (and our) attention from 'the institutional core of modern society' and toward the monotonously mutating appearances of society and culture, and by stalemating history in a play of forms in which duration can be understood 'only as absolute change.' That is, Simmel draws us into a fantasia of bastard speculation, the critical theorist's conception of what a neurasthenic's paradise must be. This is not Weber's tragic polytheism, which goes along with the ethic of choice, but a gay polytheism (which goes along with the ethic of contradiction).

E. V. Walter, from an earlier generation of critical theory, has presented the most serious questioning of Simmel's failure to affirm a social totality and a progressive theory of history. For Walter (1959: 63) 'the fading of traditional extrinsic limits on power moves us to look for ways to reconstruct the lost synthesis of political theory. That synthesis, the "state" in an Aristotelian sense, is what allows men to be truly human.' It is just such a unity as the 'state' that Simmel most strenuously denies. As Tenbruck (1959: 90) notes: 'Formal sociology is incompetent to deal with the problem of a change of society itself, a change of the whole system. It cannot be otherwise, for it refuses to regard society, as conceived of as such a system, as its proper object.' Simmel's refusal to totalize society in a single privileged way is what allows him to avoid commitment, since there is no coherent context in his scheme(s) of things to which to commit oneself. If there is no social whole there can be no history of that (nonexistent) whole and, therefore, no possibility of that whole being perfected rationally. Also, we add a bit maliciously, there can be no *hope* for that whole being perfected rationally.

For Walter (1959: 151), Simmel's position leads to detachment. With regard to history, Simmel eschews 'the idea of progress,' which, for Enlightenment writers, 'supported the ethical element in political theory and provided a critical touchstone by which existing power relations might be judged.' Instead, 'his interest in history is detached and focused on epistemological problems; he is not an "involved critic." ' With regard to society, Walter (p. 156) makes a similar point by tracing Simmel's revision of Kant. Whereas for Kant 'society is a moral world as well as a phenomenal world,' Simmel's 'approach to society is that of the observer rather than that of the participant; and his perspective is dominated by the first *Critique* in which Kant's conception of society and politics is not fully developed.'

Simmel's observational stance and especially his separation of form from content, which leads to a separation of social structure from individual needs, issue in a denial of ethical judgment and ultimately in a denial of ethical responsibility. Walter (1959: 158) argues that, for Simmel, 'the forms are not judged by how they serve or deny the needs of individuals, but merely by the criteria of logic and coherence. Domination and subordination, whether benign or malevolent, are technical requirements of society and are to be accepted with resignation.' Simmel's method is, here, a vehicle for retreatism. Since he repudiates historical progress, Simmel can, according to Walter (p. 161), only see societies moving 'willy-nilly from one political form to another, according to the requirements of structure.' He is, therefore, 'skeptical . . . of all political struggles for freedom' and 'can only hope for a political structure that limits its constraint to "external matters." ' But, as Walter (p. 162) notes, 'Simmel did not foresee . . . that modern political power would develop forms which tend to deny all private "living space," and produce a mass designed to absorb the entire personality.'

In Walter's (1959: 162, 163) hands Simmel ends up being the same pathetic retreatist that he is to the other detractors, now hiding out in an internal migration. He 'arrives at a secularized form of the Lutheran theory of power' and adopts an 'attitude of tragic resignation': 'His sociology illuminates the role of power in the inexorable system-building work of society, but as a political or social philosophy, his work does not offer a satisfactory theory of power, especially for the critical tradition. It isolates the ethical realm from external relations, relinquishes freedom to the necessities of power, and ultimately dehumanizes politics.' Critical theory, or at least Walter's version of it, assumes that if there is no commitment to (the history of) totality (and the totality of history) there can only be mechanical separation of the elements of life-experience and, ultimately, quietism toward the world. Walter does not base his conclusion about Simmel's public-intellectual character/commitment on Simmel's 'life,' but on the suggestions that he gets from Simmel's writings. He gets those suggestions, not others, because he interprets Simmel as a surface abstractionist, not as Tenbruck's radical abstractionist. Walter does not allow a *positive* opposition to totalization, to Society and History. He is wedded to the modern paradigm and its exclusions.

The defense of Simmel's political-intellectual character/commitment finds its best resources in the literature in the writings of the group associated with Julien Freund and centered at the University of Strasbourg. Unlike Simmel scholars in

Germany, Britain, and North America, these writers do not produce commentaries and criticisms alone, but appropriate Simmelian concepts and methods for use in fresh analyses of contemporary social life. They are not concerned with interpreting Simmel in relation to his own times, but with using his approach here and now. They insert themselves into the contemporary European intellectual scene as (primarily) pheno-menologists, suspicious of the totalizing ambitions of critical theory and knowledgeable about and respectful of postmodernist accounts of the technoscape, but demanding more than just a margin of spontaneity from the domination of Culture. They are, for the purposes of the present writing mainly (post), but sometimes very (post)modernist. That is, they are *modernists*, not moderns. They question the grand totalizations, but not the objectivity of social interaction and, even more important, of experience. The volume of their essays on Simmel (edited by Patrick Watier) is titled, indeed, *Georg Simmel: la sociologie et l'expérience du monde moderne*. They have not, exactly, made the postmodern flip, but, unlike the critical theorists, they are aware of just what it is and seem to 'achieve' it sometimes. They are fine allies of inclusivist postmodernists against critical theory and their phenomenologies are fine examples of modernism finding its way in postmodernity; they are very helpful to the cause of inclusively postmodernized Simmel.

Maffesoli (1986: 111) provides a direct and stalemating response to the kind of position articulated by Walter. He identifies a political paradigm which is dominant in mainstream sociology: 'in its general orientation, as in its specific modalities, *being-together* [*l'être-ensemble*] could only be understood under the political horizon, which is concentrated in the projective attitude: action, the future, the remote.' Maffesoli opposes the political paradigm with an 'aesthetic paradigm' (an unfortunate choice of words) associated with Simmel's approach that reveals 'diverse expressions of contemporary sociality.' These expressions (spontaneous forms and processes of sociation that are (relatively) autonomous of 'the state') will, however, be considered 'anomic from the viewpoint of the imagination of political morality' (anomie being an alternative term for what Walter called amoralism).

Maffesoli parries the critical theorist's attack by associating the aesthetic paradigm with an oxymoronic 'ethical immoralism,' which is 'the carrier of a morality that is created collectively and not imposed in an overwhelming manner.' *Aisthesis* rests on 'shared experience' and 'favors interaction.' That is, the micro-processes of association and dissociation generate their own ethic(s), apart from the imperatives of the rationalizing and totalizing state. The difference between the political and aesthetic paradigms is (Maffesoli 1986: 113) 'qualitative': 'On one side the accent is placed on the monad and its counterpart the rational association, and on the other it is placed more on the group and its "affective cement." In other words, Politics *versus* Sociality.' In the hands of the European interactionists Simmel is transformed from a selfish retreatist into a master of forms of resistance *against* the political, which appears in contemporary society not as the totalitarian ideological state feared by Walter, but as the technoscape and mediascape (Kroker) of postmodernism. Maffesoli (pp. 109–10), indeed, calls for 'a sociology of the social imaginary,' which 'will not be a simple philosophical supplement but the heart of the reflective process.' There is modernist resistance on the postmodern (not-quite-fully-yet) culturescape: a 'political' Simmel.

The basis of the Strasbourg appropriation (interpretation) of Simmel is the notion of 'interaction,' which is understood phenomenologically as a form of experience, not metaphysically as the form of the cosmos. It is, however, privileged because it is the form of *all sociality*, what is going on regardless of what people are associating about. 'Interaction' is a detotalized form, or as Claude Javeau (1986: 180–1) puts it, it is 'formist,' not 'formalist.' Similarly to Tenbruck on radical abstraction, Javeau contrasts the view that forms are 'empty "frames" destined to be filled with behaviors and meanings' with Simmel's 'assumption of principles of regulation inscribed in duration and taking it into account.' That is, forms of sociality, including interaction, the form in which all other forms of sociality appear, are not mechanical impositions on contents but the ways in which society, as a network of reciprocal orientations, is perpetually constructed and deconstructed.

Javeau provides an understanding of interaction through Simmel's essay 'The Bridge and the Door.' There Simmel shows that interaction is inherently detotalized because it is an oscillation between the poles of unifying the separate (the bridge) and severing the united (provisionally) (the door). The web-in-process of social interaction is constituted by a decentered switching mechanism through which sociators connect with and disconnect from each other apart from the control of any master plan. The fall of tradition, thought by Walter to issue in sheer state power, leaves in its ruins for the phenomenologists the persistence of detotalized social experience, which had always been going on behind the facade of tradition but now becomes conspicuous, along with our condition (Simmel 1985: 32) of being 'at any moment – in the immediate or symbolic, in the physical or mental sense – beings who separate what is united and unite what is separate.' But, of course, in the ruins has also grown up the technological society, the Baudrillardian 'simulacrum,' which, according to exclusivist postmodernism has already permeated the 'everyday,' misceginated with it, and produced a simulation of it, fed back into home and neighborhood by the externalized imagination of the mainly electronic media of 'infotainment.'

As political-intellectual commitment Continental inter-actionism is a resistance against the predatory and hegemonic features of postmodern culture-society. For example, A. J. Haessler (1986: 149), in his appropriation-interpretation of Simmel's 'The Metropolis and Mental Life,' challenges Baudrillard, who holds that in modern social formations there is only predatory economic exchange, with Simmel's defenses/descriptions of 'gratitude, fidelity, friendship, nobility of soul, credit (sic) or respect.' For Haessler these 'phenomena of symbolic exchange configure a counter-project to a social logic dominated by economic exchange, putting the accent on the necessarily communicative function that human sociality has in the process of constituting identity and beyond that on the necessity of communion, of reciprocity of perspectives, of fusion of subjectivities.'

Similarly Freddy Raphael (1986: 262), in his discussion of the stranger and the metropolis, shows how 'microsocieties,' such as racial and ethnic ghettos are resistances of 'traditional sociability' against the metropolitan environment. Enclaves such as 'Little Italy' or 'Chinatown' 'are not simple replicas of the old countries but original creations which undergo mutations.' Abraham Moles (1986: 226) uses Simmel's form of the secret to argue that even the new information technologies provide the opportunity for capturing 'interstitial freedom' (*liberté interstitielle*). Sociologists, according to Moles, might learn to practice '*immediate analysis of the forces of the reactivity* of being to environments and of the *forms* which grasp these reactions.' Moles (p. 226) neatly exposes the vision of Continental interactionism: 'It is the indefinite play of dominance and submission, of transparency and opacity, eternally renewed, which constitutes the image that the sociologist needs to construct.'

Interactionist resistance is a (post)modernist political-intellectual commitment, sharing with inclusivist postmodernism an affirmation of detotalized forms, but privileging the spontaneity of sociality far more than any postmodernism can. Yet inclusivist postmodernism, as advanced in the present group of writings, will end up adopting a form of interactionist resistance as its commitment, the commitment of postmodernized Simmel: resistance through play-forms.

One of the Strasbourg group, Patrick Watier (1986: 247) anticipates this move in his essay on Simmel's description of the form of sociability, which 'realizes union without passing through lost tradition, and without hot or effervescent communions, and reveals the metaphysical design of Simmel to desubjectivize the individual.' The 'desubjectivized individual' is of the provenance of postmodernized Simmel, the playful appreciator. For Watier (p. 250) the play of sociation for its own sake opens the way to thinking about individuals who are 'beyond self-conservation,' who, rather than practicing selfish retreat, give themselves to the play of interaction, of connection and disconnection, of building bridges and closing and opening doors. Watier (pp. 241–2) notes that 'the conflict among values and the intersections of social circles permits one to think of a multiform individuality going from possessive individualism to aleatory identity.' The former pole is the modern individual and the latter the exclusivist postmodern(ist) individual (the Lyotardian drifter, the Derridian empirical wanderer, the Deleuzian nomad).

The postmodernized Simmelian 'desubjectivized individual' stands somewhere between these poles. For Watier (1986: 250), this (de-)subject-position even has critical-theoretic (in a broad sense) possibilities. At the point at which the 'force of the subject' is no longer 'linked to subjectivity' and the subject has not yet been 'destituted,' a 'comprehension of the individual' is revealed that 'allows us at once to describe sociability and nevertheless to take it as a fiction, or better as giving a view on the "other state" that is possible in the conflict of modern culture.' That 'other state', the *nontragic* state of play, is the locus of postmodernized Simmel's ~~political~~-intellectual character/commitment. In play resistance is sublated by engagement undertaken for itself. One defies the technosphere simply by making oneself available for *interaction*, by choosing that which remains on its margins.

It is from those margins that postmodernized Simmel makes forays into postmodernity/postmodernism, as an appreciator, an elucidator, and constituter of detotalized form(s). The playful (mainly Derridian) Simmel embraces the interactionist (phenomenological) Simmel at the margins. Salute to the French, habilitators of (the image of) the good Simmel.

MODERN(IST) SIMMEL

The defense of Simmel's political-intellectual character is not exhausted by the bio-fiction of postmodernized Simmel. There is also a modern(ist) Simmel who is presented for commendation – Simmel the great liberal. This image, no more or less 'true' than that of the detractors or our own, is at least as plausible as they are. We present it here in order to acknowledge our modern allies in the Simmel literature and their contribution to building a positive Simmel image. To our minds 'modernism' and 'postmodernism' are not exclusive alternatives but discursive domains bordering each other. We are what Henry David Thoreau called 'moss troopers,' that is, bandits working both sides of a border; what Simmel (postmodernized? modernist?) called 'boundary beings,' his name for what 'We' are. We could be working the modernist side of the border (as we have in the past) if we didn't think that the postmodernist side contained more resources for mapping present culture. We salute modern(ist) Simmel(s).

The difference between postmodernized and modern(ist) Simmels is that the latter is a foundationalist whereas the former holds foundations in question, though, in the Derridian way, does not get along without writing about or with them. The foundation(s) of the modern(ist) Simmel(s) is life-experience, interpreted by some romantically and by others phenomenologically. For the romantic faction life-experience is centered in the individual self. Here Simmel becomes a mature liberal, falling into the same broad group as Benedetto Croce, José Ortega y Gasset (Simmel's student), R. G. Collingwood, and John Dewey. For the phenomenological faction life-experience is centered in the interactive event. Here Simmel becomes a (hyper-liberal) 'existentialist,' a partisan of being-in-the-world like Martin Heidegger, Jean-Paul Sartre, and Maurice Merleau-Ponty.

Simmel as liberal modern(ist), seeking to balance Enlightenment rationalism with romantic self-expression, has been filled out by contemporary writers on Simmel's cultural theory, such as Donald Levine, Birgitta Nedelmann, and Lawrence Scaff. All of them base their interpretations of Simmel on the centrality of the ideal and value of 'individuality' in his thought: Simmel is a great defender of the modern individual against the endogenous processes of modernity that threaten to abolish that individual. For Levine, Simmel is also more, an exemplary modern individual.

The defenders of Simmel as liberal modern(ist) do not, of course, conceive of him as a neurasthenic, impressionist, and retreatist. Levine (1991), indeed, responds directly to the detractors in his study of Simmel as moral educator, countering the allegation of Simmel's 'indifferentism.' Nedelmann (1991) presents Simmel in a neo-functionalist appropriation, emphasizing the systematicity of his complex thought. Scaff (1988) places Simmel in his own intellectual milieu and shows that he was thinking through a serious problem that has contemporary relevance.

For Scaff (1988) Simmel is most adequately understood as responding to the challenge issued by Nietzsche to face up to the nihilism of modern culture and its oppressive effects on the individual. By locating Simmel in 'the context of [his] *own* discourse' (the turn-of-the-century preoccupation with the fate of modern culture), Scaff (1990: 292) is able to show that Simmel is not primarily an aestheticist but a thinker deploying multiple frames of reference: 'But if Simmel was attracted to the light of the aesthetic life and aesthetic judgment as a source of warmth, as he most certainly was, then he was also in calmer moments pulled in the direction of the cold and clear air of reflection.' Scaff's Simmel is 'self-divided and necessarily so,' and is as capable as Max Weber of choosing 'intellect over enchantment, realism over latent possibility.'

Nedelmann approaches Simmel through the problem of the relationship between culture and the individual. She (1991: 179) notes that 'in his sociological analyses, Simmel implicitly uses a normative concept of individuality, which he derives from the social norms with which modern man is confronted.' Specifically,

Simmel addresses the 'double and contradictory normative requirement to develop a unique and differentiated personality *and* to find social recognition for this uniqueness.' In Nedelmann's view Simmel is able to integrate the two requirements and to formulate an 'ethical standard guiding human interaction in all social spheres of modern society.'

In a careful, subtle, and sensitive commentary/appropriation Nedelmann shows how Simmel performs a complex balancing act based on the twin needs of protecting the objectivity of culture as a generalized mediator against hyper-individualization, and of guarding the individual against the tyranny of objective form. From her critical systems perspective Simmel is revealed as engaged in a perpetual attempt to reconcile the opposites of life-experience non-reductively, to maintain a balance between, expressivity and the demands of communication for generality. Far from being an 'impressionist' Nedelmann's Simmel is a mature liberal, free from any belief in automatic progress and aware of the experiential conditions under which individuality is possible, though he sometimes believes that those conditions have little or no chance of being actualized.

Levine has presented the fullest and most convincing portrait of Simmel the liberal modern(ist). According to him (Levine 1991: 103), 'the scattered texts where Simmel plants his diagnoses of modernity all pose the question of what effects the conditions of modern life have for the fulfillment of individual personality.' For Levine's Simmel (pp. 108, 109, 110) individuality means 'the freedom to develop a unique self,' the effort to establish 'bases for resistance' (here he draws near the French Simmelians) against 'cultural anomie and alienation,' and a 'vitalization and individualization of ethics' in which 'one's moral imperative does not remain fixed for all time, but changes in accord with the integration of emerging ethical decisions.' Far from being an aestheticist Levine's Simmel is much more a moralist for whom 'each new ethical decision affects our entire moral personality.'

Just as Nedelmann does, Levine (1991: 109) argues that Simmel articulates 'a modern ideal of personal development.' Levine finds the concrete expression of that ideal in Simmel's educational writings and practice. He (pp. 112, 114) shows how Simmel forges a pedagogical program that 'is familiar to us today under the name of "liberal education," ' in which students are engaged 'actively in a learning process' and in which what is learned increases the capacities and skills of students or enhances their ' "depth, clarity, breadth, and moral constitution." ' The goal of the Simmelian teacher (p. 113) is to help students 'to learn for themselves and to internalize a schema of intellectual connections flexible enough to facilitate the acquisition of new knowledge'; that is, 'to provide a continuous setting for overcoming the crisis of modern culture.'

Levine's Simmel is a civilized romantic liberal, anticipating progressive education and situation ethics. Not only does his writing on modernity evince 'a constant commitment to the value of human individuality and integrity' (as against Lukács and Frisby who claim 'that Simmel lacked a centre of firm commitments'), but so does his practice. Levine argues that Simmel's teaching was a good application of his liberal ideal, instancing his aporetic approach of challenging assumptions with counter-assumptions, his use of analogies to connect insights, and 'his appeal to the life experiences of listeners as a basis for deriving or exemplifying abstract notions.' Here the same characteristics that are used by detractors to mark Simmel the impressionist and by us to identify postmodernized Simmel are employed to construct the image of Simmel the liberal modern(ist). For Levine (1991: 114), these characteristics are means to the romantic liberal ideal of maximizing

> the freedom of individuals to pursue their own interests and develop their personalities in accord with their innermost dispositions and aspirations. Consistent to the end, Simmel evinced a radical respect for the individuality and the developmental capacities of each person.

Simmel as liberal modern(ist) is, in Levine's hands, the mature romantic who holds on to his version of the modern ideal in full critical awareness of the difficulties of achieving it and who develops an exemplary practice in the face of those difficulties. The defenders of postmodernized Simmel part ways with the liberal modernists on the issue of such ideas as 'innermost dispositions and aspirations.' It is not that they deny that Simmel used these terms and meant them; it is just that this Simmel is not the one that they are appropriating. They take the portrayal of the liberal modern(ist) Simmel in the literature as evidence of the complexity and variety of Simmelian subject positions, glad to nudge the image of the impressionist Simmel a bit more out of the foreground.

The little brother of the liberal modern(ist) is the (post-)liberal modernist, more raffish and less respectable than his elder, somewhat of an anarchist, an existentialist, an adventurer, as avant-garde as they come; an eroticist, perhaps a flirt. He might even be mistaken for an impressionist by the less-sensitive politically pious. If it wasn't for his stubborn commitment to life-experience (being-in-the-world) he could be mistaken for a postmodernist. (Post-)liberal modernist Simmel is tangent to postmodernized Simmel and even encroaches on the latter's domain. He just hasn't (fully) made the flip to Culture, but the rest of him is already there.

Going back to rebut the accusations that Simmel is a fragmentary and unsystematic writer, David Axelrod has fashioned yet another counteractive positive image of Simmel's intellectual character: the adventurer. Still within a broadly liberal frame of reference, Axelrod (1977: 161) grounds Simmel's intellectual character in a commitment to the individual, claiming that, for Simmel, 'the individual is the source of the highest intellectual standard.' Axelrod's Simmel (p. 163) relates everything in his writings to 'the human struggle for individuality.' Here 'individuality' takes on a slightly different stress than it did for the liberal modern(ist)s. It is not so much a question of expressing a fundamental self as of 'keeping the tensions and contradictions of life open' and engaging in 'authentic speech' – speech that is 'contained in the life of the speaker.' For (post)-liberal modernist, adventurous, Simmel 'there can be no paradigm for individuality' (Axelrod 1977: 166).

In the absence of a paradigm for self, adventurous Simmel comes close to becoming a postmodernist. At least, for Axelrod (1977: 164), he rejects foundationalism: 'Thus the fragmentary style may suggest that Simmel experienced each occasion of writing synonymously with the struggle to be free from any one particular structure or formulation.' Axelrod's Simmel is a 'non-paradigmatic author.' Though he searches for and 'struggles toward the source from which unity arises,' Simmel is finally more concerned with 'receptivity toward the experience of theorizing' than with the (ac)cumulation of results. Here Axelrod directly vindicates Simmel against his detractors. As a practitioner of authentic speech who was unwilling to dissolve the individual into the 'scientific' community, Simmel became viewed by that community (for example, by Durkheim and Weber) 'as the enemy of concerted inquiry' and as 'a metaphor for nihilism and intellectual anarchy.' For his detractors, Simmel (Axelrod 1977: 159) contributed 'neither to the achievement of a unified collectivity nor to its concrete preservation over time.' His supposed fragmentary style is not the question but, more deeply, his form of thinking, which the style incarnates and which perpetually 'reconsiders its foundations.' It is this endless questioning and relativizing that the pillars of the community find subversive and dub as impressionism.

Axelrod's Simmel connects here with the Simmel of Michael Kaern, another (post-)liberal modernist. In Kaern's (1990: 76) challenging work Simmel appears as a philosopher of the 'as-if,' holding 'the view that the human mind functions independent of nature that is outside of it, the functions of the mind are independent of nature.' In consequence, 'first, the picture that the mind creates for us when we analyze the world by using the functions of the mind is not necessarily a true reflection of reality, and second, these functions of the mind *create* reality-as-we-know-it.' In Kaern's hands Simmel becomes an almost-postmodernist, rejecting the claim that cognition can mirror nature (antifoundationalism), but still clinging to a mind that is somehow independent of discourse. Kaern's Simmel is an adventurer of inquiry: the human condition is to live by hypothesis, never by certainty, and each experiment is an adventure undertaken in the absence of any ontological confidence.

Axelrod finds his inspiration for his portrayal of Simmel's intellectual character in Simmel's (1959) essay, 'The Adventure.' Axelrod's Simmel (1977: 163) is the writer as adventurer, who makes of each fragmentary experience 'an adventurous occasion that reconsiders its foundations and struggles toward the source from which unity arises.' The key to the Simmelian adventure is the 'direct experience of the contents' of life (p. 163). It is not living second-hand through detached contemplation or anticipating the future or reminiscing about the past, but engaging the present event as something for itself, in all of its contingency and risk, and yet finding some way of endowing that event with more than peripheral significance for the self.

For Simmel (1959: 243), the adventure is distinguished from other life-experiences by its 'general form' of 'dropping out of the continuity of life.' Routine life proceeds according to its schedules and systems of expectation. In the adventure the ordinary pattern is broken and the specific contents of momentary experience become valued for themselves, in great part because the individual cannot anticipate with confidence where they will lead. To adventure is to embrace insecurity and at the same time to feel the exhilaration of testing and demonstrating one's strength and wit. The adventurer, then, is someone who gets hooked on the thrill of pursuing what Alfred North Whitehead called the momentary 'lures to feeling' offered by each experience rather than passing them over or smoothing them into the normal flow of life.

Indeed, for Simmel (1959: 256), every experience is both a potential adventure and a potential occurrence in a pattern of life: 'Seen from the center of the personality, every single experience is at once something necessary which comes from the unity of the history of the ego, and something accidental, foreign to that unity, insurmountably walled off, and colored by a very deep-lying incomprehensibility, as if it stood somewhere in the void and gravitated toward nothing.' The adventure(r) privileges the latter aspect of experience, as Simmel (p. 257) does when he proclaims: 'We are the adventurers of the earth; our life is crossed everywhere by the tensions which mark adventure.' (Post-)liberal modernist Simmel is an existential phenomenologist, locating authentic existence in an embrace of contingency and accidentality. He is a hyper-modernist who calls the philosopher (p. 249) 'the adventurer of the spirit,' who 'makes the hopeless, but not therefore meaningless, attempt to form into conceptual knowledge an attitude of the soul, its mood toward itself, the world, God. He treats this insoluble problem as if it were soluble.' Still the tragic modernist here, the vitalist/existentialist, like Unamuno, who undertakes (in the best sense) a Quixotic quest. Simmel notes how the adventurer inverts common sense and is invested with a kind of madness. When confronted with uncertainty normal people limit their 'commitment of force, hold open lines of retreat, and take each step only as if testing the ground.' In contrast adventurers stake everything on 'hovering chance,' burn bridges, and 'step into the mist, as if the road will lead (them) on, no matter what.'

Of all the adventures that people can have the erotic are, for Simmel, the most typical and representative. Eroticism, for Simmel as for Freud, is more than sex narrowly construed, but is the form of primary or nonsymbolic union among human individuals. Adventures need not be of long duration. Indeed, some of the most intense last no more than seconds, as when two people's eyes meet and both are drawn transiently into an absorbing moment of experience charged with excitement, a thrill of vulnerability, and a sense of fulfillment. Simmel surely experienced such adventures many times. Perhaps they are a 'paradigm' for his relation to experience as a whole. At least their playful delight and fleeting depth are supplementary to the cultural concerns of postmodernized Simmel. We offer in the following essay our appreciation of Simmel the existential phenomenologist. We are comfortable working the (post-)liberal modernist side of the tracks. That's where we came from, and even though we're living on the other side now, we still come back for frequent visits.

The reflection on the character issue is done. We have exposed four images of Simmel's intellectual character that are present in the literature, one of them unfavorable and three of them favorable. Surely there are even more Simmels to be discovered, and the more the better, since each one will enhance different discourses. We are not interested in defeating the detractors but in decentering them or, in a more (postmodernized) Simmelian sense, stalemating them. We have suggested three ways in which this can be done and in the process have situated our discourse in its discursive formation(s).

ON THE VISUAL CONSTITUTION OF SOCIETY: THE CONTRIBUTIONS OF GEORG SIMMEL AND JEAN-PAUL SARTRE TO A SOCIOLOGY OF THE SENSES

The topic of how society, defined in its most general sense as a complex of intermental relations, is constituted by the participants in it has been of primary concern to contributors to the traditions of classical sociology and, more broadly, those of modern social philosophy. The sociological theorists of the late nineteenth and early twentieth centuries inquired into the possibility of society, by which is meant the presuppositions of intermental community, whereas the social philosophers of that era and of later decades investigated the question of how individual selves know one another to be minded beings. One of the primary aims of the social theories that were allied with the emergence of sociology in the second half of the nineteenth century was to critique the modern doctrine, which was inherited from Cartesian philosophy, that the individual thinking ego could only know directly its own mental activity and the non-mental objects of that activity. It was thought that in order to establish society as a complex of intermental relations it was necessary to show how individuated minds could have immediate access to one another. The search for the ways in which the mentality of other selves is disclosed to the thinking individual led to a florescence of phenomenological insight into the varieties of the social bond. For the most part interest was and has continued to be directed at the constitution of society through symbolic communication in the form of ordinary language. However, a few thinkers also attempted to show that relations among minded beings are constituted non-verbally and immediately, primarily through the sense of sight. The following discussion will describe and relate two alternative and contrasting accounts of the constitution of intermental relations through vision, that of Georg Simmel and that of Jean-Paul Sartre. The aim of the commentary will be to show how, when they are taken together, Simmel's and Sartre's accounts reveal the general nature of the social relation as an uneasy compound of subjectivizing and objectivizing elements or tendencies.

The scope of the following discussion is provided by Simmel's project of a 'sociology of the senses,' by which he meant the study of the forms through which minded beings apprehend or acknowledge one another as such through the media of sensation. According to Simmel (1969) 'it is through the medium of the senses that we perceive our fellow-men.' Both Sartre and Simmel argue that not only does sensation disclose human beings to one another, but that it reveals them to one another as minded beings. Therefore, neither of the two thinkers believes that the individual ego becomes acquainted with other minded individuals through observing their external movements, perceiving the similarity of those movements to the ego's own actions which are known immediately to be minded, and inferring the existence of a mind controlling the movements of the perceived individuals. Such inference by analogy, Simmel and Sartre hold, is an artifact of the Cartesian predicament which is overcome by the immediate revelation of the other mind to the individual thinker through the senses. Both Sartre and Simmel use a phenomenological method of description to make their contributions to a sociology of the senses, but come up with different results. For Simmel vision constitutes a direct relation of union among subjects, whereas for Sartre vision constitutes relations of objectification between subjects. Each thinker fails to take account of the insight provided by the other, making necessary a more comprehensive view showing how each contribution limits the other.

Simmel on the mutual glance

In approaching the problem of how social relations are constituted primordially Simmel (1969: 358) comments that 'the union and interaction of individuals is based upon mutual glances,' and that such looking by people into one another's eyes is 'perhaps the most direct and purest reciprocity which exists anywhere.' For Simmel the fact that humans apprehend one another solely through the senses makes it necessary for sociologists to investigate precisely the kinds of knowledge of alter that ego can attain through sensory data and their constructive mental elaboration. He identifies 'appreciation' and 'comprehension' as the two modes by which subjects apprehend one another, noting that in the former mode alter induces in ego an affective response which is spontaneous and non-cognitive, the evocation of a feeling or emotion by a sensory stimulus, whereas in the latter the sense impression that ego has of alter becomes 'the medium for understanding the other,' a 'bridge' over which ego reaches alter's 'real self.' Simmel is most concerned in founding his sociology of the senses with comprehension, because, for him, the process of sociation, which constitutes regularized social relations, is made possible by individuals sharing in forms or cultural patterns that are common to them. They must, in order to plan with regard to complex systems of exchange and cooperative affairs, know with whom they are dealing and what to expect from them. Yet Simmel recognizes in the mutual glance a phenomenon of pure reciprocity that is immediate and independent of symbolization and abstraction. The mutual glance which is constituted when individuals 'look into' one another's eyes is neither an appreciative nor a comprehending apprehension because it does not involve the separation of stimulus from response or that of perception from judgment.

The basis of Simmel's sociology of vision is that the eye has the 'uniquely sociological function' of constituting society without the aid of objectified forms which are primarily rooted in language and, therefore, in the sense of sound. Simmel's description of the mutual glance resembles closely the accounts of the 'I–Thou' relation which were later developed by such social existentialists as Simmel's student Martin Buber (1958), Gabriel Marcel (1956) and William Ernest Hocking (1954). According to Simmel, the mutual glance is an intersubjective bond which does not crystallize into an objective structure: 'The unity which momentarily arises between two persons is present in the occasion and is dissolved in the function' (1969: 358). The union or relation constituted by mutual glancing is fragile and is destroyed as soon as one of the participants makes the slightest glance aside. Although the interaction of eye and eye 'dies in the moment in which the directness of the function is lost,' and 'no objective trace of this relationship is left behind' its actuality, Simmel argues that the totality of social relations 'would be changed in unpredictable ways if there occurred no glance of eye to eye.' Simmel distinguishes the phenomenon of mutual glancing, which 'signifies a wholly new and unique union' between individuals, from 'simple sight or observation of the other.' He does not explore the possibility that observation may under certain conditions constitute a different form of social relation from that of the mutual glance, one which is based upon objectification rather than upon intersubjectivity. Sartre's contribution is to show how objectification constitutes sociality.

The most important feature for Simmel of the mutual glance is its reciprocity or bidirectionality. He notes that in the very act of seeking to perceive alter, ego is opened to being perceived by alter: 'By the glance which reveals the other, one discloses himself. By the same act in which the observer seeks to know the observed, he surrenders himself to be understood by the observed.' In mutual glancing, then, neither partner can maintain reserve and each one is entrusted to the other. The social knowledge gained immediately in the glance is fully participative in the sense that it is only possible through self-deliverance or active transcendence of the self into the other's vision. Such participating knowledge cannot be attained through observation, but only by offering oneself as a gift to the other: the 'direct mutual glance' sets up an emergent relation which cannot be analyzed into components although it is made possible by the initiatives of individuals who need not have been related to one another previously in any other way. The joint act of self-surrender, self-deliverance and unreserved participation is, for Simmel, 'the most perfect reciprocity in the entire field of human relations.' Mutual glancing is both a consummation and a foundation of society. As a consummation it is the most perfect social bond, which arises only when risk and trust are justified by the participant individuals. As a foundation the mutual glance provides an immediate, though transient, union which can arise even when objectified forms of interaction or cultural patterns have lost their hold or have been pluralized into sets of competing alternatives.

The deliverance of one's being, of one's character and personality, to the other in the mutual glance is both facilitated and hindered, according to Simmel, by the fact that the human face expresses the individual's 'inner nature.' Simmel claims that the face 'as a medium of expression is entirely a theoretical organ; it does not act, as the hand, the foot, the whole body; it transacts none of the internal or practical relations of the man, it only tells about him.' Personality, then, is spontaneously made manifest externally through facial expression: 'In the face is deposited what has been precipitated from past experience as the stratum' of the individual's life. Parallel to the spontaneity of ego's self-expression through its countenance is alter's spontaneous reading of ego's face. Simmel speaks of a 'peculiar and important sociological art of "knowing" transmitted by the eye' which is 'determined by the fact that the countenance is the essential object of inter-individual sight.' The knowledge gained by immediately scanning another's face is not the kind of understanding that depends upon the analysis of a unit experience into separate traits, but an intuitive apprehension of a *gestalt*. The basis for Simmel's claim that 'a man is first known by his countenance, not by his acts,' is that individuals form immediate impressions of one another, which are not initially objects of reflective judgments, through intuiting one another's facial expressions. Simmel observes that alter's 'initial impression' of ego 'remains ever the keynote of all later knowledge of him; it is the direct perception of his individuality which his appearance, and especially his face, discloses to our glance.'

Simmel, however, observes that the visual impression that alter gains of ego's character is neither simple nor easily interpreted. Indeed, facial expression is so complex and contains so many contrasting emotions at once that scrutiny of another's face is often disquieting. According to Simmel, 'the majority of the stimuli which the face presents are often puzzling.' Spoken language, then, is more abstractive than direct vision and permits the analysis of character into discrete traits which can be recombined in a simplified image: the word is not adequate to the multiplicity contained within a single personality, but it allows individuals to reach working arrangements with one another. Simmel employs the distinction between visual and auditory knowledge of another's character to contrast the life of the metropolis with that of the small town. In the latter individuals are acquainted with nearly all the people they meet, and are able to interpret the visual data that they receive from others in terms of prior impressions and judgments formed from the data of both sight and hearing. In the metropolis, however, there is a 'great preponderance of occasions to *see* rather than to *hear* people.' The increase in the metropolis of the role of visual impressions informing judgments of character leads to greater perplexity on the parts of individuals about the personality of others, intensifying thereby 'the lack of orientation in the collective life, the sense of utter lonesomeness, and the feeling that the individual is surrounded on all sides by closed doors' (Simmel 1969: 359–60). Visual impressions, therefore, may separate as well as unite. Counterposed to the directness of the mutual glance, which involves both partners in the reciprocal creation or constitution of an emergent social bond, is the confusion generated by the complexity of the self-expressive face, even when it is intuited in a pre-reflective insight.

Simmel's account of the visual constitution of society may be used as a basis for extending his observations into a fuller discussion of the role of vision in social relations. To begin with, the aspect of visual interaction which separates rather than unites individuals may become an element in a relation that is manipulated self-consciously by one or more of the participants in it. Those who do not wish to be known by others may seek to make their faces 'expressionless' (appear to be 'dead pan' or 'poker-faced') or cultivate a fixed expression such as a conventional smile. De Beauvoir (1952: 243) notes that 'all who depend on the caprices of a master' have 'learned to turn toward him a changeless smile or an enigmatic impassivity.' The face, then, may be used as a mask to conceal or even to deceive rather than as a 'theoretical organ' which provides a pre-practical basis for sociality. Indeed, much of social dramaturgy involves such efforts to mask the countenance. The masking process is carried on deliberately and elaborately through the use of make-up, jewelry, sunglasses and beards, all of which either divert attention from facial expression or disguise or hide subjectivity. The use of mirrors allows individuals to gain control over their facial expressions by learning how to manipulate them. Looking at oneself allows one to stabilize or alter one's appearance to others, including the appearance of the 'theoretical organ.' In social positions in which guile must be used to protect interest or gain advantage the art of controlling the appearance of the countenance is highly developed. Celebrities of all sorts employ specialists to aid them in the image combat that plays so great a part in the competitive life of large-scale and impersonal societies. The fashion industry creates and merchandises 'looks,' giving individuals models to guide the masking process and, therefore, encouraging a deindividualization of facial appearance and expression.

Deindividualization through masking becomes a general cultural strategy when one social group is required to be veiled. The veil may function to enhance a sense of mystery about and to protect from being known the person who is being veiled, but it also prevents the veiled person from constituting and, therefore, from influencing the basis of visual interaction. Not-being-seen, in the case of veiling, is a disadvantage to those who might express an autonomous will and influence the judgment of others through facial expression. The veil obliterates the complexity and uniqueness of the individual who is veiled, rendering that individual less problematic and facilitating stereotyping. The insistence that members of subjugated or disadvantaged racial or ethnic groups 'all look the same' is a way of projecting a veil or a mask onto them. Being effectively masked they become instances of a type and are treated accordingly. Deindividualization through masking also prevents the emergence of spontaneous sympathy for those who are exploited or treated unjustly. They are made interchangeable members of a species or mere utensils by being deprived of the use of their 'theoretical organ.' The attempts made by people to mask themselves and the use of masking to control and exploit entire groups shows that, depending upon the context, both masking and untrammelled expressivity may work to an individual's advantage. In encounter-group, interview, inquisitorial or commune situations being unable to mask oneself may make one as vulnerable to exploitation as having to wear a veil does in some traditional or fundamentalist societies.

The face is far easier to manipulate and control than are the eyes. Those who seek to conceal from others what their eyes reveal must cover them or avert them. Simmel notes that 'shame causes a person to look at the ground to avoid the glance of the other,' not only because 'he is thus spared the visible evidence of the way in which the other regards his painful situation,' but for the 'deeper reason' that 'the lowering of the glance to a certain degree prevents the other from comprehending the extent of his confusion.' Thus, according to Simmel (1969: 358–9), the 'ostrich policy has in this explanation a real justification: who does not see the other actually conceals himself in part from the observer.' Similarly, expanding on Simmel's points, those who intend to tell a lie often avert their eyes, leading to the widespread belief that there is far more assurance of a truthful statement if the speaker 'looks one straight in the eye.' Shame indicates that one judges and feels oneself to be at a disadvantage in a social relation, whereas lying is a breach of a fundamental social norm. In the former case the one who feels shame cannot tolerate the equality of the gaze, whereas in the latter case the one who lies is not adequate to the mutuality of the glance.

The purest form of mutual glancing is the lover's look in which the two partners deliver themselves unreservedly to one another in a self-conscious commitment and 'drink' one another in with their eyes. The lover's look and the 'knowing,' 'understanding' or 'candid' look that is exchanged among friends show the equality and mutuality of glancing at their fullest in concrete social relations. The glance among lovers and friends is a way of constituting a communion and perhaps a conspiracy beyond conventional social norms. Through 'looking long' into one another's eyes lovers learn to entrust themselves to one another. Those who wish to bring another into an orbit of love or friendship may begin by casting 'furtive glances' at the other, hoping for a response. The furtive glance betrays both a feeling of inferiority (shyness) and an attempt to surmount it, because if the glance is ever returned warmly the initiator will be brought into a relation of equality. Whenever equality or mutuality is not sought attempts will be made to inhibit the glance. The power of the glance to bind individuals to one another mutually is acknowledged in impersonal public situations in which people wish to avoid involvement with one another. Hence, people hide behind newspapers on buses and subways, and look up at the floor lights in elevators. Such distancing measures alleviate the intuition of the problematicity of the other which Simmel believed is a hallmark of metropolitan life, blunt sympathy and aversion, and prevent one's being a mark for further interaction by foreclosing the possibility of being noticed. Indeed, attracting another's glance or responding to it is a primary way of initiating interaction not only among associates and acquaintances, but among strangers. The built-in suspicion of metropolitan life makes necessary an arsenal of positive measures against eye contact. Similarly the equalizing power of the glance is acknowledged in relations of domination–subordination. For example, de Beauvoir (1952) notes that French women who dared look into the eyes of a man were presumed to be sexually promiscuous and were treated accordingly, and Dollard (1937) observes that blacks in the southern United States were punished for looking whites in the eye. In both cases looking a member of the superior group in the eye was interpreted as brazenness or as an assertion of equality, of the will to be an independent and equal initiator of and participant in a social relation.

A limiting case of the glance is looking into the eyes of the dead. Here neither mutuality nor equality is possible, though there may be on the part of the living a deep wish to recover a vital relation. To seek a subject where there no longer is one is such an eerie, uncanny and disquieting experience that in the West the first act upon the bodies of the newly dead is to close their eyes, to render impossible any further attempt at primordial interaction with the dead by the living. Victims to be executed are often hooded or blind-folded, perhaps as a decisive statement that their relation to the executioner is neither mutual nor equal. Also, perhaps one reason why the blind wear dark glasses in public is to discourage attempts at visual interaction which are doomed to failure. Such negations or privative instances of visual interaction point up clearly the pervasiveness and importance of the primordial form of sociality identified by Simmel as the mutual glance.

Sartre on the objectifying gaze

Whereas Simmel's description of the constitution of the intermental relations through vision is founded on subjective mutuality which creates its own context or frame, Sartre's account of the relation between self and other is based on objectification of one subject by another. Rather than appealing to the act of 'looking into,' which requires that both minded individuals give themselves to each other through their eyes as they take from one another's eyes, Sartre is concerned with the act of 'looking at,' in which the gazer is at a distance from the one who is made an object by the gaze. The 'look,' indeed, is for Sartre the primary medium through which minded individuals are brought to acknowledge themselves as parts of the world of objects: one finds oneself in one's being as an object under the gaze of another minded individual. Sartre, then, does not only attempt to show how intermental relations are constituted through vision, but argues even more profoundly that such relations disclose to individuals an essential aspect of their being, their objectivity, which they could not otherwise apprehend. Social relations are, for Sartre, patterned by the ebb and flow of ego being objectivized by alter's gaze and then reasserting subjectivity by recapturing alter in a gaze. There is no mutuality in the Sartrian scheme, but in its place alternation. The intrinsic or inherent bond described by Simmel, which creates equality without the sacrifice of unique individuality, is replaced by Sartre with an extrinsic and accidental, though yet essential, linkage of superior to inferior, of the looker to the one who is looked at. For Sartre, vision is pre-eminently supervision: the gazer creates the frame in which the one who is gazed at appears as one object among many, with determinate relations to those objects which are fixed by the gazer's visual field and the projects orienting and focusing that field. Being objectified by another's look passes easily into becoming a means for another's ulterior ends. One might say that the Simmelian glance founds an evanescent 'kingdom of ends,' whereas the Sartrian look creates a tyranny of means.

Sartre's (1956) description of the constitution of social relations through vision appears in Part III of *Being and Nothingness* where he discusses the grounds for the possibility of 'being-for-others.' His sociology of sight is an integral part of his existential ontology in which the human existent is defined as a being whose free projection of possibilities with reference to a world of objects constitutes a movement towards an unattainable self-sufficient totality. Each human existent, then, is for itself an absolute center of subjectivity before which a world is spread out. Sartre's starting-point can be grasped by appealing to that moment of conscious life in which the individual becomes disengaged or steps back from involvement in a particular activity and surveys the field in which that activity has occurred. At the moment of survey the visual field is spread out before the individual as a set of objects unified into a perspective and relative to the center of sight which is perceiving them. As the individual previses a fresh action the objects in the visual field are organized into a hierarchy of importance, some of them as aids and others as obstacles to the germinating project. The objects in themselves are stubbornly independent of the individual, but their meaning is conferred on them by the individual's project. As the new action is initiated disengagement is lost and involvement takes its place. For example, in preparing a meal I may extend my consciousness into involvement in a particular task such as cutting up a vegetable. As I conclude the task I may observe the results of my work and begin to evaluate whether I have cut a sufficient amount of pieces, whether I should add another vegetable, and so on. At the moment of evaluation the kitchen may stand out for me as the field of my activity: I am disengaged from it at this moment and transcend it passively as an observer. As I begin to formulate a resolve to start cooking the vegetable the components of my visual field are organized in accordance with the prevised action and observation passes over into a practice or participation, only to be succeeded at another juncture by a fresh disengagement. Throughout the entire cycle the only subjectivity involved is my own, whether it is spread out among the objects or tightly focused in a survey. I do not grasp myself as an object among the others, but I simply am the subject to whom the objects are relative.

It is into the kind of vital existential solipsism just described that the other breaks in to dissolve, relativize or de-totalize the absolute subjectivity of the individual. Under the gaze of the other the individual is made aware of being part of an alien visual field structured by alien possibilities and, thus, of being an object. Sartre (1956: 263) notes:

I grasp the Other's look at the very center of my act as the solidification and alienation of my own possibilities. In fear or in anxious or prudent anticipation, I perceive that these possibilities which I *am* and which are the conditions of my transcendence are given also to another as about to be transcended in turn by his own possibilities. The Other as a look is only that – my transcendence transcended.

For Sartre the key to the objectification of ego by alter's gaze is to confer on ego an 'outside,' a delimited surface. Ego's projection of possibility, transcendence or being-for-itself (*pour-soi*) becomes, according to Sartre (p. 262), 'for whoever makes himself a witness of it (i.e. determines himself *as not being* my transcendence) a purely established transcendence, a given-transcendence; that is, it acquires a nature by the sole fact that the *Other* confers on it an outside.' For example, if, as I am cutting up my vegetables, another individual enters the kitchen and gazes at me, my subjectivity no longer dominates the field and my acts are fixed and defined within an alien perspective. As I become aware of the other's gaze I apprehend myself as an object for that gaze, or, in ordinary parlance, I become self-conscious. For Sartre, in a world of many minded individuals ego is under the permanent possibility of being objectified by an alter. The permanent possibility of the look creates the permanence of the individual's social dimension, whether or not another individual happens to be present at a certain time and place.

Sartre emphasizes that the look is a pure form of the constitution of the social relation. Ego is given an outside by an alter, not, claims Sartre (1956: 262–3), 'by any distortion or by a refraction which the Other would impose on my transcendence through his categories, but by his very being':

> If there is an Other, whatever or whoever he may be, whatever may be his relations with me, and without his acting upon me in any way except by the pure upsurge of his being – then I have an outside; I have a *nature*.

For Simmel the pure form of visual constitution of the social relation is the creation of a new emergent phenomenon of union, whereas for Sartre the pure form is the dissolution of the unity of ego's world into alter's world and ultimately the division of one world into multiple and clashing perspectives. Even more deeply, in Sartre's account ego becomes social by becoming divided within itself through alter's gaze. While maintaining its own projection of possibility ego also finds its nature as a given attribute of the particular being which it is for the Other. Whereas Simmelian sociality creates a 'we' Sartrian sociality opens up a distance which cannot be overcome between ego and alter.

The contrast between the accounts of Sartre and Simmel is most apparent in Sartre's discussion of the pure phenomenology of the gaze. According to Sartre, 'we cannot perceive the world and at the same time apprehend a look fastened upon us; it must be either one or the other': 'This is because to perceive is to *look at*, and to apprehend a look is not to apprehend a look-as-object in the world (unless the look is not directed upon us); it is to be conscious of *being looked at*.' Sartre, then, excludes the mutual gazing of Simmel in which ego and alter 'look into' one another's eyes and, thus, deliver themselves to each other's gaze, bathing themselves in their apprehension of it, while they also perceive the other's eyes. Sartre (1956: 258) claims that 'it is never when eyes are looking at you that you can find them beautiful or ugly, that you can remark on their color,' because 'the Other's look hides his eyes; he seems to go *in front of them*.' For Sartre there is none of the spontaneous trust that informs Simmel's account of the gaze: all looks are piercing. To be seen is to 'occupy a place' from which one cannot 'escape' and in which one is 'without defense.' As objects of ego's perception alter's eyes 'remain at a precise distance' which unfolds from the center of ego's perspective to them, whereas the alter's look holds ego at a distance from the center of its perspective. Gazing is a war of visual fields in which the winner is able to set up the distances between selves. It is just such distancing which is created by the Sartrian gaze that the Simmelian glance abolishes. For Sartre one can only 'look at' when one is objectifying the other and is not being objectified by the other. For Simmel perceiving can come as an accompaniment of 'looking into.'

The Sartrian account of the gaze may be expanded upon to open up for description a set of social phenomena which are heterogeneous to those revealed by extending Simmel's account of the glance. In more or less regularized social organization the Sartrian gaze is epitomized by such functions as 'supervision' and 'oversight' that refer to the control of human beings by placing them into an embracing perspective of another individual or group. The pure type of supervision was described by George

Orwell (1961: 5) in *1984*, in which people were watched in their apartments by a 'telescreen' and were surrounded by posters of 'the face of a man of about forty-five, with a heavy black mustache and ruggedly handsome features,' so contrived 'that the eyes follow you about when you move: "BIG BROTHER IS WATCHING YOU," the caption beneath [them] ran.' The telescreen, indeed, concretizes Sartre's idea of the permanent possibility of alter's gaze. So long as one 'remained within the field of vision which the metal plaque commanded,' one 'could be seen as well as heard': 'You had to live – did live, from habit that became instinct – in the assumption that every sound you made was overheard, and except in darkness, every movement scrutinized.'

Though the protagonist Winston kept his back turned to the telescreen he knew that 'even a back can be revealing.' *1984*, then, describes a society subject to the Sartrian gaze employed as a unidirectional mode of social control. 'Looking at' functions to read those at whom the gaze is directed, as a consequence of which they are made perpetually aware of themselves as relative to an alien perspective and, therefore, as objects within that perspective. The supervision described by Orwell in *1984* has its counterpart in everyday social life in all forms of visual monitoring from keeping guard in a prison to proctoring an examination, overseeing a work crew, and actually televising everyday life in lobbies, parking lots, and some stores and public streets. To be monitored is to have a limit put on one's spontaneous projection of possibility relative to a world spreading out from one's own conscious center. Organized monitoring places one in the perspective of a permanent network of rules, making one the object of those projects which are formed by the rules. Under supervision ego becomes aware of itself not as the center of its own life but as relevant to another center of projection.

The paraphernalia of supervision show the unidirectional subject–object structure of the Sartrian gaze. The overseer may wear one-way sunglasses in order to read the others but not to be read by them. In Jeremy Bentham's proposal for an ideal prison, the panopticon, the guards were at the center and could see each of the prisoners ranged around them. Just as in Orwell's *1984*, all modern regimes use pictures or posters of the leader to keep a constant symbolic watch over the citizens or at least over the functionaries. To be made an object may be comforting, as when a parking garage is monitored by television cameras, but their presence calls attention to one's possibility of being prey or predator, closing off any other spontaneous projections. The ideology of supervision transforms the 'looked at' into the 'watched over,' as in the image of the benevolent 'eye of God.' The consequence of being under the eye of God or, for that matter, under the watchful protection of a supervisor, is to be a means to an ulterior design. When being a means involves regularized exploitation and fixed qualitative characteristics of inferiority, the groups held inferior are often required to lower their eyes in the presence of superiors, not only to inhibit mutuality, but so that their gaze cannot transcend the gaze of those who subject them. In *1984*, indeed, one was looked at through the telescreen but could not look back in such a way as to dissolve the other's perspective. Students similarly are not supposed to 'look up' during an examination, but are supposed to mind their work.

Supervision in a more informal and interpersonal context has the twin possibilities of malign and benign objectification. For Sartre, to be seen by another individual is primarily to be 'found out' in one's objecthood, to be rendered self-conscious of one's contingency, particularity, and relativity, in a word, to be deflated. The clearest case of being found out is to be caught in the act of committing a deed of which one is ashamed. The other's gaze confirms one in one's shame and makes the deed escape from its perpetrator and become public property. The presence of an 'inner eye' of conscience within the individual may make for a tyranny of objectification of self as pervasive as Bentham's panopticon or Orwell's telescreen. Sartre concentrates his attention on shame and deflated pride, appealing to the experience of being seen peeking into a keyhole. However, people may seek to be objectified in another's gaze as when they appear in public to be 'seen.' William H. Whyte (1957: 389) notes that the vogue in suburban architecture of picture windows in the 1950s responded to a desire to diminish privacy, which has become identified with loneliness: 'The picture in the picture window, for example, is what is going on *inside* – or, what is going on inside other people's picture windows.' Even to become a spectacle may be a way for someone to be acknowledged, if only superficially as a certain type of exterior. In everyday speech 'keeping up appearances' refers to controlling the way in which one is objectified by others. For Sartre, of course, the wish to be an object within a web of signification is a denial of one's freedom, an exercise of bad faith. But such a judgment should not be used as a way of denying the ubiquity of the phenomenon. Indeed it may be suggested that the experience of being 'looked through,' of having one's objecthood passed by, is far more devastating for ego than being 'looked at' and therefore objectified.

The understanding of the malign possibilities of the objectifying gaze, which follows from Sartre's insights, is exemplified in the phenomenon of staring, in which the aim of making the other an object is self-conscious. In staring contests, which are frequent among children, each participant tries to stare the other down and victory is achieved by ego when alter averts the eyes, leaving alter in ego's field of vision while ego is outside of alter's field. In extreme cases, such as hypnotic states, alter is drawn into ego's gaze and loses the ability to mount independent projects. The superstition of the 'evil eye' in southern Europe is an acknowledgement in folk tradition of the power of the gaze of the other to limit one's independence as a spontaneous source of activity. The phenomenon of staring down or being stared down may be compared to Simmel's mutual glance. Whereas in the latter both participants are enhanced by their joint deliverance to each other, in the former one participant is confirmed at the expense of the other. Staring may be as pure and spontaneous a form of sociality as is mutual gazing, as is evidenced by the possibility of freezing some animals in place by staring at them. In Greek mythology Medusa's gaze turned its objects into stone. Here an alternative interpretation may be given of the practice of masking those who are to be executed: the executioner must be preserved from being dissolved into the perspective of the victim.

The power of the objectifying gaze to render its object helpless and dependent is acknowledged in special social relations in which people are encouraged to express their judgments freely for purposes of penitence or therapy. In the practice of confession in the Catholic Church the penitent is not under the gaze of the confessor. Similarly, in classical Freudian psychoanalysis the analyst sits behind the patient, who is lying down, thereby avoiding eye contact. Freud explicitly was concerned with eliminating hypnotic techniques from analysis and in avoiding the consequent influence of the therapist's suggestion on the patient. Analysis and confession may be regarded as practices in which an alter who is professional and is deemed to be objective creates a context in which ego is allowed the opportunity to objectify its subjectivity before a listener who has ego's ultimate or deeper interests in mind. That the Sartrian gaze is inhibited in these cases indicates how it forestalls such free objectification of the subjective contents. Confession and analysis are meant to constitute the individual as an end, not as a means of another human being's project and so they exclude the gaze, which makes ego an aspect of alter's field of vision. Those practices also exclude the mutual glance which would lead to a common emergent experience rather than a guided reformation of ego's experience.

CONCLUSION

The descriptions of the mutual glance and the objectifying gaze provided, respectively, by Simmel and Sartre are essential contributions to the sociology of the senses, because they show how sensation is not only a medium through which human beings gain information about their situations and circumstances, but is also a fundamental means through which their situations and circumstances are constituted. The ebb and flow of the mutual glance exemplifies the general process through which bonds of unity are forged, maintained and broken. Sight, for Simmel, is not a passive function of cognition primarily, but an activity of self-deliverance to or self-concealment from other persons. Simmel's discussion of seeing, indeed, is a pure phenomenology of the constitution of society which brackets social conventions and social forms in order to uncover essential forms of sociality grounded concretely in the lived body. Simmel's vitalistic perspective, then, produces the same sorts of insights as are found in those social descriptions offered by existential phenomenology, particularly the ideas that sensing is fundamentally participative and only secondarily contemplative, and that the basis of sociality is a preconventional I–Thou relation. Similarly, the alternation of the objectifying gaze in Sartre's account of the structure of sociality brings out how the visual field not only allows ego to perceive alter alongside other objects, but makes alter aware of its own otherness, both to ego and to itself, breaking down the native solipsism of self-centrality and enforcing the objectivity of self which is necessary for mediated social relations. The objectifying gaze is a basis, validated by phenomenological insight, for relations of competition and domination, and for hierarchical and impersonal organization. Supervision, for Sartre, is an essential element in producing, reproducing and challenging the master–servant relation which, following Hegel, he believes to be the basic social relation underlying all conventional forms of interactive conduct.

The phenomenological cogency of the descriptions given by Simmel and Sartre suggests that the possibility of society may rest on both mutuality and objectification. The immediate unity forged by the mutual glance is necessary for producing the trust to sustain cooperative relations and to revitalize continually bonds of community: it allows for a spontaneous 'we' perpetually to emerge from an 'I–Thou.' But individual responsibility and independent initiative demand a defensive and self-enclosed posture which arises when ego is made aware of its differences from alter by being made a part of alter's field. Deliberate individuality is an assertion of oneself against one's objectification by another, and, though it is ever frustrated and ultimately futile, it keeps society from degenerating into a herd. Indeed, the mutual glance only stands out as a precious consummation because it is constituted by individuals who must risk themselves in their deliverance to one another and, therefore, have already gained deliberate and determinate selves through their protest against objectification. In contrast, the vicious spiral of one transcendence outbidding the next and in turn being outbid is broken by mutuality. Whereas objectification prevents degradation of society into a herd, mutuality limits the dissolution of society into competitive egotism. What is so remarkable about vision is that it allows human beings spontaneously to achieve the equilibrated tension that characterizes society in its fullest expression.

POSTMODERNIZING SIMMEL

We are now ready for postmodern(ized) Simmel. The post-modernization project undertaken in the following clusters of essays is multiform, ranging from modern commentaries that show postmodern themes in Simmel's writings to postmodern(ist) writings that extend Simmelian discourses into discursive regions that Simmel could never have taken them. Along the way from interpretation to appropriation are many intermediate zones, defining what lies in the range of postmodern(ized) Simmel. There are also many different definitions of postmodern(ism) that appear in the essays, following along with the changes in style and critical aim.

This is, on the 'whole,' a postmodern(ist) text; that is, it is explicitly deconstructed in the sense that it lets its master name – postmodern – play freely through the text(s), adapting to its specific context, rather than attempting to impose a regime of control through the illusion of a master context or meta-context. Yet that master name remains, disciplining Simmel to confinement to its ragged boundaries. Those boundaries, of course, shift, as the term is specified differently (along with related terms), but there is a running disposition to respect the postmodern flip to the privileging of culture – or at least a half turn, the Simmelian coin standing on its edge between modern and postmodern. There is no disposition to settle some non-existent score between postmodernisms, but instead there is an effort to hook Simmel into as many of them as possible. Indeed, Simmel the manifold being comes into his own as postmodernized because in the discourses of postmodernity he is not forced to be any one thing, but can evince his complexity by becoming appropriate to many postmodernisms.

The project of postmodernizing Simmel did not originate as an abstract conception but took shape and crystallized after three of the essays that follow were written. The preceding study of the gaze shows the discursive ground that our longstanding collaboration occupied before we began postmodernizing Simmel and, obviously, our 'selves.' How postmodern we were willing to make Simmel depended on how postmodern we dared to be ourselves. That is, postmodernizing Simmel was a genuine process of change for us – the move from the existential phenomenology we had been practicing to the inclusivist postmodernism defined at the beginning of this introduction that we (mostly) practice now. We will trace that process in order to place the essays that follow within it. Read one way, this book is a case-study of how to (become) postmodernize(d).

We first became aware of the connections of Simmel to postmodernist discourses while, in the mid-1980s, we were working on a translation and introduction to Simmel's (1986) *Schopenhauer and Nietzsche*. We realized that Simmel's form(s) of philosophizing were deconstructive in the sense that they did not allow any symbolic reconciliation of textual diversity even though they seemed to be ruled by master names such as 'Subject' or

'Life.' We also found that 'deconstruction' in a metaphorical sense was an apt name for the way Simmel described 'Life' itself in his late life-philosophy. These recognitions inspired us to start taking a new look at the two Simmel texts that we had long considered to be the most theoretically important in his canon – 'The Metropolis and Mental Life' and 'The Conflict in Modern Culture.' Reading these with a view to detecting evidences of deconstruction we produced a series of three modern(ist) commentaries on the anticipations of postmodernism in them and in related texts brought in for support. The three initial essays are Chapters 4, 5, and 6 of this book, presented in the sequence in which they were written. Together they map out the poles of the Simmelian postmodern(s) that are presented in the final chapter, but we were not thinking in those terms when we wrote them.

The strategic break with modernism came after we went back to Jacques Derrida in an effort to link Simmel even more closely to deconstruction. Our new reading of Derrida in the light of Simmel led us to focus primarily on the former's essay 'Différance,' where the repudiation of control by master names is blended with a defense of symbolic play. We made a link between Derridian play and Simmelian play-form, and wrote a piece in a Derridian/Simmelian manner, attempting to engineer a rapprochement between modernism and postmodernism from the postmodern side (Chapter 3) by showing the relations between Simmel's textual strategy of stalemating in *Schopenhauer and Nietzsche* and deconstruction. This is where we made the postmodern flip (half turn), accepting the regency of 'culture,' but fighting for constitutional monarchy.

Two more writings of rapprochement quickly followed. First, we had the idea of extending Simmel into the postmodern by writing a new section on postmodern culture to his 'Conflict,' that is, moving through interpretation to respectful appropriation (indeed, tribute). That experiment (Chapter 7) brought out a mediating vision of postmodernity based on play – the third Simmelian postmodern presented in the final chapter. Next we finally felt ready to undertake our own response to the issue of Simmel's intellectual character (Chapter 2), arranging in the process a rapprochement between Simmel and Claude Lévi-Strauss. By that time the organization of the book had crystallized.

The extension of Simmel into postmodernity through our new section of 'The Conflict' involved the historization of deconstruction in terms of Simmel's notion of cultural history. That opened up the problem of 'history' for us as the modern master name, especially the historical-subject / subject-constituted-in/by-history. We wrote two deconstructive essays (Chapters 8 and 9) in which we tried to push Simmel into uncharted territory, pairing him with Nietzsche and Michel Foucault, and stretching our own limits as far as we could, going to excess at times but finally drawing back in a flurry of doubt and questioning, of undecidability, which seemed to us a (dis)comforting Simmelian state of 'mind.' We were in sight of the end of our odyssey.

All that remained was to write the part of the introduction preceding 'The Visual Constitution of Society' and then to survey the whole body of writing and discern whatever connections there might be. The result was Chapter 10, in which three Simmelian postmoderns are brought forward in a loose dialectical pattern. Compare 'The Visual Constitution' and the last section of Chapter 10, and judge for yourself what kind of difference post-modernization makes.

The organization of this book does not strictly follow the sequence of our intellectual journey. By the time that we completed the rapprochement between Simmel and Derrida on the procedure of symbolic play we had the idea of making clusters of probes into the Simmelian postmodern(s). Each cluster would constitute a particular way of postmodernizing Simmel and a separable region of issues. Future essays were planned around that broad design.

The first cluster, 'Simmel as Postmodernist,' contains the essays on Simmel's intellectual character and on the practice of symbolic play. In the former we present our own postmodern intervention into the character question, making the case that Simmel is more the Lévi-Straussian *bricoleur* than Frisby's *flâneur*, and illustrating Simmel's method of *bricolage* by a structural analysis of 'The Metropolis.' In the latter piece we show the deconstructive possibilities of Simmel's method, which are in the same strategic family as the de-totalization of the *bricoleur*. This cluster extends and deepens the preceding discussion of Simmel's intellectual character and approach, showing Simmel as postmodern methodologist.

The second cluster, 'Postmodern Simmel,' contains the first three essays that we wrote, moving from an emphasis, in the first, on the metropolis as deconstructed society, to a focus on the conflict in modern culture as the deconstruction of (Simmelian) 'Life' through vital rebellion and positive nihilism in the last. Going through these three essays one can grasp the sweep of the Simmelian postmoderns between cultural tyranny ('The Metropolis') and vital rebellion against it ('The Conflict'). In this cluster (post)modernism is presented in Simmel's own terms with allusions to current postmodernisms. This is probably the cluster that one should read first if one is not practiced in postmodern discourses. The essays here will help prepare the reader for the others.

The third cluster, 'Postmodern(ized) Simmel,' contains the essay historizing deconstruction and extending 'The Conflict' into the postmodern period of the supremacy of culture, the two essays on historization, and the conclusion. Here Simmel is appropriated for various uses in contemporary discourses that he could not have anticipated, by extending his texts into postmodernity through invention, by showing their problematicity on questions relating to the constitution of histories, and by using them to enhance current discourses. Finally, in the conclusion, there is a free appropriation of Simmel for the construction of Simmelian postmoderns.

Throughout the essays certain of Simmel's writings are visited several times, each time in a different way and with different supporting and supplementary texts. Derrida (deconstruction) plays a major role in configuring the Simmelian postmodern(s), but not so much as to prevent others, such as Arthur Kroker, Lévi-Strauss, and Foucault, from intervening in significant ways, and others, such as Jean Baudrillard and Jean-François Lyotard from leaving strong traces.

In retrospect these essays (in the strict sense of exploratory efforts) are concerned more than anything else with problematizing postmodern subjectivity, but they can also be plausibly read as reflections on historization (and surely in many other ways). That is, there is no totalization here, but there are several possibilities for bricolage, which is what (we believe) we have been able to provide ... as might be expected from Simmelian (post)modernists.

Part I

Simmel as postmodernist

Chapter 2

Georg Simmel: sociological ~~flâneur~~ bricoleur

Raising questions about the intellectual character of famous thinkers, creative artists, and even scientists, who have worked in the twentieth century, has become all the fashion. One need only think of the Heidegger-Nazi affair to grasp the shift in attention from critiquing the status and validity of propositions to criticizing the character of those who formulate them. To a lesser degree the character issue has been raised about many, if not most, of the leading figures of the twentieth-century humanities.

There is no need to deplore the change in focus from validity to virtue, but only to insist that the criticism of character be taken seriously. Current concern about character is based most deeply on an awareness that although it may not be possible to determine the truth about such things as human nature or the meaning of being, it is still necessary to reflect on one's engagement with one's circumstances. With what attitude, disposition, or manner of being-in-the-world should one engage in the humanities and, by extension, the social sciences? This is a serious question, especially if one agrees with Nietzsche and Heidegger that thinking is grounded in mood or manner of attunement (*Stimmung*). As Simmel understood, temperament becomes of primary importance when the objectivity of truth claims is thrown into doubt. One finds the only truth that one is capable of discerning in one's manner of participating in the struggles of one's life. Criticism of intellectual character, life-style, virtue, temperament, sensibility, mentality, taste, and personality becomes the path of Socratic reflexivity for the contemporary intellect.

Of course, the character issue can be and is raised in other than Socratic ways. Character assassination parades comfortably in the mask of aesthetic and moral criticism. It may be actuated by *ressentiment,* a devaluation of intellectual values in terms of conventional social and personal morality. It may function as mere name calling in interperspectival debate. It may reveal that the humanities have been permeated by the standards and sensibility of the gossip column and the scandal sheet. Whether criticism of intellectual character is high minded or a low blow is not always easy to determine. But it must be treated as if it were serious, just in case it is.

Georg Simmel has come in for his share of character criticism. In his major work on Simmel, *Sociological Impressionism,* David Frisby (1981: 68–101) discusses the question of whether or not Simmel is a sociological *flâneur,* in the sense that Walter Benjamin used that term. The term *flâneur* certainly has pejorative connotations and was not one that Simmel chose for characterizing himself. The following discussion will consider the question of Simmel's intellectual character, with the aim of presenting an alternative vision of it to Frisby's. Rather than being Benjamin's *flâneur,* Simmel will be seen to be more like Claude Lévi-Strauss's *bricoleur.* The discussion will proceed first by examining the Benjamin or Frisby definition of *flâneur* and how Frisby applies it to Simmel's sociological practice. Then a Simmelian analysis of the form of the *flâneur* will be worked up as a prelude to considering whether Simmel's 'The Metropolis and Mental Life,' his well-known and influential essay on the *flâneur's* environment, is the work of a *flâneur.* The conclusion will be that it is best understood not as the product of a *flâneur,* but as the reflexive analysis of the modern urban scene as a *bricolage,* calling for the virtues of the *bricoleur.* That is, the metropolis is the site of postmodernity, and the intellectual character most appropriate for describing it is developed in postmodernist discourse, not in the gallery of human types received from the first half of the nineteenth century.

For Frisby, Simmel is an escapist to a period of urban development earlier than the one in which he wrote. In the present writing, Simmel is an anticipator of postmodernism, presenting a thought contemporaneous to postmodernism's. That is, Simmel is a postmodernist in advance of the discourse. The recent wave of interest in his work, then, would reflect, at least in part, the relevance of that work to clarifying current circumstances, even when that interest is in discrediting his thought. Otherwise the Simmel boom would simply be an internal development of the academic scholarship industry. Perhaps it is partly that, but the presumption here will be that Frisby, at least, takes on Simmel because he believes that Simmel's thought has significance beyond some Simmel industry. Implied here is that the issue of Simmel's character is keyed to the culture war between modern progressivism and postmodern criticism, between diachrony and synchrony. There is no essential Simmel, only different Simmels read through the various positions in contemporary discourse formations. Yet the aim of criticism is to make one of the accounts more compelling than its competitors, to rely on plausibility rather than a proof, which is impossible in this field.

THE *FLÂNEUR*

The foundation of criticism of intellectual character for Benjamin and Frisby is a neo-Marxist version of the sociology of knowledge. That is, the intellectual character of someone who does not hold to some variant of a broadly defined Marxist world-perspective is a victim of class bias. More specifically, those who break with progressivism of a Marxist sort place themselves outside history, in some class-protective fantasia or *imaginaire*. The Benjamin and Frisby critique of character is a critique of ideology.

In essence, the critique is simple, at least as applied by Benjamin to Baudelaire and by Frisby to Simmel: those who de-totalize modernity, who have no coherent account of the whole of modern society, are retreatists from the great historical conflicts. Could they help themselves? Benjamin and Frisby are equivocal. But at least some intellectuals (like Benjamin and Frisby) join the progressive forces, so one might be tempted to think that some weakness in moral fiber or in intellectual competence might help to account for de-totalizing intellectuals. Benjamin and Frisby do not want to come right out and say 'character flaw,' partly, perhaps, because it would conflict with their sociological approach, which minimizes voluntarism. So they compromise by using the rhetorical technique of innuendo. In summary, they explain the de-totalizer as a victim of class bias who has, perhaps, contributed to his victimage by possessing a weak character. That the de-totalizer doesn't have the guts to commit himself to the historical struggle (at least reactionaries take a stand) is the more visceral message that Benjamin and Frisby sublimate: too timid to mix in; prone to escapism; holds himself aloof from others and has fantasies of superiority that mask his inferiority feelings. That is the diagnosis or indictment. The next move is to see how it is presented.

The rhetorical imagery providing the aesthetic dimension of Benjamin's and Frisby's critique of retreatism is the figure of the *flâneur*, a Parisian type, a kind of metropolitan persona of the mid-nineteenth century. When he associates, indeed, identifies Baudelaire with the *flâneur*, Benjamin is deprecating him. However much he may end up spiritualizing and embroidering the term so that it becomes applicable to an artist or intellectual (artist-intellectual), *'flâneur'* is at root and in its received connotations a term of opprobrium referring to someone who is not serious, indeed, someone who is socially superfluous, an idler, and, worse, a supercilious idler. Benjamin quotes Paul Ernest de Rattier's 1857 utopia, *Paris n'existe plus* to the effect that the *flâneur* is a 'nonentity,' a 'constant rubberneck,' and an 'inconsequential type,' who is 'always in search of cheap emotions' and knows about 'nothing but cobblestones, fiacres, and gas lanterns.' The *flâneur* was the kind of person who, around 1840, would take a turtle for a walk around the Paris arcades, letting the turtle, of course, set the pace (Benjamin 1973: 54). In 1845 Ferdinand von Gall says that the *flâneur* provides 'the strollers and the smokers' with their chronicler and philosopher (Benjamin 1973: 37). One gets the idea of what the *flâneur* is at the cobblestone level. To respectable opinion he is a social waste product. To the morally sensitive he is a fraud, a tin-horn aristocrat: facetious; fatuous; making sport of the city's serious business. The term cannot help but retain these associations when it is used to characterize an artist-intellectual like Baudelaire or an intellectual-artist like Simmel. They are, of course, not really *flâneurs* in the strict sense, but somehow they are like *flâneurs*, spiritually.

For Benjamin, the point in drawing an analogy (homology?) between the *flâneur* and Baudelaire is that both epitomize the mentality and sensibility of the nineteenth-century petty bourgeoisie. This class was, according to Benjamin, passing its time until its members would have to 'become aware of the commodity nature of their labour power.' In the meantime the petty bourgeoisie could seek enjoyment not *in*, but *from* the society, as semi-detached spectators of the spectacle of urban capitalism: 'If it wanted to achieve virtuosity in this kind of enjoyment, it could not spurn empathizing with commodities' (Benjamin 1973: 59). Baudelaire, then, is the virtuous *flâneur*, someone who makes it a self-conscious practice to perfect the stroller's art of observing the urban spectacle. He empathizes, for example, with the prostitute, enjoying her damage and decay at a distance. He owed his enjoyment of society to having 'already withdrawn from it' (p. 59).

In Benjamin's hands, Baudelaire's *disponibilité* of the imagination becomes empathy with the commodity, which means identification with it: Baudelaire speaks as and for the commodity. Says Benjamin (1973: 55), the 'soul' of the commodity, mentioned in jest by Marx, 'would be the most empathetic ever encountered in the realm of souls, for it would have to see in everyone the buyer in whose hand and house it wants to nestle.' Poor commodity, which doesn't want to be homeless! Poor *flâneur*/Baudelaire, by extension, who doesn't want to stroll aimlessly, semi-detached from society, superfluous! More, perhaps, to be pitied than scorned. Benjamin's (p. 58) intent is captured when he quotes approvingly Engels's indictment of the metropolis as a place where people 'crowd by one another as though they had nothing in common, nothing to do with each other, and their only agreement is the tacit one, that each keep to his own side of the pavement, so as not to delay the opposing stream of the crowd, while it occurs to no man to honour another with so much as a glance.' Engels's sentimentalism is what rules Benjamin's critique of Baudelaire as *flâneur*. Simmel, in 'The Metropolis and Mental Life,' provides a functional explanation of the urban phenomena that Engels emotes about. That does not concern Benjamin, who pities and scorns Baudelaire's failure (a failure from Benjamin's, but, perhaps, a strength from another viewpoint) to become solidary with others (the proletariat).

No one will deny the difference between the sensitivity of Baudelaire and the superficiality of the standard-issue *flâneur*. But that sensitivity only makes the pathos of retreatism more acute; the sense of a wasted life that knows itself to be such is more pathetic than the sense of a wasted life which veils its impotence in a supercilious mystique. He is more, perhaps, to be pitied than scorned. When Frisby takes up Benjamin's image of the *flâneur* and applies it to Simmel, he also takes up Benjamin's spirit.

Frisby on Simmel is more elusive than Benjamin on Baudelaire. Ironically, Frisby (1981: 77), who makes a point of noting Simmel's reputation as 'the philosopher of the "perhaps," ' introduces his discussion of Simmel/*flâneur* by suggesting that an examination of 'Simmel's manner of working and his relation to his subject matter might prompt comparison with Benjamin's analysis of the *flâneur*. It might raise the question of how far Simmel himself is a "sociological *flâneur*." ' Simmel was rarely that provisional. Indeed, Frisby never answers the question that titles his chapter: 'A Sociological *Flâneur*?' But it's probably safe to say that he wouldn't have brought up the issue if he didn't see a Simmel–*flâneur* connection.

Frisby makes that connection when he recurs to Benjamin's judgment that Baudelaire had 'half withdrawn' from society. He (1981: 79) remarks: 'Such a judgment could equally apply to many of Simmel's essays. Simmel, too, could extract from the seemingly most insignificant details of social life the most interesting connections. In this respect, we might see Simmel as a *flâneur* for the intelligentsia, providing them with the most subtle analyses of all manner of social phenomena without disturbing any of them.' 'Might' again, but all right. The association is there. Simmel is similar to the *flâneur* because he observes the details of life without disturbing them. His works, indeed, are 'harmless.' That is, they do not indicate, promote, or prescribe a commitment to and program of action, but are simply collections of intellectual miniatures catering to the aesthetic-intellectual proclivities of the refined tastes of the salon. Rather than being the chronicler and philosopher of the strollers and smokers, Simmel is provisioner and panderer to the intellectual diversions of the *haute bourgeoisie*.

Whether or not Frisby's description of Simmel's work is accurate (its accuracy will be disputed below), it is the description of the practice of a sociological *flâneur*. Frisby does not ground his judgment in any scrutiny of Simmel's texts, but supports it with quotes from Simmel's contemporaries and later commentators. Koppel, for example, calls Simmel 'the intellectual neurasthenic,' which Frisby (1981: 80) finds 'most remarkable of all' because Simmel singled out neurasthenia as a condition in which 'reality is not touched with direct confidence but with fingertips that are immediately withdrawn.' Simmel's theory of social pathology is a symptom of his own disease. By the same reasoning Frisby might turn out to be a *flâneur* himself.

Frisby follows Benjamin's example by making Simmel a victim of class bias in addition to revealing a personality defect (neurasthenia) in him. Unlike Baudelaire, Simmel cannot be called a petty bourgeois, so the analogy with the *flâneur* is more tenuous in his case. For Frisby, the most proximate social type to Simmel is the salon intellectual who values the interesting fragment or charming vignette higher than the systematic totalization. Simmel, indeed, ran a salon, and it is pointless to deny that the norms of polite conversation impacted on his writing style. Whether they governed the content of his thought is another question. The salon intellectual is made by Frisby the bourgeois equivalent of the *flâneur*. Both of them are innocuous and, finally, superfluous. In this light Simmel's sociological works become 'images of a section of the bourgeoisie that is no longer confident, that feels the need to distance itself from a reality it no longer controls' (Frisby 1981: 83). That is, just like Benjamin's petty bourgeoisie, the educated bourgeoisie in imperial Germany had nothing to do but pass its time, and it was enabled to do so by aestheticizing its reality.

The critiques of Simmel's character and of the class bias of his thought come together in Frisby's notion that Simmel is a retreatist. Alluding to Simmel's idea that the objective and subjective dimensions of culture are in conflict in modern life, Frisby (1981: 88) asserts: 'The response to this tragic contradiction is the inward retreat to subjectivism, the retreat to the *intérieur*.' There is no need to deny the cogency of a class analysis to explain aspects of Simmel's thought in order to question the characterization of him as a retreatist. Indeed, the term retreatist does not seem adequate to characterize even the *flâneur*, who makes a point of going out in the world, if only to observe it. It certainly does not provide the complexity necessary to account for why someone would study intensively that which they are determined to hold at a distance.

What is a *flâneur*, if not a retreatist? To answer this question it might first be advisable to sketch a Simmel-style formal analysis of the *flâneur* along lines consistent with Benjamin's definition of the type, though not necessarily with his interpretation of it. Although the *flâneur* does not appear in Simmel's own gallery of social forms, the type is amenable to Simmelian analysis because it shares boundary-crossing and mediating attributes with such figures as the stranger and the adventurer. The *flâneur*, according to Benjamin, takes the urban scene as a spectacle, strolling through it as though it were a diorama, that is, detached from involvement with its practical concerns and purposes. In making public places into playgrounds, the *flâneur* takes advantage of the systems of public order and control, and of production, which permit him to stroll safely and be entertained by the human comedy. He does not contribute to the maintenance or alteration of these systems, but is parasitical off them. The *flâneur* could not exist on a desert island or in the state of nature. He might be called a 'surplus value' of the city, a type made possible by industrial capitalism and inconceivable beyond the protected environment that it provides to the bourgeoisie in periods of relative stability. The *flâneur* dehistorizes the city, breaking it apart into a shower of events, primarily sights. He emphasizes synchrony over diachrony, and has no interest in systematizing the fragments of urban life. Each one is an aesthetic object to him, existing to titillate, astonish, please, or delight him. He appropriates the city as performance art, not seeking to know it and certainly not trying to reform it, but merely enjoying it.

The *flâneur*'s supercilious manner, so despised by respectable society, is necessary to protect him from being taken seriously by others. The *flâneur* is an observer, a spectator, a gazer; and, as both Simmel and Sartre have shown vividly, the glance has powerful effects on the psyche and in constituting social relations. The *flâneur* would be met with antipathy and in some cases would even be endangered if he adopted the pose of surveillance. By playing the fop he shows everyone that he is not concerned with finding them out, but, indeed, deems them unworthy of all but superficial and momentary attention. In order not to provoke fear he risks provoking scorn. He must be innocuous in order that society be innocuous for him. Too detached to be a gossip, he is not above listening to gossip as another emanation of the urban scene. The *flâneur* is an idler, but he passes his time in the midst of the world of affairs.

Benjamin is astute when he identifies the *flâneur* with Poe's 'man of the crowd,' who cannot exist apart from the presence of other human beings, but has no positive relations with them. He seeks out others with desperation, because he panics at being by himself. The *flâneur* is, perhaps, a sublimation of the man of the crowd, able at least to hold himself a bit aloof from the society that provides him with the *raison d'être* of his life. Rather than suffering from a psychosis, an implosion of self, like the man of the crowd, the *flâneur* shows signs of neurosis, of life lived as a compromise.

Perhaps the term 'neurasthenia' applies well here, since the *flâneur* does not seem to touch reality with direct confidence but with 'fingertips that are immediately withdrawn.' It is like the game that the moth plays with the flame and it might be a way of neutralizing the overload of urban stimuli, of coping with a fear of others or with a fear of one's own inadequacy in relation to others, or, more fundamentally, of coping with an ambivalence toward others, a need of and a loathing for them, the hallmark of Kant's 'unsociable social being,' the empirical self. If Simmel is called a *flâneur*, perhaps what is meant most deeply is that he has this ambivalence in an acute form, that he must toy with his fellow human beings but does not have the strength of humanity to commit himself to them. In terms of psychology, the *flâneur*/Simmel would, according to this view, be determined by inferiority feelings which had blossomed into the classical inferiority complex: airs of superiority; unwillingness to risk himself for fear of revealing his inferiority; abstention from the struggles of the community. Perhaps there is some truth to this, both as a psychology of the *flâneur* and as a diagnosis of Simmel. But there is only some truth, because there is an alternative to this character criticism.

In his treatment of the *flâneur* Benjamin quotes Simmel, not to criticize him, but for theoretical support. According to Simmel (Benjamin 1973: 37–8), 'Someone who sees without hearing is much more uneasy than someone who hears without seeing. . . . Interpersonal relationships in big cities are distinguished by a marked preponderance of the activity of the eye over the activity of the ear.' Simmel then goes on to argue that in systems of public transportation people are thrown into the position of having to look at each other for extended durations without speaking to each other. Perhaps, using one of Simmel's favorite terms, the *flâneur* should be considered the 'play-form' of the practice of refraining from verbal and gestural communication when one cannot help gazing at others and being gazed at by them. The *flâneur* perfects this restraint and makes it into a style of urban living that is productive of pleasure. From this viewpoint the *flâneur*'s practice would be play in the Foucaultian panoptic society, the neutralization or deconstruction of the scrutinizing gaze of commerce and administration, a subversion of the official society, perhaps even a kind of situationist *détournement*. As *détournement* it would not be motivated by feelings of inferiority but by recognition that the community had been eclipsed by systems of planned organization, so that there was no more community to commit oneself to, not even a progressive class.

Here is the core of the matter between Benjamin's and Frisby's modern-progressive criticism of character, and a postmodernist alternative: does the *flâneur* seek to escape from a commitment or is the kind of commitment that Benjamin and Frisby imply questionable itself? It is a problem of the strategies and tactics of engagement in modern/postmodern society, which in turn depends upon the intellectual question concerning the general form of that 'society.' That is, it is not a problem of engagement and retreat, but of different forms of engagement. It would not be so damaging to Simmel's character if it was associated with the play-form interpretation of the *flâneur* presented above. But even in that sense, Simmel is not a *flâneur*. The *flâneur* does not study society, but wanders through it, going, as Benjamin quips, 'botanizing on the asphalt,' that is, collecting experiences. Simmel is more than a collector. He seeks knowledge of his milieu, not merely diversion from it. Even Frisby admits that.

THE *BRICOLEUR*

In the most philosophical moment of his critique of Simmel's intellectual character, Frisby defines the structure of Simmel's thought process and relates it to a fundamental issue in theoretical sociology. For Frisby (1981: 81), 'It is through the examination of the particular and the fragmentary that Simmel hopes to grasp what is universal.' Here Frisby's characterization breaks away from the model of the *flâneur*. While both Simmel and the *flâneur* are concerned with the fragment, no *flâneur* would be caught dead trying to grasp what was universal about it. Simmel is at no distance from the object of knowledge; he is thoroughly engaged with it, seeking to make it yield universal significance. He lets that object be only insofar as it is necessary to do so in the interest of objectivity. Beyond that the object is left free for a disciplined conceptual play with it, the cognitive yield of which is chains of significance of diverse cultural objects. The task is to seek whatever orders of homology and analogy can be discerned in what initially appears to be radically heterogeneous. As Frisby (1981: 81) notes, 'Simmel, as the astute wanderer, can connect seemingly isolated fragments with other apparently unrelated fragments.' He is promoted from *flâneur* to astute wanderer (very near to where he belongs).

But Frisby also remarks that although, 'through sensitive reflection upon each of life's fragments one can arrive at an understanding of some aspect of society as a totality, . . . society conceived as a totality is an absent concept in Simmel's thought' (1981: 81). Here is the issue of the culture war on its philosophical plane. Can one credibly conceive of modern/postmodern society as a totality, or is it wiser to conceive of that society as a tangle of tightly and loosely coupled syntagmatic chains? As astute wanderer, Simmel chooses the latter, postmodernist, alternative. Which of the alternatives is the truer is not directly in question here. But if Simmel has some truth on his side, he might not be a *flâneur* or a neurasthenic, but simply sane and lucid. He is mapping the heterogeneous rather than revealing a deeper homogeneity, a common nature that would make diverse appearances a totality. For Simmel, it is a victory to understand 'some aspect of a society' *as a totality*, that is, to construct a totalization of society from one of the aspects in terms of which it can be totalized. There is no totalization of totalizations for him, no meta-narrative, and no deep structures. Such forms simply do not seem to him to be immanent to the complexes of modern culture that are his primary objects of study. Conflicts and stalemates are what seem to be immanent to them. In the absence of system there is the systematization of conflict, postmodern *bricolage*.

The practice of seeking generality through particularity recalls the *bricoleur* that Lévi-Strauss described in *The Savage Mind*. The meaning of *bricoleur* in French popular speech is 'someone who works with his hands and uses devious means compared to those of a craftsman' (Lévi-Strauss 1966: 16–17). That is, the *bricoleur* is a sly handyman, who accumulates a stock of items and takes from it whatever might seem to be useful to complete the job that he is presently doing:

> His universe of instruments is closed and the rules of his game are always to make do with 'whatever is at hand,' that is to stay with a set of tools and materials which is always finite and is also heterogeneous because what it contains bears no relation to the current project, or indeed to any particular project, but is the contingent result of all the occasions there have been to renew

or enrich the stock or to maintain it with the remains of previous constructions or destructions.

(Lévi-Strauss 1966: 17)

The result of the *bricoleur*'s method is a bricolage, a construction that arises from interrogating

all the heterogeneous objects [of which the *bricoleur*'s] treasury is composed to discover what each of them could 'signify' and so contribute to the definition of a set which has yet to materialize but which will ultimately differ from the instrumental set [of the craftsman or engineer] only in the internal disposition of its parts.

(Lévi-Strauss 1966: 18)

The *bricoleur* is practical and gets the job done, but it is not always or even usually the same job that was initially undertaken and is uniquely structured by the set of 'pre-constrained' elements that are selected from the treasury. A substitution of one element for another would change the form of the construction. The *bricoleur* works and plays with the stock. His parts are not standardized or invented; they are appropriated for new uses.

An intellectual *bricoleur* does not do hand work with tools and materials, but brain work with signifiers and significations. As an intellectual *bricoleur*, Simmel deploys a fixed stock of signifiers, the cultural forms that social life has taken. That is, his treasury is the stock of culture that is given to him in his social environment, and the psychological and existential responses that are generally made to it. He does not interpret culture through a utopia, nor does he develop a special technical language to describe its deep structure or to explain its dynamics. Rather, he constructs syntagmatic chains out of the stock, each of which reveals 'some aspect of a society as a totality.' These chains connect, as Frisby noted, 'seemingly isolated fragments with other apparently unrelated fragments.' Simmel's totalizations are constructions of the culture as received, not reintegrations of it. His constructions suggest order within a field of heterogeneous contents. He 'makes do' with 'whatever is at hand.'[1]

Not only is the 'set' with which Simmel works finite; it is also heterogeneous. The cultural forms that compose his stock are the 'contingent results' of life's precipitation of culture, which he uses for the new purpose of aspectival totalization. These forms were not created and are not maintained, altered, or destroyed for the project of totalization, but are the very ways in which society is constituted. If they all happened to fit within a logically coherent system, if they could be described adequately in terms of homology and logical equivalence and negation, all the better. But they cannot be so described, and the intellectual *bricoleur* is constrained to apply such thought forms and processes as analogy and qualitative opposition to the task of construction. Conceived as sociological *bricoleur*, Simmel is on a mission of cultural mapping, tracing the affinities and ruptures among the cultural complexes of the modern/postmodern metropolis. Renouncing transcendence over the given in his capacities of sociologist and cultural theorist, he finds as much order in that given as he can wrest from it by using his intellectual imagination.

Simmel as *bricoleur* is a practitioner of a demystified savage mind, a post-structuralist before the advent of structuralism. The mystified savage mind, the one that Lévi-Strauss devoted himself to describing, works with a finite and heterogeneous stock of signs, but feels compelled to reconcile the heterogeneity through metonymical and metaphorical mediations, which do not provide logical coherence, but which somehow offer satisfaction to that mind, which enjoys the symbolic reconciliation. The demystified savage mind is, in contrast, a postmodern critic, unmasking the reconciliations of the mystified savage mind, showing connections where there was supposed to be separation, and identifying rupture where mythic reconciliation was supposed to have occurred. By pointing out where the ruptures and oppositions appear in structurally based cultural complexes, the sociological *bricoleur* becomes a social diagnostician (not a shaman), who identifies the sites at which myth is most likely to arise. His surprising connections disturb the taboos of hierarchy and of seriousness ('sociability,' for example, becomes indicative of how society is fundamentally constituted), and his disconnections disturb the myths of identification. The *bricoleur* is only innocuous if people are incapable or unwilling to attend to him. Of course, he cannot compel them to entertain a better map of their circumstances. He does not have any 'divisions' to deploy, not even a holy office – only signifiers. He cannot, like Lévi-Strauss, even plead the cause of a future positive science of deep structures, since his rules of the game constrain him to describing the forms that characterize the apparent cultural complexes (within themselves, in relation to each other, and in relation to psychological/existential responses to them). That is, he constructs a *bricolage* from his stock.

METROPOLIS: *BRICOLAGE*

About a third of the way through 'The Metropolis and Mental Life' Simmel (1950b: 413) pauses from his main discussion and reflects on the import of his method:

> the general conclusions of this entire task of reflection become obvious, namely, that from each point on the surface of existence – however closely attached to the surface alone – one may drop a sounding into the depth of the psyche so that all the most banal externalities of life finally are connected with the ultimate decisions concerning the meaning and style of life.

Here is confirmation, expansion, and explanation, in Simmel's text, of Frisby's point that Simmel 'can connect seemingly isolated fragments with other apparently unrelated fragments.' Those fragments can be related to each other intelligibly because all of them are somehow also related to 'ultimate decisions concerning the meaning and style of life.' That does not mean that the psyche generates the appearances, as idealism would hold; nor that the appearances are merely organized in the unconscious mind, as Lévi-Strauss seems to hold; but that there is a relation between the surface and the interior, if only metaphorical. As *bricoleur* Simmel connects the banal externalities of life to each other, and then to what would later in the century be called existential concerns.[2] His relations are meaningful, not causal, but they do not provide a meaning for the totality: they reveal aspects of a totality that shows certain comprehensive patterns of order that answer to the problems posed by the ego-centered discourse of the existential self. But that self is de-centered by the discourse, which does not privilege, causally or ontologically, the existential self; rather, that self appears, not as the protagonist, but as an interlude in a socio-cultural *bricolage*.

As *bricolage* 'The Metropolis and Mental Life' displays a structure of analogy and opposition, metaphor and metonymy, that is, a structure of similarity in difference, and of difference in similarity. Cutting through and yet constituting the chain of discourse is the opposition between the blasé (intellectualized) self, which is interpreted as a defensive action of the self against being overwhelmed by the diverse and often adverse stimuli of the metropolitan environment; and the interior self, associated with romanticism and in rebellion against the metropolis and the defensive adaptations of the psyche to it, which demands expression and acknowledgment of, if not submission to, its unique contents. That is, the metropolis is not productive of one form of mental life, but conditions two irreconcilable, yet intelligible, mental responses to it. One of them, the protective, nurtures the calculative freedom of the rational ego (Enlightenment freedom) and the other, the expressive, is the Romantic freedom to determine one's life according to one's inner nature.

The most comprehensive structure of 'The Metropolis' is metonymic. The totality of metropolitan life is first viewed under the aspect of the defensive self and then under the aspect of the expressive self. Neither one is allowed to claim victory; they stalemate each other, and their stalemate is the synchronic analogue to diachronic theories of meaning and direction in history.[3] There is no meaningful totality: 'The metropolis reveals itself as one of those great historical formations in which opposing streams which enclose life unfold, as well as join one another with equal right' (Simmel 1950b: 423). But there is an intelligible opposition between two versions of and responses to totality, indeed, to the same totality, but with differences. (Enter Derrida and undecidability.) 'The Metropolis' is a *bricolage* in which the form of the 'metropolis' mediates between two alternative totalizations of itself. It cannot unify them, but it can bring them together by placing them on a common ground.

Although that common ground cannot be defined apart from the two aspectival totalizations of it, it is indicated metaphorically by a series of structural analogies between levels of metropolitan life that cut across the opposition between the defensive and expressive responses to the metropolis. Especially in the division of the chain devoted to the defensive self, Simmel composes a fugue, showing how the intellectualization of life, as a protection against sensory and emotional overload, corresponds to the depersonalized and calculating mentality of the money economy, which in turn corresponds to the calculative precision of the natural sciences and the need for a uniform system of mechanical time to coordinate the disparate practical activities of the metropolis. Then he does a reprise, showing how the defense mechanism of the blasé attitude corresponds to the devaluation of the objective world and, finally, of the self in a 'completely internalized money economy,' which in turn corresponds to the psychological reserve, masking mild antipathy, which is required for people to pursue their particular affairs without mutual interference. Thus, Simmel moves from the more superficial to the deeper, using successive sets of analogies between the same three levels, creating a tight weave among the elements he has taken from his stock to place in his *bricolage*.

When he turns to the expressive self, Simmel follows the same strategy of moving from periphery to core, tracing the drive to be unique and different from others first to the sheer size and specialized fragmentation of the metropolis, which makes people strive to be distinguished by each other; and then to the unmasterable 'overgrowth' of objective culture, which threatens to overwhelm individuals and provokes their efforts to summon 'the utmost in uniqueness and particularization,' in order to preserve their most personal cores. Here analogous external structures (size and specialization, and cultural mass and complexity) are related to analogous personal responses (the need to be distinguished by others and the need to distinguish oneself to oneself). Again the relations are analogical and meaningful – a *bricolage* – not homological and causal.

The 'metropolis' is, for Simmel (1950b: 409), a structure 'set up between the individual and the super-individual contents of life,' that is, a mediation between the objective culture of institutionalized pursuits, each with its autonomous standards, and the subjective culture of personal character. But in an 'overgrown' objective culture the metropolis is capable only of mediating opposition to the individual. The stock of the *bricoleur* that is appropriate to defining the most comprehensive social structure, the context of modern life, its physical and socio-cultural site, does not allow for a single and consistent totalization. One form of life, the modern (or postmodern) metropolis, gives rise to opposing responses, through which that form of life is interpreted. Neither response is sustainable as an organizing principle because each excludes what is cogent, intelligible, perhaps, justifiable in the other.

The detached and intellectualized ego, void of emotional response, confronts the expressive self, void of calculative reason. Each is an intelligible response, illuminating an aspect of the totality; but neither is a sufficient response, just because it is aspectival (presents an aspect of totality). The preferred contemporary mythology, advertising, is in large part an exercise in merging these responses, without being able to synthesize them; that is, it identifies circumspective calculation with expressive emotion, the purchase of a commodity with the core of personality. But in the absence of models of character that are appropriate to mediating engagement in a coherent objective culture, the reflective and self-critical individual is forced by the duplicitous mediation of the metropolis to become a *bricoleur*. The incoherence of the stock of signifiers indicates a built-in incoherence to modern life. The individual must cobble together whatever meaning can be wrested from the irreducible and irreconcilable fragments of reality. Even the most fateful and existential decision, that between the two forms of self and of freedom, is made within this socio-cultural horizon of elusive, unrationalizable totality. Simmel has constructed the *bricolage* that makes intelligible the strategy of being the *bricoleur* of one's own personality.

Simmel is a *bricoleur*, not a *flâneur*: he concludes 'The Metropolis' (1950b: 423–4) by asserting that in the process of the struggle between the two responses to (post)modern life and their changing entanglements

> the currents of life, whether their individual phenomena touch us sympathetically or antipathetically, entirely transcend the sphere for which the judge's attitude is appropriate. Since such forces of life have grown into the roots and into the crown of the whole of the historical life in which we, in our fleeting existence as a cell, belong only as a part, it is not our task either to accuse or to pardon, but only to understand.

Sociological progressives (and reactionaries) want to judge, and in order to do so they need to hold that society is a describable totality. Postmodernism, by negating modern historicist sociology, also negates its humanism. There is nowhere that 'man' stands to define 'himself.' Each individual is a cell in an overwhelming organism, which is divided in itself. This is not a 'tragic' view, as Frisby would have it, but something even worse from his viewpoint, a destiny or fatality. But fatality appears only from the form of sociology. For the individual there is liberation to gratuity, which can take up sacrifice or commitment as easily as it can observational play.

Doubtless, the modern self is afraid of the gratuity of any commitment with reference to its historical meaning, that is, of not knowing which side will win or even if the struggle has yet to be decided. But historical gratuity is the grace of the postmodern condition, the opportunity to be a *bricoleur*, to construct a self and strategy of living from the shards of objective culture.

Chapter 3

Simmel/Derrida
~~Deconstruction as symbolic play~~

At the end of his writing, 'Différance,' Jacques Derrida (1973) deconstructs his text by taking on an authoritative rhetorical tone. Reflecting back on his discussion of metaphysics, Derrida (1973: 160) announces 'There will be no unique name, even if it were the name of Being.' And then he takes a surprising phenomenological turn and advocates a privileged attitude or disposition towards his reflection: 'And we must think this without *nostalgia*, that is, outside the myth of a purely maternal or paternal language, a lost native country of thought. On the contrary, we must *affirm* this, in the sense in which Nietzsche puts affirmation into play, in a certain laughter and a certain step of the dance' (1973: 160).

Derrida's moment of decision, his taking a position, his exclusion of alternatives, and his move to closure occur in the brief and rounded paragraph quoted in full above. On the side of negation one is to reject nostalgia, which, although Derrida's project includes 'decapita(liza)tion,' is *italicized*. And one *must* think without it; there is some kind of necessity here, either a willed coercion or the blind force of historical circumstance. On the side of affirmation one is to affirm, with the same 'must,' Derrida's prediction, or perhaps it is an eternal counter-*logos*, that there will be no unique name. One must affirm a negation, but not in the sense of recording a disembodied judgment; one must give more than cognitive assent. One must put affirmation into *play*, laughing and dancing in a certain way.

Derrida issues the sweet command to liberated play in his decisive and sacrificial paragraph. The violence that attends deconstruction and, for Derrida, the written word itself aggresses against *nostalgia* by virtue of its very italicization, which exposes it and sets it off as the victim of the piece. Nostalgia, that backward-looking pining that preens itself, is put into play as the binary opposite of . . . play. Derrida here privileges play – play is that for the sake of which deconstruction is undertaken; deconstruction is a form of play. When one gives up the nostalgia, not even the search or the hope, for 'a lost native country of thought,' one plays. Deconstruction is the play-form of metaphysics.

'Play-form' is a term from Georg Simmel's writings. The importance, indeed, the centricity of play for Derridian deconstruction leads to the possibility that deconstruction can be enlightened by the philosophy of play, by a text that interrogates the structure of play; and that, in turn, that text can be enlightened by deconstruction. Georg Simmel is an apt figure with whom to pair Derrida. Both are socially marginalized Jews, accused by many of their respective contemporaries of being unsystematic, unserious, irresponsible, and impressionistic. Both are hyper-cosmopolitan sophisticates. And both privilege play, from a Kantian background, though neither is a Kantian. Simmel, the high modernist, and Derrida, the postmodernist, will be put into reciprocal play here through appropriate writings. They will be permitted to inform, criticize, and supplement each other, creating a field for their ideas of play, embracing both discourses but preserving the distinctiveness of each. The aim is to gain a better understanding of the import of play in philosophical discourse.

The play within and between the texts of Simmel and Derrida will proceed as a game of relays. Derrida, whose metaphysical-play and play-with-metaphysics is the frame of this writing, will pass the baton to Simmel, who will provide an exposition of play-form as a distinctive form of life in dialectical relation to its binary opposite, natural form. Then Derrida will take the baton back, with all of Simmel's tracings on it, and will offer an explication of deconstruction informed by Simmel's account of play-form. And, finally, Simmel will grasp the deconstruction-inscribed baton and have one of his metaphysical texts, embodying his textual strategies, liberated for a form of not-quite-Derridian philosophical play. The writing itself will be meant to exemplify this not-quite-Derridian play, which is the fruit of the inter-play between Simmel and Derrida. That is, by way of negation, there will be no effort to reduce the different texts to one another;

Derrida's deconstruction will not be made a simple example of Simmel's play-form, nor will Simmel's strategy of textual analysis be understood as a simple instance of Derridian deconstruction. It is merely that their 'distance' (Simmel) or 'difference' (Derrida) from each other is sufficiently small to put their texts into play with each other, to their mutual and singular intelligibility.

SYMBOLIC PLAY

When Derrida hands the baton to Simmel one is thrust back into the discourse of high modernism, which is still stamped with the metaphysics of presence. But what is held to be present to the author/reader and also, in a sense, to the text is not amenable to the imposition of a logocentric structure; that is, what is deemed to be presenced is not capable of being described without falling into logical contradictions. High-modernist philosophy is Janus-faced. It is committed to the logocentric discourse of modernity and of the West more generally, but its starting-point is a presence that cannot be consistently defined. For the Derridian sensibility, high modernism is tainted with nostalgia, the nostalgia for a discourse issuing in a writing that inscribes a 'master-name,' putting presence under control. For Simmel that master-name is 'Life,' capitalized in every sense. But not capitalized enough, since it cannot be defined so as to capture itself consistently in signifiers. The Simmelian idea of life instances Derrida's *brisure*, a severing connection. 'Life' is a flux, generating ever more of itself as process, but it also produces what exceeds itself, 'more-than-life,' which is form channeling processual content into its structures. *Life* on its own terms is an indescribable being-between more-life and more-than-life, a logically contradictory union of opposites, a figure of Camusian absurdity; the demand for unity, not pervaded by silence, but frustrated in its activity.

Simmel's discourse remains logocentric, not because of its ground but because of the language in which it interprets that ground. *Life* is conspicuous by *not* being amenable to logically consistent definition. The negation of logocentrism's aim of the intellectual intimacy of thought and its prime content is performed by affirming logocentric discourse. Nostalgia is inscribed within the high-modernist text regardless of the author's intention because the text does not problematize logocentric discourse but accepts its authority: any thought will be judged according to its success or failure in fulfilling the logocentric project of portraying a present Being with logical consistency and necessity. A presence that cannot be defined with logical consistency will appear to be important just because of its failure to fulfill logocentricism. An element of tragedy will enter the text, the tragedy of the heroic philosopher who storms Being for its *logos* and must admit failure. Yet there is another element in high modernism, which is introduced in the interstices of tragedy: Life, in the most mundane sense of that word, goes on through its configuring tragedy, and the author writes about everyday things in terms of that configuration, producing philosophies of all the topics that capture interest, including play, which is the opposite of tragic nostalgia. In Simmel one finds a logocentric analysis of play that is founded on an inability to grasp the *logos*.

The text for Simmel's philosophy of play is his essay 'Sociability,' which appeared in 1908 as a section in his *Soziologie*. Simmel imbeds his discussion of play within an early version of his dialectic of more-life and more-than-life, resting it on the binaries content/form and natural form/play-form. Play, for Simmel, will be thought under the sign of nostalgia, but just because of this it will gain a conceptual fixity that is lacking in Derridian deconstruction. The essay begins with a reprise to Simmel's fundamental categories, placed in dialectical relation. The 'contents' of life, primarily the manifold of human interests, gain relative satisfaction through patterns of their pursuit, that is, forms. For example, the human desire for food may be pursued through the socially organized form of the hunt; the hunt undertaken with the purpose of procuring food is a natural form. Natural form is privileged, made foundational, by Simmel (1950c: 41):

> On the basis of practical conditions and necessities, our intelligence, will, creativity, and feeling work on the materials that we wish to wrest from life. In accord with our purposes, we give these materials certain forms and only in these forms operate and use them as elements of our lives.   .

Natural form is practical, indeed technical: it is a device by which human interests are satisfied, exclusively.

But then Simmel introduces a complication into his text, which he calls 'the autonomization of contents.' Continuing through the paragraph just quoted, Simmel (1950c: 41) breaks with the practical viewpoint, stating:

> But it happens that these materials, these forces and interests, in a peculiar manner remove themselves from the service of life that originally produced and employed them. They become autonomous in the sense that they are no longer inseparable from the objects which they formed and thereby made available to our purposes. They come to play freely in themselves and for their own sake; they produce or make use of materials that exclusively serve their own operation or realization.

Simmel here presents his genealogy of play: In a *peculiar manner* (that is, the *logos* is breached), the contents configured in natural forms are separated from their practical ends and play freely in themselves and for their own sakes. As a preliminary indication, one might hazard that play-form 'deconstructs' natural form, rather than replacing it, by removing it from its practical import. Play-form is play within the natural form, in opposition to the use of natural form to satisfy an ulterior aim. It turns against life, as a child against a parent, making it incipiently tragic; but it also affirms life, as a child delighting a parent. Play is the transient redemption of tragedy, the possible remediation of nostalgia. It is not merely one of the many expressions of life, as it is commonly understood, but a crucial operation of Life on life, a 'peculiar' operation insofar as Life/life is essentially practical and must deconstruct itself to be something other than its essence – that is, – playful.

The deeper binary in Simmel's discussion of play-form is practical/impractical. Must the impractical be playful? Simmel appears not to be sure. As he continues his writing he instances science, art, and law as examples of the autonomization of contents. Science removes cognition from its service to 'the struggle for existence' and makes 'exact knowledge of the behavior of things' a 'value in itself'; art relieves perceptual interpretation from subservience to practical needs and renders interpretations 'purposes in themselves'; and law may forget the origins of the conduct it prescribes in practicality and make the observance of its prescriptions an end-in-itself. But Simmel does not identify any of these important instances of autonomization with play. Indeed, science, art, and law echo the serious Platonic triad of truth, beauty, and goodness. They illustrate the 'complete turnover, from the determination of the forms by the materials of life to the determination of its materials by forms that have become supreme values,' which 'is perhaps most extensively at work in the numerous phenomena that we lump together under the category of *play*' (Simmel 1950c: 42). Play occurs when auto-nomization is 'most extensively at work'; that is, science, art, law, and (might one add?) metaphysics are incomplete forms of play, still clinging to some seriousness, to something that they are called upon to accomplish, be it exact knowledge (science), faithful expression (art), or strict observance (law). They can be tragic, tyrannizing over life, as well as expressions of its florescence. And play?

In Simmelian play the forms produced by the '[a]ctual forces, needs, impulses of life' become 'independent contents within play itself or, rather, *as* play' (Simmel 1950c: 42). The other kinds of autonomization – science, art, and law – are in some way perfections of natural forms, free in the sense that they are relieved of practical purport, but bound by a (transcendent) value principle: science perfects cognition, art perfects the forms of perception, and law perfects obedience. Play does not perfect – it plays. Among other examples, Simmel instances the hunt. Here a form is 'lifted out of the flux of life' and liberated from its 'material with its inherent gravity' (p. 43). The sportive hunt is not the perfection of the natural form of hunting, as science might be considered to be the perfection of the natural form of cognition. The sportive hunt plays with practical hunting, making all of its moves but transposing them into an order of significance that privileges the pleasures and excitements of pursuit, without concern for the object of procuring food. It approaches a deconstruction of the natural form, releasing it from the spirit of gravity and infusing it with 'gaiety and symbolic significance' (p. 43). It is not tragic, either in the sense that it turns against life or in the sense that it submits its contents to a new regimen, though it must draw its 'depth and strength' from life on penalty of becoming 'empty' play. By Derridian analogy, play must bear the 'trace' of its origin without reproducing it. If gravity is a physical emblem of centricity, then play eludes centricity by removing practical ends and holding back from imposing any new (spiritual) ends.

Simmel's general remarks on play are merely prefatory sketches of the concept to guide the reader into his discussion of 'Sociability,' the essay's title. Sociability is the play-form of the process of sociation, which constitutes all the forms of society or of social life. As sociation is encountered in its natural forms of human pursuit and avoidance it is never conspicuous for itself because it is erased or written over by the practical viewpoint. It becomes conspicuous when it breaks down (as Simmel's discussion (1950b: 409–24) of 'the metropolis' illustrates) or when it becomes its own object of pursuit, when it plays with itself as a structured process with no ulterior object. Concretely, the game of sociation (sociability) is played primarily in civilized social gatherings through the counters of conversational speech. It evinces an open texture, taking up all the interests that go into natural forms and replaying their discourses as means to keeping the gathering going with gaiety, rather than pursuing their original objects. Sociability sweeps its actors into its play of itself, requiring of them a tact that substitutes for the discipline exerted by objects of natural interest:

> *Tact*, therefore, is here of such a peculiar significance: where no external or immediate egoistic interests direct the self-regulation of the individual in his personal relations with others, it is tact that fulfills this regulatory function. Perhaps its most essential task is to draw the limits, which result from the claims of others, of the individual's impulses, ego-stresses, and intellectual and material desires.

> (Simmel 1950c: 45)

Tact, indeed, is what makes sociability possible as a free play of sociation which at the same time is limited by its own inherent form. It is the ethic or ethos of social play, an inherent disciplinary code prescribing a dance in the chains of gaiety. Through tact sociability becomes the *brisure* between life and form: 'Sociability is a *symbol* of life as life emerges in the flux of a facile and happy play; yet it also is a symbol of *life*' (Simmel 1950c: 55). Simmel's play of italicized stresses marks the privilege that he gives to play as the manner in which life doubles back on itself, which cannot be described univocally, but can only be inscribed by a difference in stress marks intimating what Derrida calls *différance*.

Sociability is Simmel's paradigm for play, which, since his master-name is 'life' must be living play (*living* play and living *play*), playing-at-living/living-at-play. For Derrida, the paradigm for play is deconstructive writing, a relation of his writing to another writing, the text that he deconstructs. If he has one, Derrida's master-name is 'writing,' and he practices a form of writing that is a play-form of writing, that is the play-form of metaphysics. The baton that Simmel will pass back to Derrida will be inscribed with the ethic of tact: deconstruction is tactful writing, which takes the place of a writing disciplined by something ulterior to itself, a presence which speaks to the writer, a *logos*. Toward the end of 'Sociability' Simmel intimates the possibility of deconstruction by working his binary life/symbol into the term 'symbolic play.' In sociability 'the independent and self-regulated life, which the superficial aspects of social interaction attain,' may be regarded, from the practical viewpoint, as 'a formula-like and irrelevant lifelessness' or, from the perspective of play, as 'a symbolic play whose aesthetic claims embody the finest and subtlest dynamics of broad, rich social existence' (Simmel 1950c: 56). And just as critics may, from the vantage points of political programs, find Derridian deconstruction to be formula-like and irrelevant manipulation of texts, so more tactful writers may regard it as a pleasurable symbolic play, a writing that symbolizes writing, that plays with symbols in the absence of their referents.

DECONSTRUCTION

John W. Murphy (1984: 132) has remarked: 'Obviously, Derrida desires to "deconstruct" the tradition inspired by Saussure, so that the impulse of language is free to follow its own self-appointed destiny.' The Saussurian tradition, which Derrida identifies with 'the West,' is founded on a distinction between the thing that is signified by language and the linguistic signifier, assuming that 'an obstrusive *object* of signification exists in the world, and an equally *a priori* concept represents it' (Murphy 1984: 132). That assumption is what Derrida calls 'logocentrism,' the doctrine, to use Richard Rorty's words, that philosophy is the mirror of nature. Murphy's interpretation of Derrida's 'project' is appropriate here because he is a sociologist who appropriates Derrida for the discourse of symbolic interactionism, which was influenced greatly by Simmel's writings. He is a good mediator, able to connect Derrida to the desire to play, which demands submission to the play of language, its freedom 'to follow its own self-appointed destiny'; just as the desire to play society, to enjoy sociability, demands submission to the play of sociation. Murphy provides the clue to, or the point of fixation for, the Simmelian Derrida, for it is that Derrida who is addressed in this writing, the playful Derrida. Deconstruction is the play-form of metaphysics, now specified as the freedom of language, not the freedom of the one who speaks or writes the language; just as sociability is the freedom of sociation, not the freedom of those who sociate, who must be self-disciplined to enjoy its freedom, to participate in it.

Derrida provides a felicitous and accessible account of what might best be called the *praxis* of deconstruction in an interview with Henri Ronse (Derrida 1981), where he links his deconstructive writing to pleasure and play. The format of the interview frees Derrida to speak about writing, knowing that his speech will be inscribed into a written text. He is permitted and constrained here to engage in conversation, to be sociable enough to try to satisfy a demand for a more common intelligibility than he might want to achieve in his writings. 'Implications,' the title of the interview, is a privileged text in which one encounters Derrida on the turf of speech, off his own turf of writing but incessantly referring to it.

Derrida's (1981: 3) first approach to describing deconstruction is to call it 'a unique and differentiated textual "operation," if you will, whose unfinished movement assigns itself no absolute beginning, and which, although it is entirely consumed by the reading of other texts, in a certain fashion refers only to its own writing.' Here, at the outset of his comments, there is an approximation of deconstruction to play-form. Deconstruction which, like sociability, is open textured, an 'unfinished movement,' exhausts itself in the contents of anterior forms while referring to itself, as sociability takes up the contents of natural forms and uses them to perpetuate itself. It is an instance at least of the 'autonomization of contents,' through which elements that were regimented by a textual code are freed, at least provisionally, from that code to play. They are freed by a writing which dances within other writing. Derrida (1981: 4) continues that,

> above all it is necessary to read and reread those in whose wake I write, the 'books' in whose margins and between whose lines I mark out and read a text simultaneously almost identical and entirely other, that I would even hesitate, for obvious reasons, to call fragmentary. . . .

Here again is an approximation to Simmelian play-form. Take the example of the sportive hunt, which is almost identical to the hunt for food but entirely other from it. No more than the play-form can deconstruction detach itself from its antecedents. Deconstruction is a playing in and with texts, not apart from them; just as the play-forms are play in and with natural forms. Derrida does for writing what human beings do for sociation when they are sociable – he lets it be itself. But this Simmelian reading of Derrida brings out something perhaps unsuspected. Derrida privileges the texts in which he dances, just as Simmelian play founds itself on natural forms. Are the texts that Derrida reads and writes in like natural forms?

There can be no deconstruction without constructions to deconstruct. And just as the play-form must deny, remove itself from, and exclude from itself the ulterior object of the natural form, so deconstruction must close off from itself that to which the metaphysical text (the text of metaphysics) purports to refer. Reverting to the point of fixation of the Simmelian Derrida, deconstruction must negate the assumption that 'an obstrusive *object* of signification exists in the world, and an equally *a priori* concept represents it.' The Derridian negation of the 'metaphysics of presence,' in which the writing is a transcription of the discourse ruled by the 'master-name' (be it God, Nature, Spirit, Life, Existence, Reality, or Being), which reveals its object through itself, is not a criticism, but a displacement of writing, a tactful writing. That is, Derrida does not negate the metaphysics of presence in order to substitute a new metaphysics (which would have to be a metaphysics of presence), but refrains from obtruding any metaphysical interest he might have on the text he is deconstructing. He is thereby freed for play, but only on condition that he relieves himself of seriousness, not, perhaps, all seriousness, since tact is serious, but of the seriousness of metaphysics. And that seriousness of metaphysics is the interest of the writer in producing a transcription of the speech that speaks that to which the capitalized master-names refer or, in the supreme instance of Logocentrism, that which they *are* ('In the beginning was the word . . .'). Derridian writing 'assigns itself no absolute beginning,' whereas logocentric texts record the pursuit of absolute beginnings that lie beyond the pursuit, but somehow are supposed to, though Derrida does not allow them to, enter the texts or *be* the texts. Western metaphysics is like a natural form, prescribing a code for the pursuit of presence, which Derrida (1981: 6) takes up, abstaining from pursuit, as 'a system of fundamental constraints, conceptual oppositions outside of which philosophy becomes impracticable.' Deconstruction is play with those conceptual oppositions, such as nature/culture, reality/illusion, being/nothing, spirit/matter, existence/essence, tracing how each member of an opposed pair asserts itself, despite, indeed, in the face of, any intention by a writer to suppress one or another of them. Deconstruction is the play of the language of metaphysics, liberated from the nostalgia for presence but faithful to the 'system of fundamental constraints,' just as the sportive hunt is faithful to hunting's constraints and sociability to the demands of sociation.

Deconstruction, to remind us, is, first of all, a 'textual "operation."' But it is more than that, if by 'operation' is meant a mere technique devoid of the possibility for description in ethical discourse. By drawing out the Simmelian Derrida the ethical elements of the deconstructive operation become prominent. Perhaps 'operation' should be thought of more in terms of a medical procedure that constitutes a moral relation of agent and patient than through the notion of 'operational definition' from the philosophy of science, as has been implicit in this writing up to now. Derrida operates on texts by deconstructing them. But deconstruction is a form-of-play/play-form and, as such, is constituted by an ethic/ethos. The Derridian ethic of textual play is brought forward in a passage in the Ronse interview where Derrida elaborates on deconstruction as a writing with two hands. Noting the violence that attends deconstruction when it inscribes, through *erasure*, that 'within the text which attempted to govern it from without' (the 'master-name' of presence), he (Derrida 1981: 6) then switches to moral discourse saying: 'I try to respect as rigorously as possible the internal, regulated play of philosophemes or epistemes by making them slide – without mistreating them – to the point of their nonpertinence, their exhaustion, their closure.' Here is one of Derrida's clearest expositions of what he does when he deconstructs a text: it is framed by the 'etheme,' respect, the Kantian virtue, which, when one is playing is called tact. Deconstruction is tactful play with the text of metaphysics, which does not *mistreat* its counters, the epistemes and philosophemes, but lets them play to exhaustion, that is, until they lose the traces of their others, their binary opposites, and close in upon themselves. Then they are not pertinent – they are isolated (dead?) and ready for *erasure*. Completing the move, deconstruction is play, but it is a play that has, as one of its dialectical moments, a violence imposed from the outside, an erasure. The deconstructive operation proceeds by putting-into-play, erasing, putting-into-play again. Deconstruction is very much a surgical play, but also very much like sociability, in which themes and particular conversations are put into play and then dropped as the sociable actors circulate and recirculate.

Continuing his moral interpretation of deconstruction Derrida (1981: 6) next remarks,

> To 'deconstruct' philosophy, thus, would be to think – in the most faithful, interior way – the structured genealogy of philosophy's concepts, but at the same time to determine – from a certain exterior that is unqualifiable or unnamable by philosophy – what this history has been able to dissimulate or forbid, by making itself into a history by means of this somewhere motivated repression.

Here the virtue of fidelity is added to respect, a fidelity to the *construction* of the logocentric text, just as sociability involves loyalty to the ruling spirit of sociation, to the process of constituting society. Yet again, and here there is a difference from Simmelian play, there is the violence of an exterior determination – the erasure – because, although the text must be respected in-itself, as text, it must not be respected for-itself, as its pretensions might make it out to be. That is, Derridian play cannot affirm its 'natural form' in the way that sociability affirms sociation. There is a difference between deconstructive writing and the logocentric written that cannot be bridged because the logocentric text represses that which is not itself in the very proclamation of a 'master-name' that pretends to . . . liberate: it dissimulates or forbids in the name of freedom – a 'somewhere motivated repression.' The therapeutic element in Derridian deconstruction – the release from repression through erasure – makes it, from the vantage point of the Simmelian paradigm, an imperfect form of play. There is something ulterior about it: it must attack the text from the outside to liberate the philosophemes (even as it is faithful to the text) by 'putting into question the major determination of the meaning of Being as *presence*, the determination in which Heidegger recognized the destiny of philosophy' (Derrida 1981: 7). Sociability, by contrast, puts nothing 'into question,' but simply removes the objects of natural sociation, the natural interests, from consideration.

Yet, Derrida (1981: 7) continues, 'this simultaneously faithful and violent circulation between the inside and the outside of philosophy' produces 'a certain textual work that gives great pleasure':

> That is, a writing interested in itself which also enables us to read philosophemes – and consequently all the texts of our culture – as kinds of symptoms (a word which I suspect of course, as I explain elsewhere) of something that *could not be presented* in the history of philosophy, and which, moreover, is *nowhere present* . . .

The pleasure of deconstruction is diagnostic and, perhaps, therapeutic. Might it be figured as playing doctor with a dying (dead?) patient . . . 'the West' and the Western(ized) writer; and simultaneously keeping the patient alive beyond any intellectual dream by writing the servant-word *différance*, the other of presence, over the erasure of the master-name? Or perhaps the pleasure of deconstruction can be figured in the image of regicide, as Derrida (1981: 14) invites when he concludes his exposition of deconstruction by identifying it with play:

> To risk meaning nothing [to write *différance* as a self-prohibiting inscription (proscription)] is to start to play, and first to enter into the play of *différance* which prevents any word, any concept, any major enunciation from coming to summarize and to govern from the theological presence of a center the movement and textual spacing of differences.

Or maybe deconstruction is not exactly regicide despite Derrida's 'decapit(aliz)ation.' Derridian deconstruction is permanent revolution in the text produced by erasure and enabled by the permissive word *différance*, the joker in the pack, which permits 'the movement and textual spacing of differences' to play. And now deconstruction looks more like the Simmelian play-form, interpreted in a last approximation as the play-form of logocentrism, only possible by means of an anti-logocentric deed that preserves and emphasizes the binaries master/servant, king/joker. Doctor, regicide, servant, and joker – all of these are the Derridian deconstructionist, and none of them is privileged.

STALEMATE

When the deconstruction-inscribed baton is handed back to Simmel for the last stretch of the relay it is to the Simmel who works on texts other than his own, the textual strategist. What is in question here is the set of operations that Simmel employs when he writes about the texts of metaphysics that have so preoccupied Derrida. Is there an opening to deconstruction in Simmel's textual strategy? Does his writing on writings evince a form of play and is it a play-form of philosophy? Can the Simmelian Derrida bring forth a Derridian Simmel? The above thoughts are put as questions because Simmel, a foundationalist with the master-name *l*ife, did not explicitly treat metaphysics as pure play. Instead, he desublimated the master-names of other writers, interpreting them as the expressions of each writer's vital temperament, which had been projected into the cosmos by the form-giving intellect. That is, Simmel de-objectified metaphysics, just as other high-modernist critics and philosophers of life, such as Nietzsche, Freud, Unamuno, Dewey, and Santayana did. But he did that to let *l*ife, not writing, have its freedom. His textual work on metaphysics was a means to an ulterior end, the vindication of *l*ife as Being, which cannot be captured in any intellectual constructs, but can be articulated in paradoxes, formal contradictions, and absences. He is, in Derrida's sense, a critic, who speaks for, of, and in the presence of Being and then inscribes his master-name in a text. Metaphysics for Simmel is an expression of *l*ife, presupposing a metaphysics of *l*ife to interpret it, even if (only) as a failed effort to present Being as an intelligible unity.

If Simmel's writing is to show an opening to deconstruction, then his writing on writing must be deconstructed to free his writing about writings for play. That is, one must indicate how Simmel does something supplementary to what he claims that he will do when he works on another writer's text, that he engages in a form of deconstruction or in a textual work that supplements deconstruction or shows unsuspected possibilities in it. In one way of putting it, Simmel might permit a broader interpretation of deconstruction, freeing it from localization in Derridian texts; or put another way, Simmel might help to open a field of textual operations with family resemblances to deconstruction, ranged under the broader term symbolic play. Which way of putting the possibility of a Derridian Simmel is a matter of textual rhetoric, depending on which texts are informed and which ones are the informers. Both strategies will be used here to produce a free interplay of Derrida/Simmel in a writing on Simmel's text, *Schopenhauer and Nietzsche*, in which Simmel wrote on the two dominant philosophers of life in nineteenth-century Germany. *Schopenhauer and Nietzsche* is a privileged text because it embodies Simmel's way of treating the texts from which he extracted the materials for his own metaphysics. What is of concern here is his manner of treating the texts, not what he extracted from them or his metaphysics.

Simmel's methodological 'Preface' to *Schopenhauer and Nietzsche* stands in the way of any easy deconstructionist reading of the main text. Indeed, Simmel proposes to do everything that Derrida would try to forbear from doing. His 'Preface' is devoted to declaring and defending the project of finding for Schopenhauer and Nietzsche the 'positive core' where the 'nucleus' of each one's 'doctrine, its subjective center, coincides with the center of its objective importance, as occurs in the case of every original philosopher who answers questions about "things out there" "from his own inner depth, from the inner depth of mankind," as Goethe once remarked concerning Schopenhauer' (Simmel 1986: liv). And the 'aim' of his project is to make 'a contribution to a general cultural history of the spirit' and to emphasize 'the transhistorical importance of the two philosophers in question' (Simmel 1986: liii). Objective (transhistorical) importance, the notion of a general cultural history of the spirit as the repository of importance, and a 'subjective center' with a 'positive core' as the origin of history are just the kind of terms that define the metaphysics of presence for Derrida. Simmel firmly emplaces his writing within logocentrism, attempting to control the texts on which he will work from the outside by his own master-names, exposing, as he says, a 'philosophy about' each philosopher, based on what he finds important in them for a general cultural history of the spirit.

In order to accomplish his project Simmel announces a strategy that violates every rule of Derridian deconstruction. Admitting that Schopenhauer and Nietzsche 'very often discussed problems that were not necessarily connected to the central cores of their respective thought and were even quite distant from them,' he 'presupposes' that the 'very few *Leitmotivs* at the innermost cores of the doctrines of Schopenhauer and Nietzsche are the most objectively valuable parts of these doctrines and the parts that will endure' (Simmel 1986: liii, liv). Simmel, it seems, will not in Derridian fashion make philosophemes *slide* 'to the point of their nonpertinence, their exhaustion, their closure'; but will hold fast to them to the point of retextualizing them as a philosophy of the philosopher. His final definition of his program is to compose a philosophy 'into a single coherent picture which has no immediate counterpart in reality but which is comparable to an artistic portrait providing, instead of the real totality of the object, an ideal interpretation and a meaning derived from the method and the goal of presentation' (Simmel 1986: liv). Simmel appears to be a constructivist here, someone who plunders the texts of others for his own constructive activity, rather than a deconstructionist who respects and is faithful to a text, but who is also free to write in its margins and between its lines, and to erase its master-names. The deconstructionist does construct a new text, but it is in and around the old text, not above or beneath it.

Up to the point at which he announces his project of portraiture Simmel is a prime exemplar of logocentrism, but then he suddenly exceeds his project and prepares his text for deconstruction. He (1986: liv) continues: 'One must select from the totality of the philosopher's utterances those that form a coherent, uniform, and meaningful context of thought – and it does not matter if the totality also includes contradictions, weaknesses, and ambivalence.' Simmel's text has slid from 'central core' and 'objective importance' to 'a coherent, uniform, and meaningful context of thought' rendered in 'an ideal interpretation and a meaning derived from the method and the goal of presentation.' And then he acknowledges the field for Derridian deconstruction, the totality that 'includes contradictions, weaknesses, and ambivalence.' If one erases the words 'objective importance' from Simmel's text, his program becomes a work of composition, the portrait of the philosophical objectification of a vital temperament. And if one erases the words 'subjective center' from Simmel's text, his composition becomes one of 'utterances' (still phonocentric, but very close to Derrida), of epistemes and philosophemes. And if one then makes the pair composition/totality one grasps the possibility of deconstruction through the back door; that is, in order for Simmel to create his composition he must deconstruct the totality, respecting it for what it is, including its 'contradictions, weakness, and ambivalence,' and refusing to force on it a unity that it does not display. And here is the opening for the Derridian Simmel, in the textual work that he must do in order to extract a nucleus for his philosophy of the philosopher, in his acknowledgment that the text he works on is different, exceeds, that which he will make of it, that it does not close itself, but that he will have to close it in a different text.

Simmel, too, is a tactful writer, preserving the autonomy of the other text. He must 'respect as rigorously as possible the internal, regulated play of philosophemes or epistemes' in order to demarcate a core; he must trace contradictions, weakness, and ambivalence to compose coherence. And, as it turns out in the main text of *Schopenhauer and Nietzsche*, his composition is composed strictly within his deconstruction, his putting into play of the texts on which he works. Relieved of making a contribution to a general cultural history of the spirit, *Schopenhauer and Nietzsche* is a play within and between texts. A central core is, indeed, described (but doesn't Derrida also depend on the master-names of other texts to center his decentering?), but it is then played off against the totality of the text in which it was demarcated and against counter-texts. Simmelian deconstruction is an operation of stalemating core by recurring to periphery and counter-core. That is, while he could have simply written a straightforward exposition of the philosophy of the philosopher, he proceeded instead to put his composition into play with the textual totality from which he constructed it.

A first approximation to Simmel's textual strategy of stalemating can be made by recurring to his discussion of non-partisanship in *Soziologie*. Similar to the way in which sociability makes the process of sociation conspicuous, non-partisanship brings out the structure of the more specified process of conflict. The non-partisan is either a mediator who 'produces the concord of two colliding parties, whereby he withdraws after making the effort of creating direct contact between the unconnected or quarreling elements, or an arbiter who "balances," as it were, their contradictory claims against one another and eliminates what is incompatible in them' (Simmel 1950d: 146–7). From a reading of his program Simmel would appear to be an arbitrator, whose portrayal or philosophy of the philosopher eliminates contradictory claims, composing a coherent unity of thought. But in practice he is a mediator who brings epistemes and philosophemes into contact with each other so that they can play off each other.

There is, however, a difference between social mediation and the textual strategy of stalemating. Whereas the natural form of mediation in society has the ulterior object of a voluntary concord among the conflicting parties, the mediation of intra-and inter-textual conflict of logocentric philosophical texts does not produce concord, but a heightening of differences that cannot be reconciled and that the stalemater refuses to arbitrate. Stalemating is the play-form of philosophical mediation, the deconstruction of any Hegelian presumption to unify opposites, Hegel stripped of his dialectical *logos*. For Simmel, as for Derrida, Western metaphysics has been the effort to define 'ultimate reality' in consistent terms by privileging a master-name. The non-partisan stalemater is a tactful writer, exercising the self-prohibition against arbitrating the conflict among philosophemes by choosing one of the contending master-names or by imposing a new master-name from the outside. Instead, stalemating constructs scenarios in which contending philosophemes are continually brought into a play in which they cancel each other out continually as they displace one another from privileged spaces in the logocentric text. The stalemater perfects the ethic/ethos of Simmel's non-partisan who fuses 'personal distance from the objective significance of the quarrel [which master-name will win] with personal interest in its subjective significance' (Simmel 1950d: 150). That is, the stalemater makes sure that no master-name wins, becoming a partisan of the continuing play of the philosophemes; but finds the pursuit of the master-name significant. Stalemating is the mutual and ever-renewed canceling of master-names, metaphysical play and play with metaphysics.

Simmel sets up his scenarios for stalemating by a three-step operation that he follows throughout his specific discussions of philosophical questions in *Schopenhauer and Nietzsche*. He initially constructs his composition of the philosopher's 'own center,' understanding the philosopher as presenting an intelligible response to a genuine problematic. Remaining faithful to the text on which he works, Simmel does not at first bring any external perspective to bear on it but attempts to describe its internal meaning. He does as little synthetic reconstruction as possible, stating major doctrines clearly and avoiding efforts to reconcile contradictions while correcting the misinterpretations of other critics. But once Simmel has taken up the philosopher's position he proceeds to a second and more deconstructionist operation, showing that the very assumptions of the position permit at least one other substantive alternative than the one asserted by it to follow logically from it. By revealing that the unity of the position has not been achieved by logical necessity Simmel relieves the position of its pretension to objective truth and retextualizes it as a speculative possibility expressing the philosopher's temperament. Then, in his last move, he states what he has found to be tenable and significant in the position. The moves of retextualization and judgment about tenability are extraneous to the deconstructive operation of submitting speculative alternatives that cancel the one that appears in the analyzed text. Indeed, when the speculative alternative comes from a counter-text, as when Simmel plays off Schopenhauer and Nietzsche against one another, he becomes a purely playful mediator, at a concernful distance, putting the philosophemes of others into play and stalemating their master-names. He engages in inter-textual play, writing as Derrida does with two hands, but instead of wielding a pen and an eraser, he brandishes two pens that cancel/inscribe, inscribe/cancel, in an open process of mediating play that succeeds by virtue of its failure to reconcile the conflicting philosophemes. Simmel's play is as violent as Derrida's, but it is a non-partisan proxy violence.

At the conclusion of *Schopenhauer and Nietzsche* Simmel summarizes the stalemate that he has set up between the two philosophers. The core of Nietzsche is the 'dogmatic value-presupposition' that 'Life shall be,' whereas the core of Schopenhauer is the equally dogmatic negation that 'Life shall not be.' For Simmel (1986: 181), the stalemate of core and counter-core reveals 'the limits of logical understanding,' indicating 'an opposition of being which cannot be bridged by the intellect.' Schopenhauer's conviction that 'life is valueless, which is based on selecting from all of the diverse and non-observable meanings only monotony, the preponderance of suffering and failure' is met by Nietzsche's belief that 'life is a value and that every deficiency is but a step towards a new attainment, every monotony but an interplay of infinite vitality, and every pain inconsequential in light of the surge of values in the process of realization in being and action' (Simmel 1986: 181). Schopenhauer and Nietzsche cancel and recancel each other, making a 'search for peace' between them a 'meritless venture,' which is 'worse than useless because it falsifies the meaning of their opposition and, thus, the meaning of each one of them' (Simmel p. 181).

The tactful stalemater deconstructs to heighten difference, respectful towards and faithful to the conflict and the participants in it, a mediator of the irreconcilable. The playful mediator remains at a distance from the conflict, achieving the only unification possible here, as 'a subject who can regard both positions.' Simmel (1986: 181) closes his book with a stalemater's credo: 'By sensing the reverberations of spiritual existence in the distance opened up by these opposites, the soul grows, despite, indeed, because of the fact that it does not decide in favor of one of the parties. It finally embraces both the desperation and the jubilation of life as the poles of its own expansion, its own power, its own plenitude of forms, and it enjoys that embrace.' The mediator takes the canceled checks, the texts, and plays with their exchange. There is no ulterior Being for them to draw upon, only the pleasure of regarding the interplay of sentiments of life through the philosophemes that stand for them. The therapeutic pleasure of Derrida cedes to a more erotic pleasure between the texts in the 'distance opened up by these opposites.' Perform a Derridian erasure of 'soul' and write in the word '*différance*' and one engages in a not-quite-Derridian play, not-quite-Derridian because it also permits the sentiments to play through the philosophemes, a play of *life* taken up into philosophy. Might this not approach a Derridian thinking 'without *nostalgia*,' putting 'affirmation into play, in a certain laughter and a certain step of the dance'?

Is the stalemating operation a form of deconstruction or are they both symbolic play-forms? Does this question matter anymore?

DECONSTRUCTION AS A SYMBOLIC PLAY

Narrator: You are asked to imagine that what you will see and hear for the next fifteen minutes or so is the inside of a Derridian dream, that is, Jacques Derrida dreaming about himself in a conversation with Georg Simmel, who appears to him in the form of a woman. We find our imaginary Derrida at, of all places, a panel at the meetings of the Midwest Sociological Society, presenting a paper on deconstruction. Now, just suspend your disbelief.

Derrida: There will be no unique name, even if it were the name of Being. And we must think of this without *nostalgia*, that is, outside the myth of a purely maternal or paternal language, a lost native country of thought. On the contrary, we must *affirm* this, in the sense in which Nietzsche puts affirmation into play, in a certain laughter [Laughs] and a certain step of the dance.' [Dances] [Moves off podium] So much for my performance. Aagh! Baudrillard writes an 'Oubliez Baudrillard.' We'd just as soon have an 'Oubliez Derrida.' This farce at conference after conference. Deconstructing myself. Doing violence to free discourse by privileging play and inhibiting nostalgia. It's as though I was no more than another modern ideologist, just like Nietzsche railing against pity and thus determining himself as pit*iless*. I defame nostalgia and determine myself as *un*sentimental. What is this deconstruction of mine? Yet another season of the old logocentric medicine show? What is this play?

Simmel: [approaches Derrida from behind, touching him on the shoulder] Doubts are only natural to someone like you. I suffered them myself. It's something of a curse to be aware of multiplicity and yet to have to close it off, draw a boundary around it – as we always must.

Derrida: [turns to Simmel] And who are you?

Simmel: I'm Simmel, my dear. Free to appear to you in the form in which you'll be most susceptible to my influence.

Derrida: Simmel? The German Jewish liberal who played *flâneur* around Berlin? What do you have to do with me? I study the likes of Nietzsche, Husserl, and Heidegger. But Simmel?

Simmel: I never thought that Husserl and Heidegger were much for playfulness. Even Nietzsche talked a better game than he played. All of them were intoxicated with the theo-logos. And you, too?

Derrida: So what do you have to tell me?

Simmel: I'm only here to help. I've noticed that your precious deconstruction bears a certain affinity to, perhaps a trace of, my notion of play-form. I venture the idea that your deconstruction is nothing else but the play-form of metaphysics.

Derrida: On the face of it that's simply a reductive trick, but go on.

Simmel: Well, as I see it, life is essentially a practical affair. We have certain interests, we devise ways of satisfying them. I call those ways of satisfying interests forms. In the first case, they are natural, the means to some ulterior end . . .

Derrida: I must object. This 'life' you talk about. It's just another logocentrism, governing your text from the outside.

Simmel: Not exactly. Life, for me, is never reconciled. It is usually at odds with itself, struggling against its own forms. It carries no assurances that the real is rational.

Derrida: But it is *nostalgic* for such comfort.

Simmel: All right. Though you might do well to think that you're alive. Let's 'de-capitalize' life, as you would put it. Would you allow me to speak about form without any metaphysical prejudgments?

Derrida: Go ahead. Though you'll be making them despite your promise.

Simmel: You'll allow that we mediate our pursuit of satisfactions through forms. Well, when the practice of a form is its own satisfaction, then we have a play-form. Take what I call sociability. The general form of sociation, interaction, if you will, is normally engaged in for some ulterior purpose, for example, buying and selling. But at a party, let's say, all of these conventions of getting along with each other are performed for their own pleasure. Or take the easiest example I can think of, the hunt. As a natural form one hunts for food. As a play-form one hunts to hunt. To the point, perhaps, that one doesn't even load the gun. Or, one of my favorite themes, flirtation. One engages in nonpossessive foreplay for its own sake, not to fuse in a possessive embrace.

Derrida: So you're flirting with deconstruction?

Simmel: I could do worse. The way I see it, there's a lot of my play-form in your deconstruction. Think of sociation. The game of sociability is a language game. It is open textured, like your deconstruction, taking up all the interests that go into natural forms and replaying their discourses as means to keeping the interaction going with gaiety, rather than pursuing their original objects.

Derrida: I won't deny that your analogy is appropriate.

Simmel: And, most important, sociability is regulated by a special morality – tact. Where no external or immediate egoistic interests direct the self-regulation of individuals in their personal relations with others, tact steps in to regulate. It draws the limits, which result from the claims of others, of the individual's impulses, ego-stresses, and intellectual and material desires. Tact, my dear. Is your deconstruction tactful? Don't you set up a social, a moral, relation with the texts on which, to use your word, you 'operate?'

Derrida: *Touché*, Simmel. However we might differ on the way that we interpret metaphysics, we are at one in a certain fastidiousness that you can call morality if you want. I have always been concerned to distinguish between deconstruction and destruction. Your play-form shows how that distinction can be made clear.

Simmel: Yes. The play-form. Metaphysics is that all-too-serious business of thinking one's way into what I call a central idea and what you call a master name, a word that somehow makes a direct contact with . . . With what? Let's call it the noumenon and be done with it.

Derrida: That's the problem with you. You have to call 'it' something. You have to learn to erase those words like Being, Reality, Spirit, Matter; Life, for that matter. Here, let me explain. I know how to play with your play-form better than you!

Simmel: Yes, Master Name!

Derrida: You were correct about the similarity between deconstruction and sociability. Deconstruction is a textual operation, whose unfinished movement assigns itself no absolute beginning and, which, although it is entirely consumed by the reading of other texts, refers only to itself. That's just like your sociability, in which the contents of natural forms – anything that might be talked about for practical purposes – are taken up to perpetuate sociability itself. Sociability is a conversational dance – deconstruction is a writing which dances within other writing.

Simmel: I'll admit that I never wrote in such a way. I wrote about play, but I never played with writing.

Derrida: You were too captivated by logocentrism. You were one of those who understood that the language of metaphysics did not refer to some ulterior controlling power, but you tried to find a function for it nonetheless – in the philosopher's temperament. That was how you came to your own tragic logocentrism: your Life – capitalized with the entire Western tradition – was the fundamental drive to reflect and contain itself in a commodious form. But no form was commodious enough. Each one projected his or her own temperament on to the ulterior. You were a metaphysical expressionist, regimenting language to a self. But, of course, you tried to float above temperament or, better, to embrace all temperaments. But that couldn't work – you got stuck with a tragic sense of Life.

Simmel: *Touché*, Derrida. I didn't make my writing a play-form. I didn't think it was writing – I thought it was metaphysics. Perhaps writing mastered me just because I took it for granted as my faithful servant.

Derrida: Well, not to blame yourself too much. You went a long way down the road to dethroning the master-names. You showed how each pair of metaphysical terms contained irreducible opposites – that neither one nor the other could ever assert regency over discourse: neither nature nor culture, reality nor illusion, being nor nothing, spirit nor matter, essence nor existence. I simply made it clear that metaphysical texts themselves contain the assertion of each member of an opposed pair despite, indeed, in the face of, any intention by a writer to suppress one or another of them. That's a rather simple matter. More clearing away some refuse than making some new or even unfamiliar point.

Simmel: I just never took play-form *seriously* enough.

Derrida: And perhaps you can teach me to take ethics more playfully and, therefore, more seriously. You're right that I'm tactful when I deconstruct, damned tactful. I try to respect as rigorously as possible the internal, regulated play of philosophemes or epistemes (you'd simply call them 'ideas') within the text by making them slide – without mistreating them – to the point of their nonpertinence, their exhaustion, their closure. There seems to be an 'etheme' regulating my writing here – good old Kantian respect. The respect of tact.

Simmel: So, what you're saying is stop making sense. Stop trying to use writing to make sense. Let it make senses, all kinds of senses. So, that's deconstruction – letting go of those sense-making forms that never give the satisfaction that they promise anyway. I'll admit it. I had a terrible case of nostalgia for those sense-making forms.

Derrida: Indeed. To risk meaning nothing is to start to play, and first to enter into the play which prevents any word, any concept, any major enunciation from coming to summarize and to govern from the theological presence of a center the movement and textual spacing of differences. But here I am speaking in that impossible language of mine again. It's as simple as this. Just as in sociable conversation one never lets one's convictions get the better of one's tact, so in deconstruction one never lets any convictions get the better of the text.

Simmel: Except, perhaps, the conviction that writing should be freed to wander through what you call the general text, the arche-writing.

Derrida: Perhaps so. I am always the one to cherish indeterminacy, undecidability. And you are the one who insists always on the necessity of determination. I know that, strangely enough, even though I sometimes call myself an empiricist – of the text – you will find me to be a Platonist in disguise. That's what gets me so deflated now and again.

Simmel: Let me declare a stalemate between us. I have begun to understand that when I did my explication of metaphysical texts I was engaged in an operation very much like deconstruction, though not exactly the same. Had I relieved myself of nostalgia I could have carried the play-form into metaphysics. All the moves in the game were already there.

Derrida: So, you're proposing that there might be a broader interpretation of deconstruction, freeing it from localization in my texts; or, alternatively, a field of textual operations with family resemblances to deconstruction – a number of forms of what you call symbolic play.

Simmel: Yes, that's the kind of thing I'm getting at. Take my methodological preface to my book *Schopenhauer and Nietzsche*. I'm a hopeless modernist there, in my programmatic posturing, but I'm postmodernist, perhaps, in my practice. Just look at how I begin, saying that I will find the 'positive core' where the 'nucleus' of each philosopher's doctrine, its subjective center, coincides with the center of its *objective* importance, as occurs in the case of every original philosopher who answers questions about 'things out there' 'from his own inner depth, from the inner depth of mankind,' as Goethe once remarked concerning Schopenhauer. Hardly a playful approach to the matter.

Derrida: Yes, dear Simmel. It's just that kind of chatter that I've sought to discredit a bit in my pronunciamentos against logocentrism. You even resorted to the inner depth of *mankind*. You see how logocentric you could get.

Simmel: Mea culpa. I even claimed to be making a contribution to a general history of the spirit and at the transhistorical importance of Schopenhauer and Nietzsche. I wasn't going to let philosophemes slide to the point of nonpertinence. On the contrary, I was going to exclude from consideration everything that didn't fit into my notion of what belonged to the positive core of the doctrines. I was going to build a new text above or beneath the old ones, not – as the deconstructionist does – in and around them.

Derrida: Yes, there is such a thing as logocentrism.

Simmel: But for all of my romantic pomposity, I didn't let my program get the better of me. In determining the so-called positive core I said that it did not matter if the totality included contradictions, weaknesses, and ambivalence. That is, just like you, I acknowledged that the texts that I worked on exceeded any unilateral interpretation. I still defined the positive core of each philosopher's doctrine, but I played it off against the totality of the text in which it was demarcated and against counter-texts. My deconstruction is an operation of stalemating core by recurring to periphery and counter-core.

Derrida: I can see how what you ended up doing is similar to deconstruction. After all, I depend on the master-names of other texts to center my decentering. I don't see why it's not as fruitful for you to define a philosophy of the philosopher, as long as you proceed to deconstruct it forthwith.

Simmel: And that's just what I did in *Schopenhauer and Nietzsche*. Not only did I show the excesses within each text, but when I pitted the two philosophers against each other I made sure that neither one's master name triumphed over the other's. Each philosopher cancels and recancels the other's pretensions. This is how it worked on the largest issue between them. The core of Nietzsche is the dogmatic value-presupposition that 'Life shall be,' whereas the core of Schopenhauer is the equally dogmatic negation that 'Life shall not be.' The stalemate of core and counter-core reveals the limits of logical understanding, indicating an opposition of being which cannot be bridged by the intellect. Schopenhauer and Nietzsche cancel and recancel each other. The issue between them is, as your deconstruction has it, *undecidable*. As I wrote, any 'search for peace' between Schopenhauer and Nietzsche is a 'meritless venture,' 'worse than useless because it falsifies the meaning of their opposition and, thus, the meaning of each one of them.'

Derrida: And can the same be said of us. Is the search for peace between us a meritless venture or have we already found that peace?

Simmel: You mean, is that stalemating operation a form of deconstruction or are they both symbolic play-forms?

Derrida: You know it goes deeper than that. Are you nostalgic and, therefore, still alive? And am I lifeless and, therefore, free?

Simmel: Perhaps. We might end our encounter with the words that I wrote to conclude *Schopenhauer and Nietzsche*: 'By sensing the reverberations of spiritual existence in the distance opened up by these opposites, the soul grows, despite, indeed, because of the fact that it does not decide in favor of one of the parties. It finally embraces both the desperation and the jubilation of life as the poles of its own expansion, its own power, its own plenitude of forms, and it enjoys that embrace.'

[Simmel withdraws. Derrida is left alone to awaken from his dream.]

Derrida: The self, the self. It's not the self which is powerful, which holds a plenitude of forms. It's the text. To risk meaning nothing is to start to play. 'Good day, sunshine.'

Part II

Postmodern Simmel

Chapter 4

Simmel and the dialectic of the double boundary
The case of 'the metropolis and mental life'

The recent revival of interest in Georg Simmel's contribution to sociology calls for and makes possible a rethinking of his approach to the study of society. Simmel has been characterized as an 'interactionist,' who derives society from the mutual responsiveness of individuals; as a 'formalist,' who describes the patterns through which relations among human beings are mediated; as a 'functionalist,' who shows how even conflict contributes to the constitution of society; and more recently as an 'impressionist,' who provides insight into distinctive phases of social life without uniting them systematically. There are good grounds in aspects of Simmel's work for each of these characterizations, but none of them is fundamental enough to exhibit the unity of his sociological project. That unity is found in a distinctive form of dialectical thinking which permeates Simmel's thought as a whole and not only his sociology.

Among the widely acknowledged founders of the discipline of sociology Simmel is the only one who did not devote himself primarily to the human sciences. Indeed, in his own generation he gained recognition mainly as a philosopher who took up the task of synthesizing the Kantian legacy with the new philosophies of life. He occupied a place in German thought analogous to that of Henri Bergson in France, William James in the United States, and Miguel de Unamuno in Spain. Albert Mamelet (1914), who published the first comprehensive study of Simmel's thought, believed that Simmel merited the rank of one of the leading philosophers in the Western tradition. However, after World War I vitalism and radical pragmatism fell into disrepute and Simmel's philosophical reputation faded in part because philosophies of life were adopted in vulgarized forms by fascist and racialist movements.

With the exception of J. Loewenberg, Simmel did not find any followers among American philosophers. Instead, beginning with Albion Small and continuing with Robert Park, he became known in the United States as a sociologist. The American reception of Simmel in the inter-war period focused on the results of his thinking, for example, his description of social relations in the metropolis, rather than its form. The bias toward studying the content of Simmel's sociology has persisted into the present, leading to a lack of appreciation of its integrity, most recently evidenced in David Frisby's (1981) idea that Simmel was a 'sociological impressionist.' Frisby's valuable study of Simmel's thought in relation to the historical period of high modernism provides a significant insight into the context in which his ideas were developed. However, Frisby (p. ix) argues that Simmel was a sociological *flâneur*, who explored a wide variety of subjects without integrating them into a systematic coherence. The following discussion is intended to pose an alternative to Frisby's interpretation, without slighting his contribution, and will argue that Simmel's sociology and philosophy display a systematic form.

The current interest in Simmel's thought provides an opportunity to reconsider the character of his sociology in a wider context. Translations of some of his major philosophical works are now available (Simmel 1977, 1978, 1980a, 1984, 1986), which allows the sociological studies to be read in a more adequate frame of reference. An examination of the sociology in tandem with the philosophy reveals that Simmel's entire thought is integrated by a subtle dialectic betraying fundamental irony in the human condition in each of its dimensions and as a whole. That is not to say that Simmel's sociology is 'philosophical' rather than 'scientific,' in the sense that its results are determined a priori by certain substantive premises about human need and nature, or the motive forces of history. Instead, both the sociology and the philosophy are informed by the same pattern or form of thinking, and, therefore, enrich one another and sometimes even blend together. For example, in the masterwork, *The Philosophy of Money*, the theory of value is clarified by inquiring into the operative social relations of the modern capitalist economy. Simmel, then, applied the same dialectical pattern or operation of thinking, a master form, to each of the subjects and problems that he addressed. That dialectic is not exposed most clearly in his studies of society, which, perhaps, is why it has not been previously isolated and identified by commentators on Simmel's sociology.

HUMAN BEINGS ON THE BOUNDARY

Simmel's master form only comes fully to light in his last major philosophical work, 'Lebensanschauung' (1971d), though it guides all of his earlier thought. In this work, he constructs a bridge between the philosophies of life of the early twentieth century and the existential phenomenologies of the inter-war period, particularly Martin Heidegger's (1962) *Dasein* analysis. Simmel grounds his exposition of the category of 'Life' in a description of 'man's position in the world,' what Heidegger called 'being-in-the-world.' For Simmel, the being who investigates its own being does not find, after Heidegger's fashion, estrangement, but irresolution, incompletion, and paradox. The 'formal structure of our existence,' which is manifested 'in countless ways in the diverse provinces, activities, and destinies of human life,' is to stand 'at every moment between two boundaries.' Following Soren Kierkegaard, Simmel places the human being at the juncture of the infinite and the finite, but he adds that all of the traditional metaphysical dualities, such as richness and determinacy, and the unconditional and the conditional also constitute boundaries of the existent rather than properties of the cosmos. Indeed, the more fundamental dualities have their counterparts, within the apparently finite sphere of everyday life, in such relations as higher and lower, greater and less, and better and worse. No aspect of our existence can be defined unilaterally: 'By virtue of the fact that we *have* boundaries everywhere and always, so accordingly we *are* boundaries' (Simmel 1971d: 353).

The idea that 'we are boundaries' is both the most difficult and the most important or foundational component of Simmel's philosophy. It may be clarified and explicated by the simple insight that if we are always between two boundaries we must ourselves be a boundary or mediator between them. We are, for Simmel, essentially mediative beings, which condition accounts for our stubborn incompletion. The basic human condition of being a boundary between the boundaries of the infinite and the finite is a special one; in Martin Heidegger's language it is ontological or fundamental rather than ontic or founded. Indeed, the infinite does not seem to be a boundary at all, but a recognition of boundlessness. Yet as Simmel (1986) states in his *Schopenhauer and Nietzsche*, the infinite is a boundary, just because it is able to be 'encircled' by a name. That word, 'infinite,' however, does not refer to anything that is discriminable: its function is to allow us to comprehend our incompletion and, therefore, to exist with it, without nullifying, negating, or denying it.

Within our basic condition of bounding the infinite and the finite we perform further acts of bounding the infinite with mental forms which circumscribe it. Each ideal determination of the infinite generates a special finite sphere of human life, such as the religious, the ethical, the aesthetic, the metaphysical, and the social. Each of these primary forms of living purports to embrace the totality of life, to resolve its irresolution, but is itself bounded by the others and, therefore, never achieves its desired completion. Further, each of the primary forms is interpreted by sub-forms within it – for example, the various criteria for beauty within the aesthetic realm – which, in turn, are bounded by each other and by the primary form. Human life is, therefore, an endless mediative process of creating oneself as a boundary between two finite boundaries within a basic condition of bounding the infinite and the finite. As a dialectician of mediation Simmel is a thoroughly systematic thinker, only he does not create a closed system which, to use Heidegger's phrase, 'names the holy.'

That the very essence of our existence is to be boundaries does not mean, for Simmel, that we are determinate or fixed, incarcerated within rigid limits. Boundary as such cannot be evaded, but 'every single determinate boundary can be stepped over,' creating a new one:

> The pair of statements – that the boundary is unconditional, in that its existence is constitutive of our given position in the world, but that no boundary is unconditional, since every one can on principle be altered, reached over, gotten around – this pair of statements appears as the explication of the inner unity of vital action.

(Simmel 1971d: 354)

All determinate boundaries, therefore, are provisional and only the boundary between the infinite (indeterminate) and the finite (determinate) is fixed, though even it is transcended through thinking it. What Simmel (1971d: 355) calls the 'essential fluidity of our boundaries' means that our existence can only be described in such paradoxical terms as 'we are bounded in every direction, and we are bounded in no direction,' and 'man is the limited being that has no limit.' He is aware that such characterizations seem to present logical contradictions, but he cannot abandon them because they are the only ways we can express accurately the complexity of our being: we are not things or phenomena, but unified acts of life, whose integrity eludes consistent linguistic description.

THE MASTER FORM OF DOUBLE BOUNDARY

The condition of being boundaries, which, for Simmel, is implicated in having them, is not a state of affairs that exists apart from knowledge of it. The fluidity of boundaries, their inherent susceptibility to being surpassed, implies that they are known. And at this point in his discussion Simmel (1971d: 355) articulates the master form of his dialectic: 'For only whoever stands outside his boundary in some sense knows that he stands within it, that is knows it as a boundary.' Here Simmel has transposed the Kantian critique of knowledge into the key of existential phenomenology, just as Karl Jaspers (1956: 204) did in his definition of the *Grenzsituationen* (ultimate situations) and Heidegger (1962) did in his analysis of the 'existentials' which are constitutive of 'being-in-the-world.' Immanuel Kant's 'transcendental critique' of knowledge involved the possibility that 'the world might not wholly enter the forms of our cognition.' Paradoxically, according to Simmel (1971d: 357), this very acknowledgment of a boundary opens the way to a transcendence of it: 'the fact that even in a purely problematical way we can think of something given in the world which we just cannot think of – this represents a movement of the mental life over itself.' The Kantian revolution is, for Simmel, a surpassing 'not only of a single boundary, but of the mind's limits altogether'; a standing outside cognition which cognizes 'the immanent limits of cognition, no matter whether these limits are actual or only possible' (1971d: 357).

In light of the human ability to transcend mental limits while also remaining within them, no other set of boundaries in human existence can be exempted from the possibility of being surpassed, since it will have to be infected by mentality. Any boundary will have been formed by a mental act of determination. Indeed, any phase of human existence can only be known from a position that is outside it and yet remains within it. This general rule holds true for the study of society, which is only possible, in Simmel's view, for someone who keeps one foot inside it and one foot outside. The dialectic of boundary and not any monadic presupposition about human nature is responsible for the individualistic strain in Simmel's thought. Indeed, Simmel holds that society is one of those encompassing boundaries that human beings cannot escape and yet that they must be able to distance themselves from, even isolate themselves from, in order even to participate in it. Society is on the boundary between nature and convention. We neither belong to it as members of an organism nor do we contrive it out of our isolated individualities. Instead, we co-constitute society as a boundary that we continually transcend as we remain within its confines. We cannot dispense with it, but we do dispense with it. Using the dialectic of boundary to illuminate Simmel's sociology, it becomes clear that his special studies of society are not fundamentally interactionist or functionalist, formalist or impressionist, but elucidate the way in which a mutable yet terribly resistant dimension of existence is constituted.

THE DOUBLE BOUNDARY IN SIMMEL'S SOCIOLOGY

The dialectic of the double boundary is constitutive of Simmel's special studies of society. The following discussion will focus on Simmel's 1903 essay 'The Metropolis and Mental Life,' which is the analogue in his work to the forms of society presented by his contemporaries Émile Durkheim (mechanical and organic solidarity) and Ferdinand Tönnies (*Gemeinschaft* and *Gesellschaft*), displaying how Simmel applies his dialectic and in the process revealing that he worked out a theory of modernization which anticipates contemporary postmodernist thought. The same approach could be taken to many of his other sociological inquiries, showing similar systematization, the elucidation of his theory of modernization being in that respect exemplary.

Simmel's development as a thinker followed a line of increasing self-lucidity and originality until, at the end of his career, during World War I, he achieved clarity about his fundamental presuppositions. The *Lebensanschauung*, written at the end of his life, is one of a series of writings in which, suffering from a terminal cancer, he strove to bring together his ideas in as systematic a fashion as possible. During the same period in which he articulated his basic idea of the human being as a boundary between two boundaries he also presented his clearest conception of the ground of society. In his *Grundfragen der Soziologie* Simmel (1950a: 58) stated that the 'really practical problem of society is the relation between its forces and forms and the individual's own life.' It is in terms of that 'practical problem' and its dialectical exposition that Simmel's investigation into the types of society can be most precisely understood.

The boundary of individual and society

Interpreted through the dialectic of the double boundary, Simmel grounds the possibility of society in the human being. The individual is a boundary between his own drive or tendency to complete himself through developing his full capacities and the society's demand, expressed through social components inherent within the individual, that 'he employ all his strength in the service of the special function which he has to exercise as a member of it' in order to round out society or complete it as an organic (functional) unit. The tension between society and individual can never be resolved because it 'inheres in the general form of individual life' (Simmel 1950a: 59). As a boundary between society's bid for self-completion and his drive for his own self-completion the individual can only exist in a state of conflict among his component parts: 'This conflict between the whole, which imposes the one-sidedness of partial function upon its elements, and the part which itself strives to be a whole, is insoluble' (p. 59).

It is most important to note here that Simmel does not take the classical individualist position that there is an ' "anti-social," individual interest.' Rather, within each human being there is a pull toward submergence in one's station and its duties based on the human capacity to decompose oneself into parts and to feel any one of these as one's 'proper self,' and a counter pull to satisfy a wider range of impulses, interests, and aspirations than any restricted function permits. The war between individual and society is a struggle within the individual between the contents of life that can be absorbed within social function and those which cannot, just as the more basic tension between infinite and finite is not a structure of the cosmos but of the individual life. One can seek completion as a part of a greater whole (the social motive) or as a whole unto oneself (the individual motive). In choosing either of these alternatives at the expense of the other one makes a genuine sacrifice and, indeed, people are so constituted that they can never escape being boundaries between themselves as members of society and themselves as self-enclosed lives.

It would not be going too far to say that for Simmel society is an aspect of the struggle between individual and society, that is, between the social components of the individual and those components of that particular individual which cannot be expressed adequately through accessible social form. Each type of society, then, structures into the individual a different balance between the demand for its own completion and the individual's impulse to a unique wholeness. Simmel's theory of modernization differs from that of Durkheim because, for Simmel, the individual is ever-resistant to absorption into any social totality, which means, by virtue of the fact that society is a mediation between individuals, that society never achieves totality.

The boundary in the metropolis

Having shown how Simmel describes the double boundary of individual–society as a general structure in his late work, it is now possible to turn back to his famous essay 'The Metropolis and Mental Life' and exhibit the application of the dialectic of boundary to the theme of modernization. For Simmel the metropolis is the site of modernity, its characteristic and all-comprehending structure. Indeed, in metropolitan man the dialectic of individual–society is for the first time in history revealed fully as a root condition of human life. Modernity is not merely another era in history but is the self-revelation of the human condition. As Simmel (1950a) states in *Grundfragen*, the tension between the drives to social and to individual self-completion is a general characteristic of the human predicament. However, it can only be known fully to be such in the metropolis.

'The Metropolis and Mental Life' is known in American sociology primarily as a founding work in urban sociology, but it will be considered here as a compact symbolization of the modern spirit. And, at its core, that spirit turns out to be the intense and acute experience of the boundary between individual and society. Although Simmel had not yet self-consciously formulated the idea that we are boundaries between two boundaries, his essay on the metropolis is formed by that conception. For Simmel (1971c: 338), the metropolis is the site of a cultural crisis, which he summarizes in the phrase 'the atrophy of individual culture through the hypertrophy of objective culture.' That is, the hallmark of modernity is the development of a 'social-technological mechanism' through which the capacities of human life have become differentiated into specialized operations. This is the concrete historical expression of the tendency of society to complete itself. Indeed, it is another way of putting what Durkheim hailed as 'organic solidarity.' But, in Simmel's view, the processes of differentiation and specialization have led to hypertrophy because there is no longer any principle for unifying the totality that can be used by individuals as a basis for the task of completing themselves as unique persons.

In the metropolis the dialectic of individual–society has been heightened but it is also being strained to the breaking point. In a social-technological mechanism any *raison d'être* for uniting with others beyond calculation of individual interest (Tönnies's *Gesellschaft*) has receded beyond the horizon of individual consciousness. Yet individual interest does not have the resources of a subjective culture to permit it to generate a coherent process of individual self-completion.

Along with *The Philosophy of Money*, 'The Metropolis and Mental Life' can be fruitfully viewed as Simmel's major contribution to the classical theories of modernization which were articulated at the turn of the twentieth century. The two of these theories which are most familiar to sociologists, Durkheim's (1933) *The Division of Labor in Society* and Tönnies's (1963) *Community and Society*, describe polar boundaries of a mature modern society, between which Simmel's dialectical reflection is suitably interpolated. For Durkheim, modernization is primarily a process through which social differentiation moves in step with the expansion of objective culture, culminating in a social organization in which the specialized contributions of individuals harmonize in a coherent whole. The individual gains integration into society through fulfilling a specialized code, whereas personal life is epitomized by commitment to a universal ethic of freedom, recalling Kant's 'categorical imperative.' In contrast, Tönnies views modernization as a movement in which community is disintegrated. Individuals are progressively released from collective norms and are forced to relate to one another through self-consciously willed contracts based on personal and group advantage. Simmel's dialectical approach balances Durkheim's emphasis on the objectivity of society and Tönnies's stress on the deracinated individual by relating the individual's isolation to the growth of hyper-differentiated culture, synthesizing the contributions of the competing modernization theories.

Thus, Simmel's interpretation of metropolitan life may be viewed as a mediation between Durkheim's 'organic solidarity' and Tönnies's *Gesellschaft*. The intensive development of 'objective culture' is directed toward the actualization of a perfected organic solidarity, whereas the atrophy of 'subjective culture' is marked by the deterioration of individuality into the calculation of self-interest in successive formalized situations. Here Simmel stands between the sociological realism of Durkheim and the more individualistic exchange theory of Tönnies, showing how each of them grasps an aspect of modernity. The pure organic solidarity is one of the boundaries of metropolitan life and the pure *Gesellschaft* of isolated individuals making temporary bargains is the other. And each 'metropolitan man' is the boundary between those boundaries.

But there is a complication and a subtlety in Simmel's dialectic of the metropolitan mentality which, perhaps, accounts for why he has not entered the sociological tradition as one of the major theorists of modernization. Whereas Durkheim and Tönnies developed their types of modern society as though they were self-consistent, Simmel, the dialectician of unresolved mediation, holds that neither one of them has coherence, either by itself or in relation to the other one.

The 'hypertrophy of objective culture' means that specialization and differentiation have gone so far that society has outrun its own tendency for organic self-completion. In the metropolis there is simply too much diversity for the possibility of organizing the contents of life into an objective whole to be taken seriously. There is no society in which the individual can be a member, but in its stead a social-technological mechanism. Hence, paradoxically, as society has become more 'organic' (functionally specialized) it has lost its character as an organism with a substantive unity of purpose. Society has burst through its own tendency to self-completion. Simultaneously, the consequence of the hypertrophy of objective culture has been the atrophy of subjective culture, which means that the individual is left without any materials for creating a completed personal self. Society has exploded and the self has imploded, threatening the dialectical tension which Simmel holds to be constitutive of individuality. In Simmel's discussion of the metropolis human beings appear to be boundaries between boundaries, but on closer inspection those boundaries vanish. One might say that for Simmel the modern is the impossible possibility.

The metropolis as deconstruction of type

The metropolis, then, is not so much a completed 'type' as it is the deconstruction of any type or, perhaps better, the outgrowing of type. Simmel does not devote much attention to pre-modern society, the 'mechanical solidarity' or the *Gemeinschaft*, but he alludes to 'the most elementary stage of social organization,' which is the self-enclosed 'small circle' which imposes a conformity of we against they. The small circle with its 'rigorous setting of boundaries and a centripetal unity' sacrifices subjective culture to objective culture, but that objective culture is narrowly cohesive rather than widely dispersed, as it is in the metropolis (Simmel 1971c: 332). The double boundary in the small circle is the social component of the individual which mediates between the individual's uniqueness and those who are outside the circle, both of which are not-we. Simmel does not romanticize non-metropolitan life, indeed, he notes 'the incessant inner and external oppression of a de-individualizing small town.' Of all the classical sociologists he is the greatest partisan of modernity. Yet modernity is also oppressive, but by virtue of its variety, disjointedness, and abstraction, rather than uniformity, cohesion, and concrete particularity.

What metropolitan life lacks that the small circle has is qualitative unity and a confidence in the significance of its struggles to perpetuate itself. In the metropolis nobody is an outsider, but, then, nobody is an insider either. Each is a stranger to the others, a participant in sociation yet detached from and objective about that sociation. The metropolis is society in the absence of a society – Simmel is a postmodernist at the height of modernism. There are not two types of society but one type of society, the closed circle, and one deconstructed society, the metropolis, the name for the site of a life that has lost qualitative unity.

Characteristics of the metropolis

The specific characteristics by which Simmel defines the metropolitan mentality follow from its formative structure of the double boundary. Hyper-stimulation, the multiplicity of segmented contacts, and rapid change are all the results of specialization and differentiation. The hypertrophy of objective culture reaches a point at which society as an abstraction seems to confront the individual as an external antagonist, though it does not have an effective coherence. Indeed, as Simmel describes it, the metropolitan mentality is a reaction against objective culture, a protective defense against it: subjective culture is exhausted in defense mechanisms. Here is where the readily observable phenomena of the blasé attitude, the calculative mentality, the intellectualization of life, and the metropolitan man's reserve and the antipathy toward others lying beneath it gain intelligibility within a dialectical structure. They are all ways in which the individual holds out against dispersion into the fragments of objective culture. And, similarly, the eccentricities and the 'specifically metropolitan extravagances of self-distanciation,' all of which signify a clinging to the 'form of "being different" ' rather than an interest in any content, are bids for individuation and for affirmation of one's individuality by others in a vacancy of subjective culture.

Far from being the observations of an 'impressionist' Simmel's descriptions of the metropolitan mentality exemplify his root idea that 'the development of modern culture is characterised by the predominance of what one can call the objective spirit over the subjective' (Simmel 1971c: 337). The mental life of the metropolis may be understood as a deprived form or what Heidegger called a 'privative mode' of subjective culture. It is most deeply interpreted as a schizophrenic culture constituted by defense mechanisms, used up in defense, but normal in the sense of psychopathology because it is an intelligible adaptation to a general environing condition: normal schizophrenia, mild and, indeed, functional schizophrenia.

THE METROPOLIS AS MODERNITY

Simmel concludes 'The Metropolis and Mental Life' with the observation that it is 'the function of the metropolis to make a place for the conflict and for the attempts at unification' of the root tendencies toward identification of the individual with a 'general human quality' and toward the individual's expression of uniqueness and difference from others. Each individual in the metropolis constitutes the metropolis by being the boundary between those two tendencies. And each one is a measure of how well the 'really practical problem of society' – the relation between its forces and forms and the individual's own life – has been handled, since it can never be resolved. Modernity is not, for Simmel, as it was for Durkheim, another way of living with its own coherence, but a challenge to live in the absence of a restrictive coherence based on the need to defend a closed group against an adverse environment. Indeed, the struggle is now centered where it always was, but could not be acknowledged to be when the group imposed a qualitative unity on the individual. The site of conflict is the individual, who has now become the unit of defense in an environment of incipient hostility.

With the insight that has come from the fusion of psychoanalytic and sociological thinking in the generations since Simmel wrote 'The Metropolis,' we can say that the grave danger of metropolitan life, even graver now than it was eighty years ago, is the intensification of the mild schizophrenia inherent in it. The mental life of the metropolis tends to degenerate into a series of defense mechanisms, the boundary becomes a fortified wall behind which hides an over-inflated self without spiritual resources. It is just that eventuality which Simmel foresaw in his 1918 essay, 'The Conflict in Modern Culture,' and which we now confront in the wake of the 'me generation.'

Georg Simmel gained his philosophical autonomy in a great burst of thinking just before his death. With his dialectic of the double boundary he was able to make sense of the root understanding of life that he had striven to express and communicate throughout his career. An informed interpretation of his thought in all fields, but particularly in sociology where he made the most various of his contributions, should reveal its systematic structure based on his own mature philosophical reflections. Simmel was systematic, even when he was as yet unable to articulate his ground conceptions with self-conscious precision, but he was never systemic. In this regard he is more similar to contemporary thinkers such as Derrida, Deleuze, Baudrillard, and Lyotard than are any of the other classical sociologists. Perhaps only now can we begin to appreciate the depth and complexity of his thought because we and the society we are constituting are beginning to catch up to it.

Chapter 5

Dimensions of conflict: Georg Simmel on modern life

Among the founders of sociology as a distinctive discipline at the turn of the twentieth century Georg Simmel is distinguished from other major figures such as Émile Durkheim, Vilfredo Pareto, Ferdinand Tönnies, and Max Weber by his breadth of intellectual interests and contributions. In continental Europe sociology ordinarily arose as an outgrowth of the generalization of more specialized concerns about social relations into comprehensive accounts of social organization. Durkheim's use of anthropology to ground his visions of society, Tönnies's expansion of modern classical political thought to interpret the social bond, Pareto's synthesis of economic rationality and non-logical motives in a general sociology, and Max Weber's amplification of economic history into the study of types of social organization are all exemplary of the emergence of sociology as a coherent discursive formation. Simmel, too, constituted sociology through its relation to other fields of knowledge, but alone among the founders his primal discourse was philosophy, which provided him with a totalizing viewpoint from which he could enter a wide variety of areas and place them in dialectical reciprocity with each other.

Although he is best known in the United States as a sociologist, Simmel viewed the category of society as one of several embracing concepts through which human beings necessarily ordered the whole of their existence, some of the others being aesthetic completion, moral obligation, metaphysical vision, and religious faith. He investigated each of those embracing concepts or master forms, holding the others relative to the one that interested him at a particular time and then moving to the next. His procedure was to place an embracing idea, such as a religious ideal, in the foreground, and then to interpret the contents of life as its background. Once he was done, often in the same essay, he would shift the focus of nearness and distance, placing another idea, such as society, in the foreground and would interpret the original master form in terms of the new one. All of the master forms were, for him, equiprimordial except for a root conception of man which he progressively clarified through his intellectual career. Each embracing concept could be used to interpret all of human life but none of them could satisfactorily subsume the others under its meaning. Unlike the other founders of sociology Simmel relativized the study of society as one perspective, albeit a decisive one, for enlightening human reality, which, perhaps, is why he has occupied an equivocal position in the discipline.

Simmel was not a philosophical sociologist in the sense that he derived his descriptions of social relations from a set of prior assumptions about the nature or character of social existence. Rather, his philosophy led him to consider each master form of human life on its own terms and to explore it in an unprejudiced phenomenological spirit. That proclivity to practice Edmund Husserl's approach of going 'back to the things themselves' is responsible for his sensitive aesthetic criticism, his original interpretation of the category of life in his late work, and the many brilliant descriptions of social forms for which he is famous. Simmel did not achieve unity in his thought through system building but sought unification for it by mediating between the various dimensions of human experience. Philosophy, for example, might offer an account of society in the context of a metaphysical vision of reality, but sociology might then turn the tables and derive that vision from the character of social relations when it was enunciated. Neither interpretation would be final, since each one would express an inherent and irreducible human capacity, but each one would reveal a truth on its own terms. In his study of nineteenth-century philosophies of life, *Schopenhauer and Nietzsche*, Simmel (1986: 15) calls man a 'manifold being' whose relation to things 'is presented in the multiplicity of modes of perception in each individual, in the entanglement of each individual in more than just a single series of interests and concepts, of images and meanings.' The only meaningful unity for human existence is the formal concept of multiplicity: 'The basis for all philosophy is the fact that things overflow any single determination' (p. 15).

Despite his deep acknowledgment of man as the 'manifold

being,' it is still fair to ask whether Simmel achieved any more substantial unification of his thought, since he follows that definition with the observation that the 'irregular multiplicity of our interpretations and apperceptions of things' is eventually gathered in a 'single theme' (Simmel 1986: 15). In Simmel's case that unitary theme only became clear at the end of his philosophical career when, under the horizon of a terminal cancer, he sought to make sense of his intellectual life. In his 1918 essay 'The Conflict in Modern Culture' Simmel was at last able to give a comprehensive interpretation of modernity from the perspective of cultural history, which may be understood as the embracing standpoint from which the rest of his work gains the most complete, though not exhaustive, intelligibility. Cultural history is the grand mediation between Simmel's philosophical and sociological inquiries, providing a common ground for them without imposing any substantive principles on their autonomy.

The following discussion will interpret 'The Conflict in Modern Culture' through its philosophical and sociological background, illuminating the continuities between Simmel's most mature reflections and his earlier thought; that is, showing the intellectual possibility of his critical cultural history in his philosophy and sociology. In the process a far more integral image of Simmel will emerge than the one which dominates most of the commentaries on his work. The interpretation will also suggest that Simmel's sociology is a decisive and necessary element in his total vision, not as a derivation from philosophical presuppositions or cultural criticism, but as an independent ground offering and contributing its own irreplaceable knowledge. The discussion will build up to 'The Conflict' by initially presenting Simmel's sociological description of the structural determinants of the modern mentality in his well-known 1903 essay 'The Metropolis and Mental Life' and then moving on to sketch his image of man in relation to how the philosophical question of the meaning of life is posed. The sociological and philosophical descriptions taken from the middle period of his work (1900–10) will then be used to enrich and to clarify the interpretation of cultural history that he gives in 'The Conflict.' Underlying the discussion will be the principle that each element of the triad sociology–philosophy–cultural history informs the others and receives enlightenment from them, but that cultural history is ultimate in the restricted sense that it mediates between philosophy's emphasis on the individual and sociology's stress on the group, collective, or network of relations.

The metropolitan mentality

Simmel's 1900 masterwork, *The Philosophy of Money*, marked the decisive shift in his intellectual career from adherence to nineteenth-century positivistic and evolutionary perspectives on socio-cultural change to a more descriptive and phenomenological approach stressing the analysis of cultural forms. In *The Philosophy* Simmel had performed a Copernican revolution or inversion of evolutionary thought through working out the insight that societies embodied philosophies of value in their institutional life. Whereas neo-Darwinist theories had derived philosophical ideas from processes of economic, political, or technological development to which they gave their own progressive philosophical interpretations, Simmel sought philosophy directly in the practice of social relations; that is, he reached the understanding that doctrines such as Marx's, Spencer's, and Comte's were themselves dogmatic philosophies which served as ideologies to mask the effective standards of judgment in modern society. *The Philosophy of Money* described and criticized the operative axiology or value theory of a money economy, which is why Simmel called it a philosophy and not a sociology: his work was an analysis of a living value theory which, despite the hopes of progressivism, had, through the medium of money, elevated quantitative value over any qualitative standards. *The Philosophy* anticipated Simmel's late move to cultural history but it remained in the sphere of philosophical inquiry by virtue of its demystifying intention: it was the seedbed out of which his later and more precise investigations grew.

As Simmel cultivated the ground that he had worked in *The Philosophy* during the first decade of the twentieth century he turned his attention to what Karl Mannheim would later call the 'sociology of mind'; that is, he endeavored to trace the mentality that he had found inherent in the money economy to its most general structural determinants. The major result of his effort was 'The Metropolis and Mental Life,' which exposes the functional relation of the modern mind to modern social organization. Here Simmel turned the tables on his project in *The Philosophy*, but he did not return to evolutionary naturalism. Rather, he undertook a phenomenological description of the social conditions in which the distinctive features of the urban mentality appeared. 'The Metropolis' gives the sociological answer to the question of how a philosophy of money is possible by showing what it is about social life that has favored the triumph of quantitative over qualitative judgment and what the consequences of that victory are for individual subjectivity. In his return to seeking a social ground for mentality Simmel voided sociological theory of any teleological import and freed it from any demystifying intention. He simply gave a pure description of urban society and its characteristic mentality, and provided a functional interpretation of their interrelations.

'The Metropolis and Mental Life' might have been better entitled 'The Conflict in Modern Society.' The great theme of the essay, which would be reworked in 'The Conflict in Modern Culture,' is the struggle between individual and society, interpreted as an agonizing tension between what Simmel called 'objective' and 'subjective' culture. 'The Metropolis' is the story of how the development of modern social relations, culminating in the site of the metropolis, has deprived the individual of any intelligible or meaningful unity to life; it is the sociological road that Simmel traveled to what Albert Camus called 'the absurd.' Simmel's overriding project in 'The Metropolis' is to inquire into 'the inner meaning of specifically modern life and its products, into the soul of the cultural body,' but he proposes to execute it indirectly and sociologically by solving 'the equation which structures like the metropolis set up between the individual and the super-individual contents of life' (Simmel 1950b: 409). Social structure here is the mediator between objectivity and subjectivity, the bridge between circumstance and self: it is the master form occupying the foreground, the provisional unity to which disparate contents are held relative. Simmel's proximate aim in the essay is to 'answer the question of how the personality accommodates itself in the adjustments to external forces,' since 'the deepest problems of modern life derive from the claim of the individual to preserve the autonomy and individuality of his existence in the face of overwhelming social forces, of historical heritage, of external culture, and of the technique of life' (p. 409).

The metropolis is the site of a culture explosion. Having liberated history from any unilinear teleology Simmel is free to interpret the story of modernization as the sheer expansion, differentiation, and objectification of the capacities of man the manifold being. Human development begins with the small local group which is closed in upon itself from the outside and imposes upon the individuals within it a uniformity of behavior and temperament. In the closed circle there is a relatively small array of cultural objects which fit together such that their use and consumption reinforce the creation of the type of personality that is characteristic of the group: the objective culture of available usages and the subjective culture of personal integrity are congruent and they are stabilized by the discipline exerted on the members of the circle by one another. In their original social condition human beings gain a cohesiveness and familiarity with each other at the price of a relatively impoverished set of possibilities for connecting with the world (objective culture) and of drastically limited opportunities for the unique expression of individuality (subjective culture). The original condition is disrupted as soon as the group expands from within or begins to become receptive to external contacts. From that time on two processes are set into motion: objective culture becomes more diverse and differentiated, particularly through the onset of intensive division of labor, and subjective culture becomes ever more the province of the private individual. The two processes work in tandem: 'For we maintain factual as well as historical validity for the following connection: the most extensive and the most general contents and forms of life are most intimately connected with the most individual ones' (Simmel 1950b: 418).

In the metropolis the tendency toward diversification and generalization, and the drive to uniquely personal development reach their culmination. Objective culture explodes to the point at which all imaginable human capacities have been exteriorized and crystallized into differentiated cultural complexes, each one with its own internal standards of perfection; and each individual is left free to construct whatever personal integrity he can achieve out of the objectivized fragments of human potential and from his own inward vision. The substantive mediation between objectivity and subjectivity, the social personality enforced by the lateral discipline of the small circle, has vanished, leaving a stark tension between fragmented functional complexes and dispersed and self-enclosed individuals, which is bridged only by the impersonal, calculative, and contractual relations of the money economy, devoid of emotional substance and, as Simmel notes, harshly 'matter of fact.' The sheer variety of objective culture imposes on social organization a need to create a network of segmented, transient, and multiple contacts which exert upon the individual's sensibility an overload of stimuli. The differentiation of objective culture, the tendency of each functional complex to regulate itself according to autonomous standards which are indifferent to any particular individual's personal development, leaves the individual spiritually isolated from the public life, at too great a distance from it to create an inward integrity out of its resources. Modern society has become a profound and, perhaps, irreconcilable conflict between the tendencies toward objective differentiation and subjective individualization, each of which has become so extreme that it can only be mediated with the other in the most tenuous and abstract manner. The metropolis is the 'arena,' not the 'circle,' in which tentative and often failed mediations emerge in the context of struggle. In Freud's sense it is society as 'compromise formation,' not solidarity.

The mental life of the metropolis is a series of compensations for the inadequacy of objective culture to the individual's subjective demand for an integral personality. The impact of a continuous stream of various stimuli upon the sensibility drives the individual into a posture of self-protection which is maintained by a multiplicity of defense mechanisms. The sheer impossibility coupled with the danger of responding to each stimulus emotionally results in an intellectual attitude toward persons and things which sets up a distance between inwardness and external circumstance and which dovetails with the requirement of the money economy that value be reduced to calculative judgments of quantity. A further emotional distancing is achieved in the blasé attitude toward life, 'burnout' in today's parlance, which proceeds from a sensibility that has been jaded by too much sensory and emotional stimulation. The self-adjustment of individuals to the metropolis carries over into the tone of their relations with each other, which are marked by a reserve masking a mild hostility, aversion, and antipathy. Aversive reserve is, ironically, the functional equivalent in the metropolis for the imposition of a common social character in the closed circle; rather than enforcing a commitment to a common life upon one another, the participants in the metropolitan arena enforce a distance between each other that allows them to conduct their segmental and transitory affairs, and to preserve their unique inwardness. Here is Simmel's solution to the 'equation' set up by the metropolis between the individual and super-individual contents of life. The metropolis is a structure of negative mediation in contrast to the positive mediation of the closed circle: it is a deconstructed community, what human beings must be toward each other when they no longer share a common focus for life, can no longer acknowledge themselves as belonging together, and no longer have a commitment to hold one another to substantive standards of behavior and temperament. It is society of the absurd, social bonding as anti-bonding in the absence of any unifying meaning for life.

But the metropolis is ultimately a failed mediation. Modern society is not a coherent type but a fragile and unsatisfying compromise between the warring tendencies of objective and subjective culture. Individuals may be able to protect themselves from the assault upon sensibility by taking up the intellectual posture and the blasé attitude, and by maintaining aversive reserve toward each other, but, at least in many cases, they are unable or unwilling to give up their drive toward an inward expressive unity of personal life. The very defense mechanisms that allow the individual to participate in metropolitan life exact a terrible cost in subjective expression, excluding 'those irrational, instinctive, sovereign traits and impulses which aim at determining the mode of life from within, instead of receiving the general and precisely schematized form of life from without' (Simmel 1950b: 413). When the urge to determine an integral life from within becomes too insistent the compensatory mechanisms of the metropolitan mentality collapse and confrontation replaces compensation, neurosis cedes to psychosis. In the absence of a meaningful horizon for individual life figures such as Ruskin and Nietzsche appear who nurse hatred for the metropolis. Finding themselves at an extreme distance from objective culture they reject all of the mediations of the metropolis and proclaim 'the value of life alone in the unschematized existence which cannot be defined with precision for all alike' (p. 413). In 'The Metropolis and Mental Life' the emergence of this vital solipsism or positive nihilism is the cautionary counterpoint to the deadening compensatory defense mechanisms of normal neurosis. A decade later, in 'The Conflict in Modern Culture,' Simmel finds that the apotheosis of unformed life has pervaded modernity as its dominant theme. The individual takes revenge against objective culture and sociology cedes to cultural history, as the fragile mediations of the metropolis break apart in the effort of subjectivity to constitute itself as self-sufficient in the absence of cultural form.

MAN THE INDIRECT BEING

Simmel took up his inquiry into 'the soul of the cultural body' on many occasions during the first decade of the twentieth century, but engaged the theme most precisely from the viewpoint of the individual's search for a meaning to life in the early pages of his *Schopenhauer and Nietzsche* of 1907. Here Simmel presents a concise description of the objective culture of the metropolis as the isolated individual confronts it, providing an intelligible mediation between the sociological perspective of 'The Metropolis' and the cultural history of 'The Conflict.' Tracing the same pattern of human development that he did in 'The Metropolis,' but now from the individual's angle of vision, Simmel names man 'the indirect being' whose nature is to multiply and ramify the middle term of the primal triad of practical life: desire–means–end. Just as in 'The Metropolis' he showed that objective culture had become liberated from and often indifferent to the subjective demand for personal integrity, Simmel (1986: 3) now argues that as human life expands 'the complex of means is itself turned into a multiplicity in which the most important means are constituted by other means and these again by others.' Finally the proliferation of means reaches the point at which objective culture in its technological form becomes adverse to the individual's subjective demand for meaning. Human consciousness gets 'bound up with the means, whereas the final goals which import sense and meaning into the intermediate steps are pushed toward our inner horizon and finally beyond it' (pp. 3–4). Here the metropolis appears in the striking image of 'a criss-crossing jungle of enterprises and institutions in which the final and definitely valuable goals are missing altogether' (p. 4). Only when technology, 'the sum total of the means of civilized existence,' has become 'the essential object of struggle and evaluation,' that is, when the activities and interests which had been endowed with absolute value 'become transparent in their character of being just means,' does the need to search for 'a final goal and meaning for life' arise (p. 4). Man the indirect being becomes lost in the detours of objective culture, in a technological order of his own fabrication which in itself has no unifying purpose, and this is the absurd of technology.

Simmel observes that the crisis of meaning had occurred in Western history once before, in the times immediately preceding the Christian era. Christianity resolved 'the disquieted search' for the meaning of life in Greco-Roman culture by bringing 'redemption and fulfillment.' In the modern era, however, Christianity has 'lost its appeal to and power over innumerable people,' but 'life has retained a deep desire for an absolute goal, especially now that the content has been excluded which allowed habituation to this inner form of existence' (Simmel 1986: 5). The legacy of Christianity is the need for a unitary meaning of life, which now persists as 'an empty urge for a goal which has become inaccessible' (p. 5). For Simmel, Schopenhauer and Nietzsche represent the self-conscious recognition of the crisis of meaning because they are the first thinkers to have made of life its own object. Schopenhauer makes the 'empty urge' for meaning definitive of life's essence, providing an apt description of contemporary culture. But under the influence of Darwin's evolutionism Nietzsche goes a step farther and removes 'the meaning-giving goal of life from its illusionary position outside of life and (puts) that goal back into life itself': 'There was no more radical way to do this than through a vision of life in which self-directed augmentation is but the realization of what life provides as potential, including means and values' (p. 6). For Nietzsche, 'life can become the goal of life.' And so the stage is set for 'The Conflict in Modern Culture' where modern history culminates in the breakout of Nietzsche from the study and into the streets, and Western man seeks his redemption out of his own vital impulses.

LIFE AS FORM-GIVING ACTIVITY

None of Georg Simmel's works should be considered in abstraction from the others if one wishes to gain an adequate understanding of the systematic coherence of his thought. Even in his most exhaustive treatments of a theme, such as nineteenth-century philosophies of life in *Schopenhauer and Nietzsche*, he is proceeding within the confines of a single master form, pushing it, indeed, to its limits and even a bit beyond, but always remaining conscious that other embracing ideas would interpret the matter at hand differently. In 'The Metropolis,' for example, the individual appears at the conclusion of the essay as a transient 'cell' in the social organism, fated to struggle for subjectivity itself under the assault of a fragmented and autonomous objective culture. Indeed, within the metropolis the individual may be so overwhelmed by stimuli and so disjointed by the differentiation of conduct that he cannot even hear his inner voice. In contrast, in the discussion of man the indirect being in *Schopenhauer and Nietzsche*, the individual is the protagonist confronting the problem of life's meaning in the metropolitan context and falling back upon the inward experience of dynamic life to secure a purchase on reality. The basic message of the sociological and philosophical interpretations of modern mental life is the same: that the cultural forms of modernity have become, to use José Ortega y Gasset's (1956) term, so 'dehumanized,' so distant from the individual's demand for personal integrity, that the individual is forced to build a character without cultural resources; but each interpretation places a different aspect of the modern mentality in the foreground. From the sociological perspective, individual experience is a defensive adaptation to social and cultural forces, whereas for philosophy that same experience is the active initiative to gain meaning from pure inwardness. Both accounts are, for Simmel, true, but neither one is exhaustive and there is no third and totalizing viewpoint from which to integrate them. An adequate understanding of the broken whole is achieved only by shuttling back and forth between the master forms, exhausting the interpretative resources of each one while keeping in mind that there is no final word: unification is gained in real or lived time through the process of relativizing perspectives against each other.

When Simmel engages the problem of the modern mentality for the last time in 'The Conflict in Modern Culture' he applies yet another master form – cultural history – which is, perhaps, the one most congenial to his intellect. Cultural history in the grand manner is the history of those ideas through which human beings have attempted to unify their manifold capacities: 'In every single epoch, the central idea resides wherever the most perfect being, the most absolute and metaphysical phase of reality joins with the highest values, with the most absolute demands on ourselves and on the world' (Simmel 1971b: 378). A 'central idea' always proceeds from one of the master forms of life and strives to include all of the others under its sovereignty, always unsuccessfully. Cultural history is the story of the replacement of one central idea by another over time, but it has no unifying central idea of its own to substitute for those which it analyzes. Indeed, it is the same sort of negative mediation that the metropolis is in sociological inquiry, the ground for its possibility being the insight that life must create cultural forms through which to express itself, but then must rebel against them because no objectification of vital capacity into culture is capacious enough to satisfy life's manifold and restless essence. The struggle of life for and against form is both the ontological and methodological presupposition of cultural history; it is Simmel's most complete acknowledgment of the absurd, indeed, his acceptance of it, rendering intelligible the deprivation of subjective culture in 'The Metropolis' and the individual's failed search for meaning in *Schopenhauer and Nietzsche*, without providing any reconciliation.

Cultural history, as Simmel understood it, is far more in tune with current postmodernist thinking than it was with the 'cultural pessimism' that swept German thought in the first quarter of the twentieth century. Cultural pessimism, for example, as it appeared in Max Weber's account of the rationalization of the world, was always nostalgic for a lost unity. Simmel, in contrast, did not take a stand in the debate over optimism and pessimism, but was a partisan of modernity who was hyper-conscious of its terrible costs and, perhaps, of its ultimate hostility to deeply rooted human need. Cultural history, indeed, could explain its own historical possibility through the absence of a meaningful unity in modern culture; that is, cultural history could not have appeared as a possibility for thought if human beings could still share a belief in and a commitment to a central idea that they held to be regulative over their belief, conduct, and temperament. In the presence of such a central idea there is no cultural history, but instead there is history interpreted through the dominant master form which generated the central idea – the history of divine providence in a religious age, the history of reason in an era of rationalism, the history of social progress in an epoch of society. The sociological import of cultural history is to announce the irrevocable explosion of the closed circle with its substantial unity of meaning into the metropolis, and its philosophical significance is to declare the bankruptcy of metaphysical solutions to the quest for personal meaning in the face of a fragmented objective culture.

Cultural history, however, is not merely the negativity of what remains to thought after it has lost the cultural basis for a unification of social and personal life. Simmel's brief account in 'The Conflict' of the central ideas which have guided Western culture through its history culminates in the dominance of the idea of 'life' in his own time. Life, in Simmel's hands, becomes the substantial negative mediation between subjective and objective culture which accompanies the formal mediation of cultural history and provides it with ontological grounding. But it is an inherently failed mediation, the reflection or objectification of 'the deepest internal contradictions of the spirit' disguised as its own self-sufficiency. According to Simmel (1971b: 393) the cultural dominance of the idea of life is the objective expression of a rebellion of life against itself, a form signifying the will of life 'to transcend all forms and to appear in its naked immediacy.' In the past the incessant rebellions of life against the forms which it had created to express its manifold capacities and to harmonize those expressions into personal integrity had been undertaken in the name of new forms which were deemed to disclose a deeper truth and a higher value than the old ones. In each case life recommitted itself to a central idea which it held to be regulative over itself. Only at the height of modernity do human beings finally grasp that all of the central ideas which had informed life in the past were simply objectifications of life itself, fragments of it which were given an illusory independence from and domination over it. Man at last confronts himself as the form-giver to himself, but in the acknowledgment of his creative generativity he finds himself incapable of pledging himself to a meaning of his own construction. He responds to the disclosure of the truth about himself by making the form-giving process itself, that is, life, the form to which he pledges fealty. The idea of life, then, is not a meaning for life, which might give it focus, direction, and unity, but a name for its own restless activity of form-giving marking the insatiable urge to keep giving coupled with the unwillingness or inability to accept any of the gifts. This is not a cultural pessimism which is nostalgic over the exhaustion of forms, but a positive nihilism, a continual nihilation of forms spinning in a tragic circle of vital solipsism.

The revolt of the form-giving activity against any of its own creations, which is Simmel's profound extension of Nietzsche's more optimistic notion of value creation, is the revenge of subjectivity against modern culture, in which technology has become the essential object of struggle and evaluation. In 'The Metropolis' Simmel (1950b: 413) had shown that modern culture had generated its own dialectical negation in isolated thinkers such as Nietzsche and Ruskin, who demanded that the value of life be found solely in 'the unschematized existence which cannot be defined with precision for all alike.' In 'The Conflict' that unschematized existence is reinterpreted more clearly and positively as the form-giving activity, which seeks to reproduce itself endlessly; in the terms of Husserl's phenomenology noesis has become its own noema. But, for Simmel (1971b: 393), this desperate attempt of subjectivity to recover itself through making its own process its object, a move which is intelligible in terms of the fragmentation and recession of objective culture, must fail: 'Yet the processes of thinking, wishing, and forming can only substitute one form for another. They can never replace the form as such by life which as such transcends the form.' The spread of the Nietzschian rebellion against the metropolis to every sphere of modern culture has made 'the chronic conflict between form and life' an acute crisis revealing life to be 'a struggle in the absolute sense of the term which encompasses the relative contrast between war and peace: that absolute peace which might encompass this contrast remains an eternal (gottlich) secret to us' (Simmel 1971b: 393).

Yet within its vital self-contradiction modern life creates its own peculiar forms of failed mediation. The greater part of 'The Conflict' is devoted to how the idea of life is expressed in some of the great regions of culture such as art, philosophy, and religion. In each case the form-giving activity strives to make its object immanent to itself. Here Simmel inverts his procedure in 'The Metropolis,' where subjectivity was analyzed as a series of compensatory adaptations to objectivity. Now it is objectivity which must adapt to the demands of a rampant and nihilating subjectivity. In expressionist art the painter rejects any perceptual or cultural models and strives to manifest his inner emotions in his work 'exactly as he experiences them.' Similarly, in pragmatic philosophy truth is absorbed into imagination and is defined as those imaginations which contribute to the maintenance and expansion of the life process, thereby losing the status of a form of reality. And, finally, religion tends to lose any attachment to systems of belief and dissolves into a function of life, a mystical or pietistic emotion coloring life's other contents with its tone. Under the reign of the idea of life culture becomes as subjective as it can possibly be, but not in the form of an unfolding personal integrity: it is the nihilating subjective culture of vital solipsism, the positive nihilism of a life which refuses to allow autonomy to its own creations and, therefore, repudiates their influence and any possible contribution they might make to its integrity.

Modern culture culminates for Simmel in the jealous will of life to possess the forms that it creates. But in order to possess them it must continually destroy them. That is, modern culture is the project of its own deconstruction, carried through by the impulse to make sheer constructivity self-sufficient. Form is carried back to its origin in the form-giving activity and is held fast to that activity and never allowed to become regulative over it. In light of 'The Metropolis' the positive nihilism of deconstruction is a rebellion against the tyranny of objective culture, particularly in its dehumanizing technological expression. That rebellion has intensified since Simmel wrote 'The Conflict,' thoroughly penetrating the humanistic sectors of the Western academic world and, what is more important, the Western psyche. The vast array of psycho-therapies and their popularizations in the mass media substitute for the extinct subjective culture of the nineteenth century a plethora of functional self-images to allow the individual to negotiate an ever more alien 'jungle' of means. Only today, perhaps, can Simmel's thought be fully appropriated because only today have enough of us come to live his problematic in sufficient depth to decipher his text.

Chapter 6

Simmel and the theory of postmodern society

The revival of interest in Georg Simmel's thought that has occurred in the English-speaking world since the early 1970s has brought to the forefront of attention his contributions to cultural theory. Among the commentators on Simmel's work Donald Levine (1971) has integrated Simmel's sociological studies and his philosophy of life around the dialectical tension between 'life' and 'form'; Peter Lawrence (1976) has provided fresh translations of some of Simmel's major essays on culture and has interpreted them in the context of the European civilization of his time; and David Frisby (1981) has given a careful and rich account of Simmel's intellectual spirit in light of contemporary hermeneutical categories. The growing literature on Simmel's legacy is characterized by a welcome tendency to consider his thought as a whole rather than to abstract from it particular substantive or methodological contributions to sociological inquiry, and to establish firmly that a concern with the problematicity of modern culture is a unifying theme in his varied studies in philosophy, aesthetics, and sociology. Contemporary Simmel scholarship offers a sound basis for a further project of making some of the critical nuances of his reflections on culture more precise. A more intensive examination of key aspects of Simmel's cultural theory will not only provide a more adequate picture of his thought, but will show its relevance to present interpretations of culture.

Current scholarship on Simmel is characterized by the legitimate aim of placing his work in the context of the times in which it was written. The approach of cultural history performs the salutary function of preventing misplaced abstractions, but it often fails to grasp the significance of a thinker for future generations. Any thinker is embedded in his age, sharing with his contemporaries participation in distinctive discursive formations which are intelligible both in terms of regnant social conditions and the given level of cultural development in all of the phases of what Simmel called, in the manner of Hegel, 'spiritual life.' However, a thinker may also push beyond the confines of his era and anticipate the problems which will preoccupy future reflection.[4] Cultural history, as it is practiced today, with the guiding intention of circumstantializing a thinker, tends to neglect fruitful anticipations. Although it is difficult both to make a thinker intelligible through his socio-cultural circumstances and to show how he transcended them those two endeavors are essential to a complete interpretation: history must strive to be adequate to the temporal determinations of its object, but historiography rejoins that the past is necessarily interpreted through present concerns.

Lawrence (1976: 5) evinces the present direction of Simmel scholarship when he writes that 'Simmel is of interest as a representative, though not always a typical representative, of both European culture before the war of 1914–18 and of Wilhelminian Germany, though there is some opposition between these two environmental forces.' That understanding of Simmel will tend to assimilate his thought to the special problems of German national unification and the 'cultural pessimism' which arose in Germany as the Bismarckian formula of a thinly disguised authoritarianism fell apart in the years preceding World War I. Frisby (1981), indeed, makes Simmel into the arch cultural pessimist by interpreting his spirit through the free-floating retreatism of Robert Musil's Ulrich, 'the man without qualities.' One need not deny that Simmel reacted painfully against 'the First World War which shattered the civilization he revered,' or even that he sometimes 'displayed a characteristically German apathy towards contemporary politics' (Lawrence 1976: 6). Much of Simmel's temperament is fully attuned to his period and he acknowledges that fact in his late writings. However, among his famous contemporaries such as Max Weber, Ferdinand Tönnies, and Werner Sombart he was distinguished by a decided lack of nostalgia and by a penetrating interest in emerging cultural phenomena, for example, expressionism in art and pragmatism in philosophy, which casts doubt on the picture of him as a man who could not summon the nerve to engage himself in the great struggles of his time. If Simmel was a representative of his epoch, both as German and as European, he was also a pathfinder beyond it, most particularly in his late works on cultural theory, written during World War I. As Georg Stauth and Bryan Turner (1988: 16) note, he 'may be regarded as the first sociologist of post-modernity.'

The anticipations of future discourses in Simmel's work are articulated with greatest precision in two of his most sensitive essays on cultural theory, 'The Crisis of Culture' (1976a) and 'The Conflict of Modern Culture' (1976b). In these writings Simmel emerges not as a cultural pessimist but as an internal critic of modernism, anticipating in 'The Crisis' the existentialism of Martin Heidegger and in 'The Conflict' contemporary 'postmodernist' perspectives. The following discussion will suggest that far from suffering a failure of the will to engagement, Simmel in his later years struggled deeply with the tensions of modern life, agonizing over them and introjecting them into the core of his intellectual personality, and seeking restlessly, though unsuccessfully, to overcome them. Simmel's unwillingness or inability to take a stand in any of the movements of his period or to found a school or a movement of his own do not bespeak, as Frisby (1981) has it, the spirit of the *flâneur* or the impressionist, who distances himself from the currents of life because he finds them too multifarious and fluctuating to embrace in a consistent praxis; or, as Lawrence (1976) claims, a 'characteristically German apathy.' Instead, the absence of partisan commitment in his intellectual life stems from his placement of the problematicity of modernity in cultural conflict rather than in economic, political, or social dynamics. Simmel traced the crisis of modernity to an internal contradiction in culture and he strove to discern signs of its possible reconciliation: he was not so much 'the man without qualities,' the victim of a cultural pathology, as a Nietzschian diagnostician and therapist seeking cultural health, an agonistic healer, similar to his Spanish contemporary Unamuno.

The following discussion will interpret 'The Crisis of Culture' and 'The Conflict of Modern Culture' as parallel texts which address the same phenomena of modernist culture – expressionism, post-metaphysical philosophy, and post-Christian religiosity – in distinctively different ways. 'The Crisis,' which is Simmel's most careful reflection on World War I, interprets modernism in terms of the categories of his pre-war thinking, recalling *The Philosophy of Money* and 'The Metropolis and Mental Life' but infusing those categories with a moral commitment leading out to the existentialism of the post-war generation. Here Simmel's thought is a bridge between the past and the immediate future, anticipating the drive away from relativism and skepticism, and toward commitment that would mark the inter-war period. 'The Conflict,' which is the most original work in Simmel's canon, pushes beyond the parameters of his other writings, leaving off from the past and breaking entirely new ground in its profound acknowledgment of the positivity of modernism and of its essential failure: in this text the postmodernist discourse erupts. In 'The Crisis' Simmel is still a representative, though certainly not a typical one, of his generation, though he is struggling painfully beyond it. In 'The Conflict' he is intellectually contemporaneous with our own cultural situation, which gives us the privilege of understanding him more fully than previous generations have been able to do.

THE EXHAUSTION OF FORM

'The Crisis of Culture,' which is one of four essays collected in Simmel's *The War and Spiritual Decisions*, has been generally ignored by commentators, who find the notes of German nationalism that are sounded in his writings on World War I to be uncharacteristic of his supposed cosmopolitan bias and, perhaps, embarrassing. Lawrence (1976), however, points out that Simmel's 'war enthusiasm' in 'The Crisis' is 'reasoned rather than rabid.' The essay, indeed, far from being a defense of the war spirit is exemplary of Simmel's late cultural theory, framed in the context of how the war affects the basic dialectical tensions in modern life. Simmel shows in 'The Crisis' how war reveals the presuppositions of peacetime life in a 'highly developed objective culture.' His project is similar to that of 'The Metropolis and Mental Life' (1971c), in which he traced the impact of the social form of the modern urban setting on individual subjectivity, only now the form mediating cultural conflict is war. The basic terms of that conflict are the same in both essays – the opposition between objective and subjective culture – and recur to his masterwork *The Philosophy of Money* (1978).

Throughout his mature writings on culture, until the radical break which he makes in 'The Conflict,' Simmel's fundamental description of modernity is constituted by the tension between objective and subjective culture. Working within the parameters of a naturalized Hegelian dialectic he defines man as a being who objectifies his life in cultural forms, such as technology, science, art, philosophy, and religion, which then demand that life conform to their constraints and standards. Under ideal conditions the form-giving activity of human life is able to appropriate its objectified creations to fill out and enhance individual subjectivity, that is, the objective culture of things serves the subjective culture of personal development. In 'The Crisis' Simmel (1976a: 253) gives one of his best accounts of the normative grounds of his cultural theory, arguing that 'improvement of the soul' is culturally achieved indirectly 'by way of the intellectual achievements of the species, the products of its history: knowledge, life-styles, art, the state, a man's profession and experience of life – these constitute the path of culture by which the subjective spirit returns to itself in a higher, improved state.' The foundation of Simmel's cultural theory, then, is a triadic relation of form creation–objectivized form–form appreciation, which functions ideally as a self-reinforcing process through which human products come back to their creators to enrich their lives. Simmel's descriptive analyses and his criticisms of culture all trade off his normative ideal, showing the various ways in which the reciprocal relation between the three moments of the fundamental dialectic is broken in modern life.

Had Simmel followed in Hegel's footsteps he would have endeavored to show how the idealized dialectic of culture was the actual form of historical development, but his deepest insight into human life was that the three terms of the relation were inherently unbalanced. 'The Crisis' culminates Simmel's tragic sense of culture by bringing together his major arguments about how the objective culture of modernity fails to serve the development of the individual's personality. His radical claim is that the form-giving activity tends to perfect its objective creations indefinitely through differentiating them into autonomous cultural realms, which then are developed according to their own inherent norms, and through generating ever more intensive and extensive means to fulfill those norms. Meanwhile finite individual subjectivity remains bound within its natural limits and becomes progressively incapable of assimilating and appropriating the vast array of cultural objects for its own perfection, and increasingly lost within the jungle of means to the point at which it even loses sight of its native goal. The crisis of an impoverished subjectivity confronting an overwhelming objectivity is further exacerbated by the demands for service that each realm of objective culture makes upon the individual spirit. Objective culture, rather than serving the individual as it is supposed to in the normative order, becomes the oppressive master of subjectivity in the actual order of historical development. According to Simmel there is no exit from this tragic predicament, which is grounded in the relation between the indefinite perfectibility of objective culture and the inherent limits of individual subjectivity: the highly developed objective culture is in a state of 'chronic crisis.'

The crisis of culture is enacted in a wrenching conflict within the individual between the demands of objective culture and the struggle of the self for its own expression of its life. The typical reaction of subjectivity to chronic crisis is defensive and protective, that is, to withdraw into a blasé attitude and to withhold commitment to objective forms. The forms become exhausted of any meaning that they might once have had for individual life and various pathologies appear such as the equation of technological with cultural progress, overt covetousness and craving for pleasure, and a desire for money that far exceeds the desire for the things it can buy. Subjectivity trivializes itself as a defense mechanism against the demands of the objective spirit, suffering from a sense of futility rather than caring for its own enrichment. But it also initiates more positive resistances such as war, which provides an overriding end of group survival for life, and modernism, which in 'The Crisis' is a struggle for subjective culture in an age of exhausted forms. War, for Simmel, is a temporary recovery of vitality and seriousness in the persistent context of futility, and in the midst of its devastation it may reveal to people how their values have been inverted by their resentment against the overbearing demands of a fragmented objective culture. Modernism, in contrast, is the extreme pathology of peacetime life, the self-contradicted resistance of impoverished subjectivity, the flaring up of an endemic cultural disease.

Although Simmel does not use the term 'modernism' he identifies 'a number of contemporary cultural phenomena' which would later be grouped under that term. Indeed, he may be considered as one of the first to discover the affinity between the various tendencies in diverse spheres of culture that self-consciously attempt to rupture received conventions and to give free play to immanent creative process. In 'The Crisis' he interprets such phenomena as futurist art, post-Christian religiosity, and post-metaphysical philosophy, as responses to an environment of inherited cultural forms which were 'eroded and lacking in self-assurance.' Modernism here is the kind of creativity that occurs when there is 'a passionate desire for the expression of life, for which traditional forms are inadequate, but for which no new forms have been devised, and which therefore seeks pure expression in a negation of form, or in forms that are almost provocatively abstruse' (1976a: 257). The modernist impulse is described here negatively as a spirit in a cultural interregnum that has lost allegiance to old models but that is incapable of creating new ones. In light of its deprivation it falls back upon itself and seeks to present itself 'formless and naked.' But such an effort, according to Simmel (p. 257), is doomed to failure because the inner life can only be expressed 'in forms which have their own laws, purpose and stability arising from a degree of autonomy independent of the spiritual dynamics which created them.' Expressionism, which tries to objectify psychological processes directly, ends in 'a chaos of fragmentary vestiges of form as a substitute for a form which is unified.' Futurism, which is Simmel's touchstone in 'The Crisis,' has created 'prisons,' not 'pure expression.'

Post-Christian religiosity, which is best exemplified by a 'formless mysticism' through which the soul attempts to stand 'naked' before its God or to be 'its own inmost metaphysical life not moulded by any forms of faith whatever' is also traced by Simmel (1976a: 259) to a 'historical moment when inner life can no longer be accommodated in the forms it has occupied hitherto, and because it is unable to create other, adequate forms, concludes that it must exist without any form at all.' Simmel (p. 258) places the new piety, which would later resonate in the movement of process theology, against the backdrop of pre-war culture, a 'peaceful age of gradual transitions, of hybrid forms, of that pleasant twilit zone where one can indulge alternately even in mutually exclusive attitudes.' He believes that the war has ended that era of trivialized faith and ushered in a time which 'demands from each and every man a decision as to where he ultimately stands.' Anticipating Heidegger's notion of 'resolute choice' in *Being and Time* (1962), Simmel hopes that the 'resoluteness' that the Germans have shown in the war effort 'will also penetrate to this inmost area of decision.' Here Simmel adopts a decidedly existentialist outlook, speaking of a 'radical eruption of man's religious depths.' He is moving along the line of Karl Jaspers's *Existenz* and Paul Tillich's 'ultimate concern,' breaking out of the idea of religion as a cultural form without falling prey to 'formless mysticism.' With his notion of radical choice he is on the brink of discovering the forms of personal existence, such as Heidegger's 'existentials' and Jaspers's 'ultimate situations,' both of which were forged in the effort to renew culture in the wake of its collapse by revealing intimately real forms.

The idea that modernism is a sign of what Heidegger called the interregnum between gods, that it bespeaks the impotent yearning for new forms, carries over into Simmel's discussion of post-metaphysical philosophy. Anticipating Heidegger, Simmel suggests that the system of philosophy which has been 'elaborated since classical antiquity' is 'beginning to become an empty shell.' Ideal antinomies such as free will and determinism, and absolute and relative 'no longer permit a clear decision to allocate any dubious case definitely to the one concept or the other' (Simmel 1976a: 260). There is a 'demand for an as yet indefinable third possibility,' because 'our resources for mastering reality by giving it intellectual expression are no longer adequate to their task.' The 'philosophical instinct' quests for 'new forms, which as yet announce their arcane presence only as intuition or perplexity, desire or clumsy gropings.' In the inter-war period there would be an effort throughout the West to engender those new forms. Ludwig Wittgenstein would find in ordinary language the matrix out of which philosophical abstractions escaped, Heidegger and later existential phenomenologists would coordinate the classical antinomies in the category of being-in-the-world, and the late Heidegger would make the daring attempt to break through metaphysics altogether to the thought of Being itself. None of those efforts has proven adequate to the traditional task of philosophy, which, for Simmel, is to make reality intelligible, but they show that the very problem he identified during the war would become the center of philosophical reflection after it was over.

The discussion of modernism in 'The Crisis' is framed within the primal understandings of the exhaustion of received cultural forms and of the deprivation of subjective culture. Modernism, as a failed mediation between form-creating activity and form appreciation, occupies a gap between a past and a possible future culture, both of which provide a modicum of satisfaction to the subjective demand for coherent personal development. Although the essay concludes with an assertion that the 'chronic crisis' of highly developed objective culture cannot be reversed in the long run Simmel (1976a: 265) still nurses a hope that the tendency of such a culture to 'disintegrate into futility and paradox' will be recurrently arrested by 'the fundamental dynamic unity of life.' He senses that the 'concept of *life* now seems to permeate a multitude of spheres and to have begun to give, as it were, a more unified rhythm to their heartbeat' (p. 263). Simmel here endows the form-giving activity of life with its own meaningful integrity, its own inherent pre-intellectual and self-preservative and self-renewing direction. The crisis of culture is the exhaustion of form and its pathological manifestations are the currents of modernism which attempt to dispense with form only because they are unable to create it. Indeed, in 'The Crisis' life and form are held in tension with each other in a 'process of interaction'; they are not antithetical forces, but are defined reciprocally in terms of the polarity flux and fixed, each one a necessary moment in the totality of the life process. The real antithesis here, as it is through all of Simmel's work from *The Philosophy of Money* until 'The Conflict of Modern Culture,' is between objective culture (objectivized form) and subjective culture (form appreciation). Life itself as form-giving activity is not problematized and, thus, can be dogmatized, can remain a repository of hope for spontaneous renewal, encircling the tragic opposition between the two cultures. In 'The Conflict,' however, the ground shifts altogether and Simmel problematizes the relation of form-giving activity to objectivized form, abandoning the last vestiges of his metaphysical optimism and opening the door to postmodernist perspectives on culture. He abandons the waiting game of the interregnum and enters the age of radically contradicted life.

THE REBELLION OF LIFE

Georg Simmel was the leading philosopher of life in Germany in his generation, performing the function of assimilating the idealist tradition into the ground of lived experience as it is seized directly from within by a conscious finite self. Like his French contemporary, Henri Bergson, with whom he is often compared, he philosophized from a vision of life's structure which he achieved by a reflective review of the various human activities, guided by his intuition of life's process. Far from taking the pose of the detached ego who floats above life observing it indifferently or of the *flâneur* who mingles in society but can take it or leave it, he experienced to the depth all of the conflicts of his time. He was acutely aware of the multiplicity and relativity of forms, but he took each one of them seriously, pondering its internal meaning and its relations to the others. He did not commit himself to the perfection of any special form as a Weberian vocation, but concerned himself with the problematicity of form itself; he was, on the contemplative side, a cultural theorist, and, on the active side, a cultural critic. He was a man of forms, not of form; a man of many qualities, not a man without them. He understood and was loyal to a moral ideal of a culture in which human beings express their lives in objects which return to them to fortify their personal development, but he did not believe that this ideal was capable of realization. Rather, in his review of life as a whole he discovered irremediable paradoxes, ironies, and contradictions.

Simmel's vision of the dialectic of 'form creation–objectivized form–form appreciation' governed his entire mature intellectual development, but he placed emphasis on different tensions within that dialectic over time. Through the middle period of his career (1900–10) he was concerned with the conflict between objectivized form and form appreciation, arguing that the objective culture of things had outrun the ability of individuals to incorporate it into a satisfying subjective culture of personal enrichment. He did not attend during this period to the moment of form-giving life, leaving it as an unanalyzed ground and taking for granted the 'chronic crisis' of the highly developed objective modern culture. In his late writings, however, a decisive shift in his focus occurs which culminates in 'The Conflict of Modern Culture.' Whereas in the preceding phase of his thought objectivized form was the protagonist overwhelming form appreciation, which adopted a multitude of compensatory and defensive measures to maintain some semblance of integrity, in his thought during the war period the form-giving activity of life itself becomes the protagonist, seeking to deconstruct objectivized form: to capture it, assert sovereignty over it, and assimilate it into itself. Concern with subjective culture drops out of his thinking, as though it had become anachronistic, and the creative spirit confronts its products without the mediation of the appreciation of culture: creative life seeks to become the self-sufficient appreciator of itself, of its own creativity.

Simmel began 'The Crisis of Culture' by defining culture subjectively as 'the improvement of the soul' attained indirectly through 'the intellectual achievements of the species.' The ground shifts decisively in 'The Conflict,' which he initiates with the reflection that 'we speak of culture when the creative dynamism of life produces certain artefacts which provide it with forms of expression and actualization, and which in their turn absorb the constant flow of life, giving it form and content, scope and order' (1976b: 223). Culture is here primarily a product of creative life, not an object of appreciative life. In light of this new focus the site of the conflict of culture moves to an antagonism between creativity and its creations. According to Simmel (p. 223), form-giving life produces objectivized forms which 'have their own logic and laws, their own significance and resilience arising from a certain degree of detachment and independence *vis-à-vis* the spiritual dynamism which gave them life.' The independence of objectivized form from the life which creates it is the root of cultural theory. The forms created by the life process stand over against it, demanding that the process contain itself within them. Life as creative activity, however, immediately departs from them and seeks to engender new forms in which to express itself. Objectivized form necessarily tends to become hostile to life, which constitutes itself as cultural history by ceaselessly creating and abandoning a succession of forms, none of which ever fully satisfies its restless and multifarious drive for self-expression.

The history of spiritual life, which is cultural history, does not have, for Simmel, a formal unity or meaning, but it does reach an intelligible crisis in the twentieth century. Until the present era the conflict of culture had been fought out by the replacement of one form of meaning by another, each one commanding obedience as an objective imperative and then ceding to others after a struggle. But during the nineteenth century a unique and far-reaching eruption occurred in modern culture: life began to take itself as its own object of meaning, first in the thought of such philosophers as Schopenhauer and Nietzsche (cf. Simmel 1986), and then in every region of culture; that is, life at last understood itself as the generator of all of the forms to which it had pledged obedience, and could no longer tolerate subservience to objectivized form which it knew to be its own product. By the twentieth century cultural movements were in process that not only sought to replace exhausted forms with new ones, but that rebelled against the submission to any objective demand: 'We are at present experiencing this new phase of the age-old struggle, which is no longer the struggle of a new, life-imbued form against an old, lifeless one, but the struggle against form itself, against the very principle of form' (Simmel 1976b: 225). Simmel here breaks through the confines of the 'cultural pessimism' of much of his generation. He no longer interprets modern history through the exhaustion of form but has discovered the rebellion of life, toward which he experiences a deep ambivalence. Indeed, Simmel's cultural theory in 'The Conflict' is an expression of that ambivalence.

Just as his contemporary Unamuno (1954) was the agonist of Christianity, Simmel is the agonist of modern culture. His agony cuts as deeply as can be possibly imagined. His great sensitivity enabled or, perhaps, condemned him to experience the spiritual currents of his time more profoundly than his contemporaries did, and his brilliant intellect allowed or even coerced him to express those currents with acute clarity. He was the premier German philosopher of life in his generation, that is, he did more than most others to propagate the rebellion of life, yet he understood that the fate of life was to submit itself, even if only temporarily, to its own products. An uncompromising will to truth prevented him from seeking comfort in the aestheticism of dwelling in the exhausted forms, but he also had to acknowledge the special or, as he called it, 'peculiar,' quality of form, its demand to constrain life. So, he could not embrace the modernist rebellion against the principle of form, its normative autonomy. And, further, he could not, like Émile Durkheim, take normative constraint for granted as constitutive of actual culture because, somehow, it was not. In his thought, just as in Unamuno's, lucidity bred agony and paradox, from which he could not escape, but which he could express by a strategic distancing in the form of cultural history and criticism.

As Simmel turns in 'The Conflict' to a fresh interpretation of the currents of modernism which he had analyzed in 'The Crisis' he breaks through to the set of ideas that are associated with the contemporary rubric of 'deconstruction.' His criticism is not itself deconstructionist – it is a pure descriptive analysis – but it details how the modernist movements are themselves deconstructions of their objects or, better, of the objectivity of their objects. The essence of modernism is the deconstruction or de-objectivization of objectivized form; the attempt to assimilate form to the process which generates it and to keep it there, immanent to the process, so that it can never gain sufficient independence to constrain creative expression. In general, modernist deconstruction proceeds by the two-step process of rejecting the objectivity of form and then of striving to make form an immanent function of life. Simmel's ambivalence shows through in his description of the impulse to make form subservient to form-giving life. In his discussions of expressionist art, pragmatic and vitalist philosophy, and post-Christian piety he is careful to affirm their intelligibility in terms of their positive vitality, but he is equally concerned to show the problematicity of their rebellion against the principle of form. His interpretation is an articulation, an objectivization, of his ambivalence as a philosopher of life, a step, therefore, beyond the modernist pretension and into a postmodernist acceptance of broken form, failed mediation, and a subjectivity decentered by the irreconcilable motives that constitute it. As he wrote in concluding 'The Crisis,' cultural conflict is 'consciously or not, the crisis of our own soul.'

Simmel's ambivalence appears clearly in his interpretation of expressionist art, which, unlike his treatment of it in 'The Crisis,' is sensitive and even approving when it is contrasted to impressionism, which retains the immediately perceived datum as an objective model. Expressionism performs its deconstruction of objectivized forms of art by taking seriously 'the insight that a cause and its effect can have wholly dissimilar external manifestations, that the dynamic relationship between them is purely internal and need not produce any visual affinity' (1976b: 230). The expressionist artist 'replaces the "model" by the "occasion," ' translating the impulse awakened in him by a datum into a representation rather than attempting to communicate the significance of the datum for itself. Although the product of expressionist art is necessarily a form it does not have the conventional work of art's 'significance in itself,' which requires 'creative life merely as the basis of its actualization.' Instead, the expressionist's form is an 'unavoidable extraneous appendage' of the form-giving process: form is present, but it has been deconstructed, deprived of independence from creativity and, therefore, of regulatory authority over it – it is a by-product of the function of expressivity. The positivity of vital impulse here gains a triumph, but at a severe cost: 'Life, anxious only to express itself, has, as it were, jealously withheld . . . meaning from its product' (1976b: 230).

The same pattern appears in such currents of post-metaphysical philosophy as pragmatism and vitalism. In this phase of his discussion Simmel replaces his reflection in 'The Crisis' on the exhaustion of classical metaphysical categories with a positive account of the deconstruction of what Jacques Derrida (1974) calls the 'metaphysics of presence,' the description of a realm of objective truth which the knower must acknowledge and seek to discover. Pragmatism, according to Simmel, denies 'the independence of truth' by interpreting the object of knowledge not as a descriptor of an autonomous reality but as an imagined idea which is called true if it supports vital demands and false if it does not. The pragmatic philosopher carries out the same sort of procedure of de-objectivization as the expressionist artist, holding that 'our ideas are dependent on our mental make-up, they are by no means a mechanical reflection of the reality with which our practical life is interwoven' (Simmel 1976b: 234). There is, then, 'no independent, pre-existent truth which is merely later incorporated, as it were, into the stream of life in order to guide its course.' Instead, life seeks to guide itself through an imagination disciplined by the consequences of its hypotheses: it reasserts 'its sovereignty over a sphere which hitherto appeared to be separate and independent of it.' Here Simmel does not even enter a reservation about the modernist impulse to deconstruct objectivized form and to engender forms which are fully immanent functions of its own vital dynamic. Indeed, his own philosophical doctrine of the objectification of life into form was a contribution to modernism, differing from the pragmatic interpretation mainly in its insistence on the 'peculiar' autonomous imperative of form and not on any independent realm of truth.

Simmel concludes his interpretation of modernist tendencies with a reflection on post-Christian piety, which also displays a deconstructionist impulse, this time aimed at any articles or doctrines of faith which would command the believer's assent. Here the deconstruction proceeds even more radically than it did in the cases of expressionism and pragmatism, to the point at which life would 'itself produce the sense of absolute value which, in the past, appeared to be derived from the specific forms of religious life, the particular articles of faith in which it had crystallized' (1976b: 238). Religious modernism seeks to make faith an 'intransitive concept'; it is life seeking to produce out of itself 'that unique inner blend of humility and exaltation, tension and peace, vulnerability and consecration, which we can describe in no other way than as religious' (p. 238). Simmel shrinks from the implication of this tendency, which is simply narcissism, the self-worship of life. At the only point in 'The Conflict' at which he retreats to the interregnum thinking of 'The Crisis' Simmel (p. 239) doubts

> whether a fundamental religious need does not inevitably re-quire an object . . . whether this is not merely an interlude of an ideal nature which can never become reality, the symptom of a situation where existing religious forms are being repudiated by the inner religious life, which is, however, unable to replace them with new ones.

Religious modernism poses such a challenge to Simmel because for him, as for Unamuno, a sentiment of life is at the core of religion and there have always been mystics who have rejected its objectification into imagery and doctrine. A mysticism of life, the final and radical outcome of modernist deconstruction, would substitute immanent feeling for transcendent meaning, putting into question the necessity of Simmel's dialectical vision of the inevitable tension between life and form, the need for life to confront itself as other to itself. It is just that tension which is questioned and problematized by certain postmodern thinkers who recur to Nietzsche (Allison 1985). The conflict in modern culture persists today, perhaps even more intensely than when Simmel wrote.

Simmel ends 'The Conflict' equivocally and far more soberly than he did 'The Crisis.' No longer does he repose any trust in a 'unified dynamic' of life to heal even temporarily the modern agony, which is not a struggle between two forms of culture but of life against what is deemed to be its own inherent structure, an attempt of life to deconstruct itself. In 'The Crisis' he had suggested the most 'perilous' project: 'to salvage the values of the former life and carry them over into the new life' (1976a: 260). At the end of 'The Conflict' he observes that 'the link between the past and the future hardly ever seems so completely shattered as at present, apparently leaving only intrinsically formless life to bridge the gap' (1976b: 241). But then he adds that 'it is equally certain that the movement is towards the typical evolution of culture, the creation of new forms appropriate to present energies.' That has not happened in the generations since his death. Indeed, those generations have witnessed ever renewed attempts of life to enslave form. One need only think of the totalitarian rejections of the independence of law and their milder counterparts in the industrialized democracies to grasp the expansion of the rebellion against autonomous and demanding form, or of mass entertainment in which life seeks an undemanding appreciation of itself through the replication of its vanity. The rebellion of life has become far more extensive since Simmel's time. Indeed, one might conclude that autonomous form is not a need of the vital spirit but one of its greatest goods, which must be self-consciously affirmed if it is to exist at all.

Part III

Postmodern(ized) Simmel

Chapter 7

Deconstruction as cultural history/ the cultural history of deconstruction

Among those diverse writers who are conveniently gathered under the post-structuralist umbrella Jacques Derrida is, perhaps, the most serious. The Derridian critique of 'the West' is a critique in the terms of the logocentric discourse into which he intervenes, purports to be radical in the sense of getting at the root of what the West means. Derrida performs that critique according to the standard of seriousness that he believes has been set by the historical West, that is, the privileging of metaphysical inquiry. It may seem paradoxical or even perverse to call Derrida serious when he urges one to be playful. Yet play, for him, is the consummation of textual work which liberates him from the hegemony of metaphysical absolutes, which he calls 'master-names.' Derrida transmutes the practice of metaphysics into the play of master-names. He pits them all against his unique word *différance*, which holds the place occupied by master-names, not to control them in a new metaphysics pretending to mirror an ulterior Being, but to permit them to play within and between texts. Derrida takes metaphysics, which was meant to provide an opening of Being to language and of language to Being, and encloses it into self-dependent textuality. The deconstructive move is either postmodern play or modern seriousness, depending upon one's perspective.

Derrida's thought will be taken here as paradigmatic of the contemporary moment of Western culture, specifically the culture of the modern West. The aim will be to historicize his thought, not in order to fit it into a teleological pattern which shows it to follow from previously temporalized moments, but to expose it as an intelligible development from an earlier thought on similar themes. That prior thought will be Georg Simmel's emblematic critique of the serious business of metaphysics. His critique did not cause deconstruction to be thought and written according to some mysterious dialectic of ideas. Rather, Simmel anticipates the deconstructive move, which makes his modernism and his reflection on history particularly appropriate for a rapprochement with postmodernism. His hyper-modernism provides the historization of postmodernity.

Simmel, the playful modernist, will be deployed in this writing to place Derrida's thought in a modernist discourse, and Derrida will be deployed to extend Simmel's discourse on and of cultural history into the current postmodern moment of Western culture. The result will be a Simmelian history with Derridian content and a Derridian deconstruction with historical import. The extrinsic intention of this writing will be to configure what is called postmodernism in a cultural history.

CENTRAL IDEAS/LIFE

In his late work Georg Simmel stood on the boundary between cultural history and metaphysics. His most ambitious philosophical work, 'Lebensanschauung', deployed the hot discourse of metaphysics, seeking a Derridian master- name to define that which is present and extra-linguistic, and using that word, 'Life,' to control his text, as Derrida says, 'from the outside.' But in 'The Conflict in Modern Culture,' his very last work, Simmel (1971a) deployed the cool discourse of intellectual history to interpret all master-names, including his own, as 'central ideas' that characterize cultural epochs. In his cultural history the master-names were not, as they were for Hegel, tokens of a progressive struggle of Being to achieve self-lucidity, but operators functioning to integrate the diverse regions of culture. Central ideas work culturally to bestow meaning on human pursuits. As long as they perform that function it does not matter if they have named some ulterior Being inaccurately.

Simmel did not make as clear a distinction between metaphysics and cultural history as was made above. He sought to control the text of 'The Conflict in Modern Culture' from the outside by appealing to his metaphysics of Life as its foundation. In order to make Simmel's text available for informing Derrida's writing with a historical dimension that text must be deconstructed to free cultural history from its metaphysical foundation. At the outset of 'The Conflict' Simmel (1971b: 375–6) discusses 'the ultimate reason why culture has a history,' summarizing his metaphysical thesis that 'life, having become spirit,' perpetually creates forms in which to express itself. These forms, 'which become self-enclosed and demand permanence,' eventually fail to satisfy life, the essence of which is a 'restless rhythm' opposing 'the fixed duration of any particular form.' What might be called normal history for Simmel is the ceaseless supplanting of one form by another over time: when life is constrained and frustrated by a regnant form, it creates another in which to express more adequately its current condition, in an unending process. When, however, life becomes conscious of itself as form-giving activity, as it does in Simmel's metaphysics, history enters an abnormal phase. Life, acknowledging that no form can ever provide permanent satisfaction, rebels against the submission to any form, putting a tragic stalemate into play, since the rebellion against form cannot cancel the essential need of life to express itself in form. The conflict in modern culture is that of life against itself, of form-giving activity against submission to its own creations, leading to chronic frustration and dissatisfaction.

The deconstruction of Simmel's text finds its purchase point in that text's nostalgia for a normal history. At the root of normal history is Simmel's understanding that history has been a dialectic of illusion and reality that he has succeeded in demythologizing. Up until his writing, history has proceeded by life creating a series of forms, each of which was thought to define a Being comprehending and fulfilling life, though actually it was only an expression of vital impulse. Metaphysics has been life's veiling of itself in myth, but in Simmel's text it becomes its own demythologization, revealing its presence to itself. In Derridian terms, 'life' is the master-name of Simmel's 'metaphysics of presence,' controlling all of the differences in his text from the outside. Indeed, Simmel often capitalizes 'Life,' using it to embrace the interplay of life and form, as though he were able to get beyond the conflict. According to Derrida, metaphysics, especially the tradition of modern rationalism from Descartes to Hegel, always tries to get outside the conflict or play within the text by embracing it in a name. But that name, for Derrida, is 'logocentric,' articulating dispersion in a specious unity. Simmel's 'Life' provides no such unity, but merely names the dispersion specifically as a 'conflict.' His metaphysics is the self-denial of the pretensions of logocentric writing within the affirmation of the logocentric form. It is almost a deconstruction of metaphysics, but not quite. It stalemates logocentrism by proclaiming that Being (Life) is inherently opposed to itself. It is an anti-logocentrism, a vital skepticism, which remains bound to logocentrism through nostalgia expressed in the form of tragedy. Being, for Simmel, is tragic. There is a reason for the differences, even if that reason is Life's inherent nonconformity to rationality. A deconstruction of Simmel's text lets go of the tragedy by decapitalizing 'life' and leaving the difference(s) between life and form to play within the text. 'Life' becomes another master-name to be taken up into cultural history.

In the deconstructed text of 'The Conflict' life and form are no longer mediated by privileging life as Life. Uncapitalized life may, indeed, be the generator of form (and there may also be a dialectical opposition between life and form), but there is no greater Life, controlling the text from the outside, to inform that opposition with tragedy. In the play of the text life has its pretensions to self-expression and form has its pretensions to express life. What allows these differences to be is unnamed, the place of 'Life' in the text being taken by the permissive prohibition *différance*. Tragedy need not be eternal and is freed for interpretation as a moment of cultural history.

What does cultural history become in Simmel's text if it is lifted out of its foundation in his metaphysics of presence? It is no longer the struggle of life with and against form, but the successive displacement of master-names or 'central ideas,' each of them controlling discourses and practices in the various regions of culture. Simmel, indeed, anticipates Michel Foucault's (1970) discussion of 'epistemes' by defining cultural history not as an intelligible order but as 'the displacement of an old form by a new one' (Simmel 1971b: 376). The deconstruction of his text opens the possibility that the contradictions and paradoxes ranged under the master-name 'Life' are characteristics of the discourse controlled by that master-name and are not indicative of a permanent structure of Being, albeit the structure of destructuration. 'Life' itself may be subject to displacement by other 'central ideas' or there may have been an end, for the time being or indefinitely, to 'central ideas.' Simmel's own cultural history, relieved of its foundationalist backing, opens the way to just such possibilities, to a post-structuralist or Derridian reading.

Simmel's discussion of 'central ideas' as cool cultural history has strong resemblances to current post-structuralist interpretations of language, discourse, writing, and text as modes of cultural control. Divested of the metaphysics of life, the 'central ideas' are operators in discourses and texts that perform the function of regulation through centric unification. Simmel brings the notion of 'central ideas' into his text after he has laid the foundation for cultural history in his metaphysics of life. As he turns to cultural history proper, 'the arena of the history of ideas,' he makes a textual jump that will make him 'range a little further afield.' In fact, Simmel (1971b: 378) enters a new field, grounding cultural history in a specific cultural object, the master-name of metaphysics: 'In every important cultural epoch, one can perceive a central idea from which spiritual movements originate and towards which they seem to be oriented.' From the viewpoint of the metaphysics of life the central idea is a product of 'Life's' tragic struggle, but from the standpoint of cultural history 'Life' is but a central idea, to be analyzed in terms of its intellectual content (the idea of tragic struggle) and its adequacy in fulfilling the requirements of a central idea, the rules by which a central idea is constituted. Simmel's text stalemates itself by grounding cultural history in Life and then by making 'Life' a moment in cultural history. Deconstruction is not an operation imposed on his text, but a move that is proper to it and a name for what happens within it.

Simmel (1971b: 378) states that although the central idea of an epoch is 'modified, obscured, and opposed in innumerable ways,' it 'represents the "secret being" of the epoch.' The structure of that secret, the uniqueness of the central idea as a cultural object, is its joining of 'the most perfect being, the most absolute and metaphysical phase of reality' with 'the highest values, the most absolute demands on ourselves and on the world.' The central idea performs the same function for spiritual culture in general that the master-name performs for the text of metaphysics: it exerts control over spiritual culture from the outside by purporting to give spiritual culture a foundation ulterior to itself and a regulative aim beyond itself. For the metaphysics of Life, the central idea is an expression of life through which life interprets itself as other than itself, according to the contents taken up into a form. But for cultural history the central idea is a mode of discipline through which spiritual culture is organized. Having discerned the form of the central idea behind its shifting historical contents, Simmel deconstructs it, just as Derrida deconstructs the master-names. He notes that the central idea is constituted by a contradiction: 'Whatever is unconditionally real does not require to be realized nor can one evidently say that an existing most unquestioned being is only supposed to come into being.' Here the tragic Simmel cedes to the playful Simmel. Remarking that 'Weltanschauungen in their ultimate perfections do not concern themselves with such conceptual difficulties,' he advises that whenever ultimate 'is' and absolute 'ought' are joined 'one can be assured to locate a really central idea of the respective world view.' As a cultural historian Simmel is a deconstructionist.

The major portion of 'The Conflict' is devoted to a discussion of how the central idea of 'Life' can interpret the spiritual culture of the West in Simmel's own time, the early twentieth century. He notes briefly how 'being,' 'God,' 'nature,' 'ego,' and 'society' have successively displaced one another as central ideas in Western history, but he configures no orderly progression of them. When he turns to discuss the central idea of 'Life' he treats that idea as an expression of philosophical culture and not as his own master-name. Retextualizing the discourse of 'Life' as a phase of cultural history, Simmel repeats his metaphysical theses but now takes an ironic distance from them. He concludes his remarks by placing the movement toward 'Life' as a central idea in 'the most general cultural perspective.' In that context 'Life' indicates 'a turn away from classicism as the absolute ideal of human culture' (Simmel 1971b: 388). As 'the ideology of form,' classicism 'regards itself as the ultimate norm for life and creation.' It is the binary opposite of 'Life,' the most direct contender with it for cultural mastery – indeed, the master-name of its ideology is 'Form' or perhaps 'Culture.' Here Simmel deconstructs his own metaphysics by stalemating its hegemonic pretensions. He remarks that 'nothing more adequate or refined has taken the place of the old ideal,' but then reminds us that the 'attack against classicism is not concerned with the introduction of new cultural forms': 'Instead self-assured life wishes to liberate itself from the yoke of form as such of which classicism is a historical representation.' Although Simmel believes *that* 'Life' is the central idea of his time he does not here believe *in* that idea, as he seems to do in his metaphysics. He knows that it excludes the discourse of classicism, of the regency of 'Culture,' and in 'The Conflict' he places himself in the 'arena of the history of ideas,' where 'Culture' is king. As Derrida advises, one should compare title to text. Simmel's metaphysics of Life is an incident within 'The Conflict in Modern Culture.' And the text stalemates the metaphysics.

Considered strictly as a central idea, 'Life' is not adequate to the requirements of such an idea; that is, it cannot join the 'is' and the 'ought' because 'oughts' are always constituted in forms and the idea of 'Life' 'wishes to liberate itself from the yoke of form as such.' The idea of 'Life' prescribes that the form-giving activity, which is essential to 'Life,' never submit to any of its own creations. Yet submission to 'Form' is just what a central idea is supposed to engender. 'Life' is that peculiar central idea which deconstructs the notion of the central idea as a cultural operator. Rather than unifying culture it disperses it into the manifold loci of its creation, signaling an end of cultural discipline and control. As Simmel traces how the idea of 'Life' has worked its way through the spiritual culture of his time he illustrates how the form-giving activity strives to possess, indeed absorb, its creations in a frustrated effort to be simply itself. 'Normal history' has ended and perhaps with it the idea of history itself.

The irony within Simmel's cultural criticism is that life is 'self-assured' and yet doomed in its rebellion against form. The tone he takes when he describes expressionism in art, popular mysticism in religion, 'the new morality' in sexual relations, and pragmatism in philosophy is one of ironic compassion, not tragedy. He reports on the tragic conflict; he is not a partisan within it. At each point he stalemates the movement towards 'Life' with the counter-play of autonomous form. Expressionist art is a denial of the necessity 'for the identity between the form of the cause and that of the effect,' of the assumption 'that a successful artistic response must be morphologically similar to the stimulus that evoked it' (Simmel 1971b: 382). Instead of representing the stimulus, the expressionist follows the inner impulse evoked by that stimulus, creating an exteriorization of feeling rather than a publicly available meaning. Similarly, the pragmatist denies autonomous standards of cognitive validity and interprets truth as a function of success; the 'new moralist' rejects the general forms of erotic gratification (marriage and prostitution) in favor of free love; and the popular mystic replaces faith in transcendent order and obligation with the feeling of piety. In each case the cultural moment of high modernism is an assertion of life against form, a denial of the autonomy of form. Simmel's final judgment on all of these cultural tendencies is that they display a wish of life 'to obtain something which it cannot reach': 'It desires to transcend all forms and to appear in its naked immediacy. Yet the processes of thinking, wishing, and forming can only substitute one form for another' (1971b: 393). The reign of 'Life' as the central idea is contingent on the desire that it expresses. Were that desire to be displaced by another there would be a new central idea or, perhaps, none at all. Or, perhaps, the desire for a central idea might simply be lost.

The command of 'Life' that life submit to itself is self-contradictory because life is formless and yet inherently creates forms. This is not the same kind of contradiction that attended all of the preceding central ideas, which from the viewpoint of 'Life,' made certain contents of 'Life' its origin and aim. 'Life' has no aim to reach, but it is not adequate to itself when it is made its own object. Its contradiction is not productive of an illusion which permits it to sustain itself, but is the frustration of all illusions, ever repeated as long as it retains 'self-assurance,' which is its own illusion or, better, delusion. Is cultural history still in the moment of 'Life?' Has 'Life' been displaced by other central ideas? Does culture now do without central ideas? Enter Derrida, the postmodernist.

MASTER-NAMES/*DIFFÉRANCE*

Considered as an exemplar of a moment of modern cultural history, that of high modernism, Simmel epitomizes the struggle between romanticism and classicism for cultural supremacy. Although Simmel described his moment as one in which self-assured life struggled to liberate itself from the yoke of form, a view of that moment from the current epoch sees it differently. Simmel's own thought is hardly self-assured, but is, on the contrary, agonized by frustration. That frustration took material shape in the ideological warfare and wars of ideology of the 1930s and 1940s; for ideology is merely political expressionism, the effort, as José Ortega y Gasset argued in *The Revolt of the Masses*, to do without standards. The moment of high modernism is that of the agony of the West, the final revolt of romance, fighting under the master-name Life, against constraints of the mind. Freud's Eros/Thanatos, Unamuno's Reason/Faith–Life–Experience–Imagination, and Simmel's Life/Form were the counters in that serious game. That game ended after World War II and may have been replaced by another, defining a postmodern epoch. From this epoch, high modernism appears for philosophical culture as a war of classical and romantic words, not as the tragic destiny of the romantic words. As a high modernist, Simmel's thought is Janus-faced. He has made the conflict between classicism and romanticism self-conscious and has shown that it cannot be resolved. But then he enters the conflict as a partisan, on the side of Life, transmuting irreconcilability into a tragic essence of Life. Simmel the cultural historian adumbrates conflict. Simmel the metaphysician enters into that conflict on one side. But the metaphysician fails to achieve victory over the cultural historian. The *best* he can do is stalemate classicism. But he *can* stalemate classicism. Postmodernism will not amount to a revival of classical prescriptions founded in central ideas purporting to record ultimate presence. High modernism revealed metaphysics to be a cultural form and no more. In a postmodern period, non-classical culture will be king, if it is possible to speak of cultural regency.

Whereas high-modernist philosophers practiced tragic metaphysics in the wake of the modern comedy of successive classicisms attempting to control romanticism, Derrida, the postmodernist, deconstructs the texts of metaphysics to liberate them from the control of their master-names, so that the words within them can play freely through their differences. That is, for Derrida, what Simmel called 'central ideas' are reinterpreted as terms which regulate discourses. It is no longer a question of whether or not the master-names refer to, mirror, or record some ulterior and foundational Being, as they were meant to do; because Derrida's critique of metaphysics aims at disestablishing definitively any such pretensions of language to, in Heidegger's words, 'name the Holy.' As a critic of modernity, Derrida presents an anti-metaphysics, which denies the metaphysical project of naming Being, rather than a contra-metaphysics, as Simmel's was, which reinterprets other metaphysical texts in terms of a new text with its own master-names, such as Life, tragedy, and temperament.

Derrida's (1973) anti-metaphysics is based on a single and

straightforward argument which he presents with special lucidity in his published address, 'La Différance.' His claim is that Western metaphysics has been founded on the assumption that there is an originary and irreducibly simple presence which thought can capture in a name that will be able to control all discourses and texts from the outside: every signifier will be derived from the master-name and will be led back to it, fusing ground and goal in much the same way as Simmel asserted that the central idea functioned. Derrida (1973: 143) negates the metaphysical pretension by arguing for

> a primordial, and irreducibly nonsimple and, therefore, in the strict sense nonprimordial, synthesis of traces, retentions, and protentions (to reproduce here analogically and provisionally, a phenomenological and transcendental language that will presently be revealed as inadequate) that I propose to call protowriting, prototrace, or différance.

For Derrida, there are texts that bear/bare the traces of that which makes these texts possible but which these texts can never capture, because the extra-linguistic holds itself back from the text, permitting its signifiers to differ in a play of signification. The possibility for such play in the text is grounded in the prohibition of presence: the interval that constitutes 'what is called the present' must not only separate the present from what it is not, but 'must, also and by the same token, divide the present in itself, thus, dividing, along with the present, everything that can be conceived on its basis, that is, every being – in particular for our metaphysical language, the substance or subject' (Derrida 1973: 143). Deconstruction is founded on metaphysical negation, not on linguistic theory. It is a metaphysical prohibition that prohibits metaphysics by putting forward the metaphysical proposition that the interval which constitutes the present as present MUST 'divide the present in itself.' But what grounds does Derrida have for denying a unitary present, such as, for example, a Simmelian intuition of life (Life)? There are none. The *best* he can do is to stalemate the metaphysics of presence, but he *can* stalemate it.

Putting the necessity of denying a unitary present into question deconstructs Derrida's text. Rather than ending metaphysical discourse he shows that it can be prohibited by an alternative speculative possibility to the assumption of that discourse. Yet his prohibition can be stalemated by just the claim that he prohibits.

What is at stake in Derrida's thought is not the question of the meaning of Being or even the possibility of raising that question, but the textual politics of freedom and control. Derrida has understood that the master-names of the metaphysical tradition function to control discourses and texts, and, as a partisan of freedom, he seeks to displace them with the word *différance*, which holds the place that they occupied, but denies the perquisite of that place to provide the *logos* of the extra-linguistic. There is nothing to stop *différance* from being displaced by one of its old antagonists or a new one. Had he pursued a stalemating strategy deliberately he would have argued that the interval which constitutes the present as present MIGHT divide the present in and of itself. But just as Simmel was not content to let classicism and romanticism play with and against each other, and took up the romantic lance, so Derrida is not willing to play off the metaphysics of presence and its antithesis, but takes the side of liberated writing against the written about. His thought is emblematic of a moment in cultural history that privileges . . . culture.

Derrida is a partisan of the freedom of culture, not the cultural freedom of the subject, self, or individual; but the freedom of cultural practices, especially writing, to follow their own ways without constraint 'from the outside.' To accept the prohibition-permission of *différance* is to opt for play against discipline imposed from the outside to regulate cultural practices. According to Derrida (1973: 135), 'everything is a matter of strategy and risk' in the text of *différance*:

> It is a question of strategy because no transcendent truth pres-
> ent outside the sphere of writing can theologically command
> the totality of the field. It is hazardous because this strategy is
> not simply one in the sense that we say that strategy orients the
> tactics according to a final aim, a *telos* or the theme of a domi-
> nation, a mastery or an ultimate reappropriation of movement
> and field.

The strategic aspect of *différance* is the prohibition: it blocks any pretenders to transcendent truth. The hazardous aspect of *différance* is the permission: it leaves the field of writing free from reappropriation and free for play, for 'a strategy without finality . . . blind tactics . . .' Derrida (1973: 135) privileges 'play' even more than he does *différance*. He asserts that 'the concept of *play* [*jeu*]' is beyond the opposition of philosophical-logical discourse and 'its integral and symmetrical opposite, logico-empirical speech,' designating, 'on the eve and aftermath of philosophy . . . the unity of chance and necessity in an endless calculus.' 'We know,' according to Derrida (1973: 159), 'that there has never been and never will be a unique word, a master name.' The 'unnameable' is not 'some ineffable Being that cannot be approached by a name,' but simply 'the play that brings about the nominal effects, the relatively unitary and atomic structures we call names, or chains of substitutions for names. In these, for example, the nominal effect of *différance* is itself *involved*, carried off, and reinscribed, just as the false beginning or end of a game is still part of the game, a function of the system.'

Différance is the permission to play in and with the cultural form of metaphysics and, if metaphysics has been the center of the control of culture and of cultural control, the permission to play in and with all cultural forms. Metaphysics has interpreted itself as a serious quest for the meaning of Being, but when it is deconstructed it becomes the risk of meaning nothing. The purport of Derrida's project (1981: 14) is summarized neatly in his interview with Henri Ronse:

> To risk meaning nothing is to start to play and first to enter into the play of *différance* which prevents any word, any concept, any major enunciation from coming to summarize and to govern from the theological presence of a center the movement and textual spacing of differences.

The play is indeterminate and objectless; it is its own excuse for being; it need not be justified: it is culture asserting its autonomy from . . . life (Life), not the expressive life of high modernism, but life as the effort to control culture, which high modernism became when it took the form of the ideological bureaucracy. Deconstruction (postmodernism) signals not 'the eve of philosophy' but the rebellion of culture against the efforts of life to constrain it. It seeks to turn life, with all its practicalities and purposes into, as Kant called it in *The Critique of Judgment*, 'purposeless purposiveness,' into play.

From the viewpoint of a Simmelian-style cultural history postmodernism is the riposte of culture against life; it is the next moment in 'the conflict in modern culture,' which Simmel could not anticipate – the moment of self-distrustful life seeking liberation from its essential frustration by alienating itself in the free play of forms, voided of any import that they might have for any ulterior interests. Derridian thought is emblematic of how the revolt of culture plays itself out in philosophy, which is to say that no claim is made here that Derrida intends to liberate all forms of culture into forms of play. What Derrida does to, with, for(?) metaphysics is being done throughout contemporary culture. The importance of his thought for cultural history is simply the significance that Simmel accords to 'central ideas,' the significance of metaphysics as control through fusion of the 'is' and the 'ought' (even when it appears as an anti-metaphysics).

Derrida's (1973: 135) text lends itself to the historization being done here. He remarks that 'the efficacy of this thematics of *différance* very well may, and even one day must, be sublated, i.e., lend itself, if not to its own replacement, at least to involvement in a series of events which in fact it never commanded.' It is just such an 'involvement' that is accomplished when *différance* is made an emblem of the current moment of cultural history. *Différance* is not replaced, but retextualized by the stalemating strategy of revealing that it can do no more than stalemate. Deconstruction is not the 'eve of philosophy,' but the dawn of the philosophy of play, another philosophy among many, but compelling because it is the philosophy of the present, if not of the presence. And here Simmel, in another guise, provides the concept for opening Derrida's text into a discourse on the contemporary cultural moment, a supplement to Simmel's own discourse on cultural history.

PLAY-FORM

In his sociological writings, prior to his turn to cultural theory, Simmel described just the sort of liberation of culture that Derrida undertakes. Under the notion of 'play-form,' Simmel discussed a number of cultural forms which are detached from the practical aims of life. His brief text on the notion of play in its relation to life allows a Simmelian interpretation of Derrida which permits an understanding of the current cultural situation from within Simmel's text of 'The Conflict of Modern Culture.'

In his sociological writings Simmel specified and restricted his master-binary 'life/form' as a cultural-binary 'natural form'/ 'play-form.' 'Life' here is defined as the dynamic of human experience as a whole, which is impelled by passion, interest, and desire. Out of the dynamic life-experience forms are created which regulate through an intelligible pattern how desires and interests are to be pursued, and passions are to be expressed. The initial forms created in or by life are means to aims ulterior to themselves, at first sensuous and practical, later more idealized or ideal. Cognition, for example, begins as a servomechanism for practical tasks and may later become science, which is autonomous from any practical-sensuous end, but which has the ulterior objective of true cognitions according to a standard of truth or episteme. Science 'autonomizes' the contents of practical cognition, making true cognition an end-in-itself. For Simmel, practical cognition is clearly a 'natural form' developed by or in life to satisfy vital impulse. Science, however, transcends practicality by elaborating autonomous standards for ordering cognitive contents. It is, adding a term to the lexicon of Simmel's text, a 'spiritual form,' which does not escape nature but reorganizes what the natural forms have given.[4] Both natural and spiritual forms have their aims exterior to themselves. Adding another term, they can be ranged under a category called 'transitive form.' But, according to Simmel, the destiny of form is not exhausted in transitivity. Form can order contents so that they are made fully immanent to itself, creating a play-form with no object but its own perpetuation and the pleasure which that perpetuation gives. In the play-form life submits to form for its own delight, a sweet triumph of form, the polar opposite of the tragic effort of life to absorb form into itself.

Simmel (1950c: 42) defines the play-form along the axis transitivity–immanence. All the play-forms are 'lifted out of the flux of life and freed of their material with its inherent gravity': 'On their own decision, they choose or create the objects in which they prove or embody themselves in their purity.' In play-forms the flux of life (transitivity) persists, but it is gathered into the display of the form for its own sake, giving 'play both its gaiety and the symbolic significance by which it is distinguished from mere joke.' The immanence of life to play-form is illustrated by one of Simmel's examples, the hunt. The natural form of the hunt is a means to procuring food, whereas the play-form of hunting, the sport of hunting, is undertaken for the pleasures of and attending to the enactment of that form for its own sake. Life submits gladly to one of its own creations without endowing that creation with any transcendence to itself. Indeed, life is pleased to acknowledge its authorship of the play-form. It would ruin the play if life referred the play-form to something transcendent, as it does when it refers the 'central ideas' of metaphysical discourse to the presence of Being.

In terms of Simmel's discussion of play, Derridian deconstruction may be interpreted as the play-form of metaphysics. For a Derridian Simmel, metaphysics is a spiritual form which seeks to articulate a 'central idea' which joins the orders of 'is' and 'ought.' Although Simmel does not identify a natural form that metaphysics spiritualizes, Derrida provides, through his critique of metaphysics, the hypothesis that the natural form of metaphysics is the practice of controlling discourse with master-names. In the natural form of discursive control any word that succeeds in achieving the closure of discourse from the outside will do. Metaphysics takes up the contents of discursive control, for example, religious conceptions, and submits them to rational analysis and synthesis, guided by the objective of enunciating presence with its proper word, the master-name. Through its denial of presence, Derridian deconstruction deprives meta-physics of its transitivity, of its ulterior object, transforming its discourse into a play of philosophemes and epistemes within written texts, the Simmelian play-form of metaphysics, which Simmel himself never glimpsed. For Simmel metaphysics remained tragic – the rebellion of creative life against its creations. For Derrida there is metaphysical play and/or play with metaphysics. For Simmel life seeks to make form immanent to itself, and the tragic structure of its effort is 'Life.' For a Simmelianized Derrida, life makes itself immanent to form and the emblem of that playful procedure is *différance*.

Derridian deconstruction provides the paradigm for describing the postmodern moment of cultural history in terms of Simmelian cultural history. The philosophical phase of postmodern spiritual culture is deconstructionist play in which the texts of metaphysics are liberated from the burden of enunciating presence so that their philosophemes and epistemes can play in a strategic and adventurous game ruled by 'a strategy without finality.' The effort to make life immanent to form is the *motive* for deconstruction. One does not transcend the metaphysical texts, but plays within them, writing, as Derrida (1981: 4) notes, in their margins and between their lines: life is expressed by playing within a given form. And the result is not a new exemplar of the old form: deconstruction does not produce metaphysics, but appropriates it as culture using 'blind tactics.' It is not, in this sense, the next moment of the metaphysical tradition, but a liberation of it from its serious aim, from its pretension to control discourse from the outside; it is similar to the sport of hunting, which frees the tactics of the hunt from the control of a desire to procure food. By displacing the master-names with *différance* Derrida articulates a far-reaching cultural program. If the spiritual form of metaphysics is stalemated by its play-form of deconstruction, and if the play-form is taken up to the exclusion of the spiritual form, then the natural forms of making discourses submit to closure are deprived of any logocentric authority. That is why deconstruction is not a move back to classicism, but a non-classical privileging of culture, a romantic privileging of culture in Simmel's sense of romantic; a privileging of flux over fixity, of the unbounded over the restricted, and of the Dionysian over the Apollonian. Life plays in its creations and all natural forms of closing discourse now become simple bids to install hegemonic discourses; Derridian play de-authorizes metaphysics and, along with it, all discourses and, even more widely, as he acknowledges, the spiritual culture of 'the West.'

When life plays in de-authorized forms it surrenders its high-modernist pretensions to express itself, but it gains, in turn, relief and release from any obligations to make form serve an external controlling objective. 'De-authorize in order to play' is the formula of the postmodern moment of cultural history. Postmodernism raises the question of whether life can reject authority in favor of play. From one viewpoint, that is not a genuine question. As long as life must struggle to survive it must deploy forms to reach ulterior objectives. But perhaps there is a more genuine question about the possibility for spiritual forms to be made play-forms, creating a culture in which play with culture is ground and goal, and in which natural forms are but practices on the way to or thwarting play. This is, perhaps, what the postmodern moment of cultural history seeks to achieve. If so, then another question follows about the fate of a culture which pits natural form against play-form without the mediation of spiritual forms. Is what George Santayana called 'the authority of things' strong enough to bind life to practicality without the 'sensitive cuticle' of belief? Can life tolerate cultural freedom, that is, the freedom of spiritual culture from the constraints of life's practicalities?

Freedom of spiritual culture is the watchword for the postmodern moment of Simmelian cultural history. The root of that freedom is in the exteriorization and concretization of spiritual form into a sensuous form, which is thereby made available for play within it. Derrida's transformation of the originary and irreducibly simple presence of metaphysical discourse into the synthesis of marks of the texts of metaphysics, in which he playfully writes, is just such an exteriorization and concretization. For the metaphysical tradition the text is an expression of the words of presence, of presence itself; but for the deconstructionist it is the play of *différance*. That is, the metaphysician creates new texts, trying to chain writing to an ulterior Being; but the deconstructionist frees writing by operating on given texts or merely by reading them without attempting to force any unity on them. The text that the deconstructionist reads is a sensuous object, pervaded with form. And the deconstructionist participates in that form by making it a play-form, by simulating its moves in 'calculations without end.' Play presupposes the externalization and concretization of spiritual form so that there will be something to play *with*. Otherwise spiritual culture demands preoccupation – the object is not all there; one must strain beyond it to grasp its import or significance.

Throughout contemporary spiritual culture there is a movement towards the exteriorization and concretization of spirit into sensuous play-forms. In the domain of appreciative culture, including the misleading binary art/entertainment, this movement is most obvious and well known. Perhaps the most significant change in spiritual culture since Simmel wrote 'The Conflict' has been the emergence of television as the dominant site of aesthetic experience. Considered as a phenomenon, as comprehensively as possible, television is the play-form of living. It is not a question here of the contents of particular programs or of the specific effects of the medium on the sensibility, but of television as a world of sensuous forms which is perpetually ready to come into being at the turn of a switch. As a whole, television takes all of the materials of vital activity and re-presents them to the viewer in a context or situation that has been voided of any necessity of reference to an ulterior object, opening up a field for a play of images in which nothing is essential. Just as Derrida erases or strikes over, the viewer can change channels or turn off the set. Just as Derrida writes in the margins and between the lines, the viewer can praise, comment, criticize, and emote at whim.[6] The viewer, indeed, participates with different degrees of emotional intensity in the play of images and meanings, which are always displacing and canceling each other. Even seriousness is but a serious tone, taken up into the governing context of the 'blind tactics' of a heterogeneous series of games bumping up against each other.

Culture here is free in the sense that even if programs, advertisements, and announcements take themselves seriously as specific meanings, they lose their seriousness when they are juxtaposed to each other. That is, life is deconstructed by television, when television is taken as a total text, as the text, and when its 'imagemes' are considered not in isolation but as bits of the incoherent totality. Life is all there, with some editing to be sure, but deprived of any seriousness, of any need to act on it. Television asks only to be watched or, even less, just to be on, or even only to be there, ready to give the play of images. It is available for the life of the viewer to become immanent to its play-form in any manner; for example, as hypnotic subject, compensating neurotic, critic, or couch potato.

From the modern and modernist viewpoints, which privilege activity, television appears to encourage passivity; but for a postmodern sensibility it is playful rather than expressive. The expressionist art that Simmel analyzed was an effort by the creator to subdue form, to make form immanent to life, which meant that in some way the object of expressionist art had to defy interpretation by its appreciators. Postmodern art, exemplified by the total text of television, and epitomized by MTV, works in the opposite direction, making life immanent to form, by presenting pre-interpreted sensuous forms in which the viewer participates vicariously. Vicarious participation is the characteristic disposition of the postmodern spirit, present in Derridian distance from metaphysics and pervasive in the distance of the viewer from all of the details of imagined and actual life given by television. The images play across the screen, just as the philosophemes and epistemes play through the text; and the viewer plays with them, just as Derrida deconstructs the text. Television is present as a perpetual context, but what runs across it is 'the spacing of differences.' To 'read' the text of television is to surrender to its juxtapositions and displacements, never allowing any image to be a master-image, providing a meaning for that text from the outside. 'Watching television,' rather than 'seeing a program,' is a paradigmatic example of postmodern play. Regardless of what is on, spirit wants to play in 'calculations without end,' an adventure, however, without risk, and without any demand to make or possibility of a practical effect. One need not even feel in a particular way or even feel at all. Derrida, one might say, is the philosopher of television. Deconstructed texts are simulacra of television.

The play-form, through which spirit participates in a form without ulterior result, is epitomized by television. The same movement towards play in and with sensuous forms is present throughout contemporary leisure and consumer culture. More than any other site of contemporary culture the shopping mall exemplifies play-in-public/public-play. Similar to television, the mall is a context in which the contents of practical life appear as sensuous objects in a manner which makes them available for play: they are on sale as what Heidegger called a 'standing reserve.' Here again, although life is more edited in the mall than it is on television, a wide array of contents are juxtaposed to one another without any coherence except the abstract one of having been selected to attract buyers. In an environment relieved of adversity the shopper, who is a potential buyer from management's and the retailer's viewpoint, is free to reject that definition and become a *flâneur*, an empirical wanderer through a theme park displaying the commercial version of the totality of life. Shopping *for* something is like seeing a program, but 'going shopping,' 'going to the mall,' is like watching television – a form of play within a field of signifiers, in this case signifiers of utility and enjoyment. One can drift from shop to shop, examining products, imagining what one might do with them, and, all the while, even if one refrained from making a purchase, allowing free play in and with the standing reserve. Simply drifting through the standing reserve is sufficient, with no ulterior reference or purpose. Life becomes immanent to the sensuous forms in which it participates, but playfully, at a distance, deconstructing the sale situation in calculations without end, but also without risk.

On the side of art the movement towards play-form has already been well documented in postmodernist criticism. Current literary movements and genres such as magic realism, meta-fiction, and the narrative essay are open for(u)ms in which the categories of standardized-modern judgment are fused with one another, juxtaposed, and transgressed. Any genres and themes can be brought together within works of the new literature, which are pre-deconstructed so as to appear already as fields for the free play of signifiers. Such pre-deconstruction is exemplified by the magic realist's insertion of fantasia within the standard version of the perceptual world, the meta-fictionist's intrusion of the activity on the construction, and the narrative essayist's shuttling between the discourses of fact and fiction. In each of these cases both the writing and the reading are playful, creating a complete immanence of life to play-form. Whereas the providers of the leisure culture's play-forms (television and the mall) are not playful themselves, the creators of the new literature are at play when they create, deconstructing literature as they supplement it. Both writer and reader wander; there is much more adventure and risk here, though, of course, the new literature is subject to the constraints of the publishing industry.

Derridian play and play-forms are present at many of the sites of contemporary culture. They operate to deprive spiritual and now material culture of any ulterior objectives, disclosing culture as mere culture, as simply sensuous form which can be removed from practical or expressive import and reappropriated as the spacing of differences among those sensuous forms (the discourses of metaphysics, the programs on television, the groups of products in the mall, and the transgressed genres in literature). At the current moment of contemporary culture it is especially difficult to elude recognition that culture is sensuous form and not the expression of spiritual entities or forces such as 'values,' 'norms,' 'intentions,' 'the spirit,' or 'the subject.' Even if those terms are not meaningless, postmodernism shows that they need not control, that it is possible to play within sensuous forms as well as to use, exploit, or control them, that the freedom of culture is available for life as one of its possibilities, at which point 'life' becomes a player in discourses and an operator in texts such as this one, losing some of its foundational confidence. Postmodernism stalemates modernism by affirming play as the destiny of form.

But surely life must do other than play. The background of postmodernist spiritual culture is a technological culture which is at the opposite pole from play. A nuclear power-plant or an operating room are not venues for a *flâneur*. They are specialized and serious, hallmarks of the adversity which life seems necessarily to encounter. By making spiritual culture a form of play, postmodernism renounces the sublimation of technological culture into systems of ulterior meaning such as religion, metaphysics, and humanized art.[7] The practical seriousness of technology now confronts a playful spiritual culture without the mediation of unplayful (serious? practical?) spiritual forms. A new conflict emerges within culture-as-culture between technology and play. Can life tolerate cultural freedom and dispense with religious, metaphysical, and aesthetic controls and mediations? Can technology be disciplined without spiritual mediations or can a spirit of play dis-tense technology?

ENVOI: DE-DECONSTRUCTION

Simmel concluded 'The Conflict' wondering whether cultural history, the empirical wandering engendered by the interplay of life and form, had not drawn to a close with the hegemony of the central-idea, the master-name 'Life.' But uncapitalized or decapitalized life proved in the following decades to lack the tenacity to hold on to itself, to assimilate the forms it had created into itself. Rather than fitfully trying to possess culture, life let it go and fell into the habit of being possessed by the artifacts of sensuous form. Simmel saw life in its youthful, upward swing of self-assurance, but now, at the *fin de siècle*, we observe its senescence. There is a new 'central idea,' Culture, which is implied in Simmel's deconstructed cultural history and displaces the 'master-name' 'Life' with itself. Deconstructed cultural history is the historization that dwells within postmodernity, not imposed on it from the outside, but generated inside it. It is not the deconstruction of deconstruction, but de-deconstruction, the seepage of history into postmodernity, of the history in/of/by/for the *Kulturwelt*, not the *Lebenswelt*.[8]

Lebenswelt history is a drama, such as Simmel portrayed as the tragedy of Life struggling through its inward tension between life and form to achieve an ever-elusive peace. Deconstructing Simmel's drama yields a cultural history lacking any extra-textual unities, but maintaining extra-textual references, the references of uncapitalized 'life.' Life (life) goes on as different from and penetrated by form, but it has no story to tell: it is de-dramatized. Nor does form have a story to tell. *Kulturwelt* history is simply the interplay of life, full of dispersed references, and form, which takes the open form or non-form, of Derridian wandering, Deleuzian rhizomatic thinking, and Lyotardian drifting. When culture itself becomes its own self-assertion or, alternatively, the self-assertion/denial of a life without self-confidence, there can be no drama of culture, nothing controlling or inspiring culture from the outside to be anything other than it simply is. That is how it becomes free for(e)play. There is no longer any motive that it serves. Rather, it absorbs all motives and makes them serve its essence of fragmentary signification. Of course, the only way that it can do this is through the mediation of a weakened life which allows culture to mean nothing but its own dispersed meanings. Culture is liberated for play because life is too weak to do anything but play. Decapitalized life does not have the strength to assert itself as 'Life' and is not sufficiently integral to make any other master-name stick. The frenzied search after fundamentalisms counterpoints postmodern spiritual culture but is finally merged into it because no fundamentalism can displace or repress the myriad others. Life (life) is too solipsistic to pay allegiance to anything but a narcissistic fundamentalism. It mainly exists without allegiance to anything, not even to its own gratification. Postmodern play is not selfish, but at most therapeutic.

Can technology be disciplined without spiritual mediations or can a spirit of play dis-tense technology? There is no discipline in postmodernity, only disciplines, which are ever vulnerable to deconstruction. Play does dis-tense technology. If life is too weak to do anything but play, if it exists merely to submit to being endlessly formed and reformed, then Culture will be liberated for play. Let life be liberated foreplay. Of course 'Humanity' (life) may die in the process. But the neutered master-name of motiveless control (play) – Culture – is king in the postmodern moment of 'Cultural' history.

Chapter 8

Simmel/Nietzsche: the historic(al) disease

In a 1904 lecture, 'On the History of Philosophy,' Simmel hooked into Nietzsche's problem(atic) with history. 'The concept of history,' said Simmel (1980b: 200), in words recalling Nietzsche's *The Use and Abuse of History,* 'has become an idol.' Nietzsche's text had hurled a challenge to German 'intellectuals' ('scholars'?) ('academic bureaucrats'?) to confront the fact that their beloved 'History' (or 'history'), in any of its multitudinous conceptual forms – each thinker, another (philosophy of) history – had become a cultural disease. For Nietzsche, 'history' was just one of those twilit idols, though it had its uses.

Living in the twilight of the idols (and the dawn of the twentieth-century simulacra of idols – it is never night in the land of mythology), Simmel had the strength of spirit, uncommon in that era, to respond to Nietzsche's challenge. He sought a cure for the disease in a form of history purified by epistemology. The disease was not 'history,' but its idolization. A de-id(e)ol(ogic)ized history (is it possible?) in Simmel's hands becomes a form of intellectual play (not a play-form of the theoretical intellect, but a primary expression of it), very similar to Derridian deconstruction and Rortian conversation. Is this a cure for the condition diagnosed by Nietzsche? Is it even the most attractive therapy, short of a cure? If not, then what next, assuming that we work within the frame of Nietzsche's diagnosis?

First step: What disease did Nietzsche diagnose and what was his cure?
Second step: What was Simmel's cure?
Third step: What about us? Are we still sick?

THE HISTORIC(AL) DISEASE

The Use and Abuse of History is a great work of what Nietzsche calls within it 'critical history,' which serves life by 'breaking up' (deconstructing?) the past. Critical historians 'bring the past to the bar of judgment, interrogate it remorselessly, and finally condemn it' (Nietzsche 1957: 21). This is what Nietzsche does. He brings nineteenth-century 'history' (in all senses, but always from the aspect of the history of 'scientific' historians) to judgment, interrogates it *remorselessly*, and then (almost) condemns it. But Nietzsche's short-fall doesn't matter. He admits that he is as sick as all the rest with the 'malady of history': 'Excess of history has attacked the plastic power of the life that no more understands how to use the past as a means of strength and nourishment' (1957: 69). Give him credit for diagnosing the disease that he did not (quite) have the strength to condemn (overcome?).

How do you say 'disease' and 'condemnation' in the same breath? Is Nietzsche just running two metaphors – the juridical and the medical – through the text or do they have a connection? Not a resolution, certainly, but a connection. The malady of history is a cultural disease, that is, it is a disease of *life* in its (spiritual?) (psychic?) (CULTURAL?) dimension, which is *undecided* between medicine and justice, and uses both for its own vital enhancement. There is no contradiction here, just a fundamental ambivalence. Part of him identifies with the herd. He is sick, too. The point is not to blame the patient but to find a cure. But the other part of Nietzsche is contemptuous of weakness, understanding that Shiva is as real as Brahma and Vishnu. Part of the cure, if there is one, is remorseless interrogation and condemnation. Condemnation is part of the pharmacopoeia of cultural medicine, which is Nietzsche's practice. Moral therapy? Therapeutic morality? Something of both? The malady of history is a *cultural disease* (spiritual disease).

If we call the disease by its cause we will call it 'excess of history,' an acute case of intellectual dyspepsia, indigestion, even gastroenteritis. Human beings in the nineteenth century are being force-fed a glut of 'history' that their systems simply cannot assimilate. Why this is happening goes back to Nietzsche's genealogy of morals, a proto-typical sketch of which appears in *The Use and Abuse*. But that is a remote cause, responsible for making history an idolatrous substitute for God, not for what happens to the acolytes when they worship the idol. The disease itself is the effect of the overdose of history on the experience of life, that is, on the personality.

Too much history causes an 'inward life [that] is too weak and ill-organized to provide a form and external expression of itself' (Nietzsche 1957: 26). That is, an excess of history makes it impossible for individuals and peoples to discern for themselves their 'true needs.' Nietzsche in *The Use and Abuse* has discovered nihilism, but has not yet turned it upon himself; he hopes that there will be an authentic expression of life, and grounds that hope on a belief in true needs. The nihilism here is observed by Nietzsche the physician in his fellow Germans, and it is not yet in its most advanced stages. In a sarcastic criticism of the German 'cult of "inwardness" ' Nietzsche (p. 26) notes that 'there is also a famous danger in their "inwardness": the internal substance cannot be seen from the outside, and so may one day take the opportunity of vanishing, and no one will notice its absence any more than its presence before.' And then, anticipating post-modernists like Jean Baudrillard and Arthur Kroker, Nietzsche (p. 26) describes, in terms befitting an evangelical preacher, what it will be like when the inward life vanishes and 'leave[s] behind it only the external life – with its vulgar pride and vain servility': 'Fearful thought! – as fearful as if the inward life still sat there, painted and rouged and disguised, become a play-actress or something worse.' The personality as history's prostitute. The simulacrum of the self as the fully cultural(ized) personality. The self as its *own* seduction: a pure sign.

The malady of history is the nihilation of the authentic self by excessive doses of history, self-administered by peoples who have lost their way back to their true needs because they have taken excessive doses of history. The disease proceeds by dis-integrating life. The self becomes dissociated into 'inner' and 'outer,' resulting in an atrophy of the interior and a hypertrophy of the exterior. The individual and the people as a whole lose confidence in their judgment because they have lost touch with their instincts. They believe that they are latecomers on the human scene, the fulfillment of the past, but impotent as creators. They compensate by deluding themselves that they possess the virtue of justice, when in actuality they have been neutered and possess at best the wan tolerance of the weak. The pervasiveness of the past in the cultural environment, without any purpose but to dredge it up as the 'truth' of the past, smothers any new beginnings in the present. Historical 'critics' will be sure to show that anything that appears to be new had a superior precedent or is diminished by its association to the character flaws of its creator.

The prognosis is grim: 'Lastly, an age reaches a dangerous condition of irony with regard to itself, and the still more dangerous state of cynicism, when a cunning egoistic theory of action is matured that maims and at last destroys the vital strength' (Nietzsche 1957: 28). The irony: we know that as we claim to be expressing ourselves, we are simulating something that is not ourselves, something cultural, historical. The cynicism: there is nothing but history anyway, so I will live to animate the culturally inscribed flesh and experience that is (not really) mine.

The therapy suggested by Nietzsche is Socratic. Each individual 'must organize the chaos in himself by "thinking himself back" to his true needs. He will want all his honesty, all the sturdiness and sincerity in his character to help him to revolt against secondhand thought, secondhand learning, secondhand action' (Nietzsche 1957: 72). In the process of revolt individuals and peoples must learn to use history in a positive way to inspire confidence in taking risks ('monumental history'), to venerate the culture that sustains them ('antiquarian history'), and to condemn the culture that disables them ('critical history'). But they must also learn that history is not their supreme frame of reference. '(T)he magic herbs and simples for the malady of history' are 'the "unhistorical" and the "super-historical"' (p. 69). The super-historical is: to have assimilated the formless excess of histories so completely that one is indifferent to history (and, therefore, to life, which is historical; so this 'poison' is taken in small doses, if at all). The unhistorical is: to be able to forget, at least for a while, so that one can act in the lived present for itself and for a fresh future to be created (which is dangerous, but which is finally privileged over any use of history, because it is how history is made). Once history is no longer made from 'unhistorical' life, the past turns against life in the form of histories, impregnating it from the outside – a 'body invader' in the Krokers' (1987) terms. The 'unhistorical' moment of confidence and risk is the presupposition of history. In its absence the past becomes an agent of nihilation, replacing authenticity, and depositing a simulacrum of the personal and collective self.

Nietzsche's challenge to those who become convinced that history is a disease is to gain the strength and wits to decenter history and to use it to serve 'life.' We leave aside now the question of whether or not his appeal to authenticity, to 'true needs,' makes any sense. The expression of life in a genuine form is one ideal of health and there might be others. In any case, Nietzsche's cure has never been taken (except, perhaps, in isolated individual instances). But the disease – historical nihilism or, as Nietzsche calls it in *The Use and Abuse*, 'infinite skepticism' – remains. Nihilation by history, the vacating of inwardness, the self as a pure sign – seductive because there is nothing behind it: these remain and are more pronounced than ever. So, authenticity becomes history for a historizing age: authenticity ended some time in the 1960s and is now a pose, another indigestible fragment, even if in some sense it is 'true.' Even Nietzsche outlived his prescription, but not the disease, the atrophy of inwardness, whatever its basis might (have) be(en). And the disease, developing ever new strains, keeps advancing and is perhaps now terminal.

PLAY TIME

Nietzsche sounded the warning of the historic(al) epidemic. For him, the disease was nihilism – the replacement of the self with a simulacrum against a void. His cure for it – the return to the self in order to inquire into its true needs – is perhaps even today effective (for those who are strong enough to take it). That is, it is part of the genuine *materia medica* of cultural medicine. But perhaps the disease has worked its way so far as to eat away inwardness to the point at which there is no longer sufficient power of imagination to represent 'true needs,' or the body has been so culturalized that it is only able to give *cultural* responses to cultural stimuli, that it has been culturally engrafted. If that is true, the disease has just advanced to the point that the organs that must assist a cure are too weak to cooperate. This is just what Nietzsche feared. Let us assume this scenario to be true on the whole, allowing for exceptional cases of individuals with sufficient vital integrity to take the Nietzschian cure. How does a weakened individual and collective life respond to the disease, how does it try to help itself?

The vast preponderance of people who suffer from the malady of history are unaware that they are sick. It takes a good deal of strength to acknowledge the dis-integrity of culture and the consequent disintegration of the 'authentic' or 'real' self. Simmel had that strength, the strength to take up Nietzsche's challenge. Nietzsche published *The Use and Abuse* in 1874. In 1892 Simmel published *The Problems of the Philosophy of History* as a 'purely epistemological' investigation, far from any concern with a malady of history. The young Simmel was not yet in Nietzsche's orbit, but firmly in Kant's. By 1904 Simmel was making Nietzschian utterances and in 1905, in the preface to the second edition of *The Problems*, he adopted a (quasi-)Nietzschian program. The mature Simmel might not have been firmly in Nietzsche's orbit, but he had fallen under Nietzsche's attraction.

In his 1904 lecture 'On the History of Philosophy' Simmel (1980b: 200) declares 'history to be an idol': 'The concept of history has become an idol. Now it has acquired the status that was once occupied by the concept of nature: reality can be exhaustively structured within the form of history. The process and the interaction of individual and social causes and motives appear as the cause and motive itself.' 'History' here is what Simmel (1971a: 378) will later call a 'central idea,' an embracing and hegemonic frame of reference for cognitive and moral judgments. The hegemonic claim of a central idea to be the context and ultimate point of reference for everything is, for Simmel, always false. There is simply too much heterogeneity for any idea to embrace it. It is normal, then, for Life to smash its idols periodically, only to contrive new ones. Idols become inhibitors, oppressors: 'each progressive moment of every historical development has only been possible through emancipation from history; through dissatisfaction with the historically given conditions and the courage to begin anew, even if with intellectual techniques that are improved by degrees' (Simmel 1980b: 200). Among the many Simmels there is Nietzsche's Simmel.

Simmel writes his version of *The Use and Abuse* in the next-to-last paragraph of the preface to the second edition of *The Problems*. He does not mention Nietzsche there, nor does Nietzsche play any significant part in the main text. But Simmel accepts Nietzsche's problematic in the preface, whether or not he is aware of doing so – he declares history to be dangerous and tries to do something to neutralize the threat. In the concluding paragraph of the preface Simmel (1977: ix) remarks that in the 1892 edition of *The Problems* he was not clear about 'the basic problem' which was to 'emancipate the mind – its formative power – from historicism in the same way that Kant freed it from nature.' He (1977: ix) wants the new edition to be 'regarded as a completely new book': 'Even the pages that were taken from the first edition now have a meaning that is more or less different from the original.' The problem is now 'historicism,' not 'historical empiricism,' as it was in 1892. The goal is to 'emancipate the mind,' not to perform 'an exercise in the philosophy of history,' the only purpose of which is to 'identify' 'the facts of historical knowledge.'

Nietzsche's Simmel does not quite belong to Nietzsche, but is a Nietzschianized Kantian Simmel or a Kantianized Nietzschian Simmel – an effort to deal with a Nietzschian problem with Kantian methods. What does that make Simmel? A 'great delayer' after the deferred event has taken place? An antidote for Nietzsche's diseases, the one he identified and some other one that he had? Is Simmel even treating (of) the same disease as Nietzsche was? How is 'historicism,' if at all, related to the malady of the excess of history?

Simmel (1977: viii) begins the next-to-last paragraph of the preface with a consideration of 'Kant's question' about the possibility of nature. He states that Kant's 'contribution to our weltanschauung' is to have shown that nature is produced by the self 'as its own idea': 'Nature is thereby subjected to the sovereign self; not, of course, to the capriciousness of the self and its concrete vacillations, but rather to the *existence* of the self and the conditions that are necessary for its existence.' Kant might not fully approve the stress on *existence*. What kind of 'self' do we have here – a place holder in the system of knowledge or some *res vera* unknown to the Kantian system? A methodological subject or a real one? If real, an inspirited flesh or a conscious animal? Simmel is at his most ambiguous here. Who (or what) is to be liberated from historicism? A Kantian subject of knowledge!? (who (or that) also *exists?*). A bit of the simulacrum has been deposited here. The full-strength animal has been denatured. The cultural animal has *regressed*. The disease is not exactly a disease, since its sufferer is not quite a life. It has been turned into a problem for . . . modern man. Enter the Nietzschianized Kantian Simmel: 'Consider the two forces which threaten modern man: nature and history . . . Both seem to suffocate the free, autonomous personality.' (It is historical asphyxiation, rather than indigestion.) Kant has provided the antidote for smothering nature, but left history to ravage. History suffocates the psyche by reducing it to 'a mere point where the social threads woven throughout history interlace. The entire productivity of the psyche is analyzed as a product of evolution.' Switch over to the Kantianized Nietzschian Simmel.

Now to the most (not-quite) Nietzschian thoughts in Simmel's reflections on history. In Kant, the 'mind frees the self from enslavement by nature': 'But this enslavement is now transformed into another: the mind enslaves itself' (Simmel 1977: viii). The dialectic:

A. 'Personality is analyzed as an historical phenomenon.'
B. But, since history is 'the history of mind' (of life as conscious and signifying), 'the personality seems to remain free from the tyranny of historical inevitability.'
C. But, the mind as historized is 'a brute fact, a reality, and a superpersonal force [that] threatens the integrity of the self quite as much as nature.'

What Simmel seems to be saying is that because history has the same mental nature as human beings, human beings generally do not experience it as constraint, as the 'force alien to the self' that it is. They are tempted 'to conceive necessity as freedom.' They *must* be disenchanted: 'It is necessary to emancipate the self from historicism in the same way that Kant freed it from naturalism' (1977: viii–ix).

The disease as Simmel diagnoses it is no longer quite the same as the one that Nietzsche identified. The victim is no longer authentic life with its 'true needs' seeking genuine expression but the free, autonomous person, not *just* in the sense of a Kantian rational being, but also as 'man,' 'man as a knowing subject,' and even 'the constitutive ego.' Simmel's lavish terminology for the self is a symptom of the excess of history in Nietzsche's sense, which is not for Simmel exactly what the disease is. For Simmel, the disease is historicism, an improper understanding of what history is; asphyxiation by a theory of history, not by a historized environment, a surfeit of histories, of precedents and criticisms that wear down confidence. Indeed, it is not clear what is to be gained from Simmel's Kantian therapy. What will happen when the self is liberated (by the mind) from historicism? The self (in which of its many definitions?) will be free. But for what? These questions are not merely rhetorical. Simmel never addresses in his writings on the philosophy of history what the fruits of emancipation are supposed to be.

The disease of historicism is a strain of Nietzsche's disease, a mild case of nihilism – as much nihilism, presumably, as Simmel could tolerate: a nihilism confined to belief that the self is a product of history, curable by an epistemological maneuver. It is a kind of hallucination: one believes that one is free when one is not, because history is of the same nature as oneself, and one is in a familiar milieu which seems to be one's own. But it is not – it is the already constituted, not the constituting. Substitute 'constituting' for 'creating' and you see the difference between Simmel and Nietzsche. Simmel has performed a Kantian sublimation of Nietzsche. Rather than a tortured turning back in a quest for 'true needs' we can get by with some epistemological maneuvering; history can be tamed with epistemological critique. It is a weaker remedy for a weaker life, in which the disease has 'progressed.' The simulacrum has made some headway.

Simmel is a notoriously complicated and, for some, complex thinker. One of his favorite metaphors for life (living) is weaving: Life is woven out of countless intersecting threads. When Life thinks about itself, it follows some particular thread as it works its way through the tapestry. Thought never grasps the pattern, if there is one, of the whole tapestry, but only some designs within regions, sometimes (almost) comprehensive. There are as many ways of seeing designs as there are threads to follow, and each thread has its own special way(s) of being seen at its ~~proper value(s)~~.

The weaving image can be applied to Simmel's thought. As a totality it is incomprehensible, probably by design. There are, however, a multitude of Simmels, each of whom is eminently comprehensible: Simmel the Nietzschianized-Kantian and Kantianized-Nietzschian, Simmel the cultural-critic-of-tragedy and tragic-cultural-critic, Simmel the formal sociologist, the philosophical biographer, the epistemologist, the aesthetician. Those are some of the threads that one can follow through the tapestry of Simmel's thought, which on the whole is not coherent, because each of these Simmels is so decided on just what he is, incapable of any compromise. Is it useful to think of Simmel as unsystematic? No. He is hyper-systematic. He is *undecidable*, the master of the undecidable, a member of the spiritual tribe to which Derrida belongs, the ones who are sensitive to *difference*. Interpreting him sympathetically means playing by his rules, not trying to force a systematization on him or complaining that he does not have one, but following the threads, one at a time, on and off, or all the way through, wherever they lead. Some of them lead to blind alleys or culs-de-sac of the past, others into the future, that is, our present.

We are with Simmel at a Kant–Nietzsche and Nietzsche–Kant moment of his thought on history. This is a short thread that intersects with a few of the longer ones. We could follow Simmel's culture theory and show how his thesis about the atrophy of subjective culture and the hypertrophy of objective culture is (nearly) as acute as Nietzsche's vision of inwardness as a void with a simulacrum stretched over it.[9] We could follow Simmel's meditation on the expressive self and show that in his late works he inverted Nietzsche's crisis of a deficit of expressive power in relation to form into a crisis of an excess of expressivity.'[10] In each of the foregoing cases we would find more-or-less Nietzsche's Simmel, the Simmel who philosophizes *crisis* and criticizes culture. But if we took up those threads we would no longer be following Simmel reflecting on history. None of the concern in the preface to the second edition of *The Problems* for 'emancipation' of the self from the suffocation of history shows up directly in the main text. But we will interpret the thread we follow in the main text in terms of that concern, taking the preface seriously so that we discern the thread that discloses Simmel's proposed cure for the malady of history.

Only one of the Simmels who appears in *The Problems* is Nietzsche's Simmel, and then only in the sense of Derrida's Nietzsche; that is, there is a Derridian thread in Simmel's philosophy of history. That is the one we will follow here. It both provides Simmel's therapy and can be woven into postmodern discourses, enriching them and identifying their limits.

The Derridian Simmel's cure for the disease of historicism is play, that is, to make history a form of free play of the mind rather than what historicism makes it out to be – a faithful reproduction of the past as it was. Simmel's general strategy is to emancipate the mind from historicism by showing how (that) the mind of the present (co-)constitutes history, how, that is, we never have the past as it was, but a version of it adapted to an interest and structured by an a priori form (a priori forms) for organizing and interpreting fact. History, for Simmel, is a theoretical practice, different from science(?) and philosophy, but no less reconstructive than they are. The 'formative power' of the mind is emancipated from historicism, which makes the mind a simple product of past mentality, by a critique of historical realism and a vindication of the freedom of the mind perpetually to reconstruct the facts about (of) the past.

In order to emancipate the mind from historicism Simmel must define history in such a way that its practice cannot (produce historicism?) (be interpreted in a historicist manner?). That is, Simmel's basic work is to *define* a (form of nonhistoricist history) (nonhistoricist interpretation of history). Simmel will sometimes argue that (each of) his definition(s) of history *is* what history *is*, that is, its *a priori* form, how it is constituted by mind. We need not follow him in this Kantian delusion (insofar as he suffers from it), but need only take his definition of history as a possible way of practicing it, a way of practicing history that (transcends?) (evades?) (avoids?) *blocks* historicism.

The Derridian Simmel places history in relation to art rather than science, even though history is a theoretic, not an aesthetic, practice (a more positivistic Simmel in *The Problems* relates history to science). The Derridian Simmel crops up most conspicuously in *The Problems* wherever freedom is mentioned. Art and freedom. And then also fact. It works this way: '(T)here is only a difference in degree between history and literature – although the historian does not enjoy the imaginative writer's freedom in structuring his narrative' (1977: 92). The imaginative writer, according to Simmel, begins with free invention, for example, of a character, but '(t)his creative invention must then be structured according to established laws of phenomena' (the character must accord 'with the average psychological experience of men' – we are talking about 'realistic' literature here). The novelist's motto: ' "We are free to make the first move, but we are servants of the second." ' 'History only transposes this motto': 'In history the first move is determined by the factual material with which the inquiry begins. In the formation of this material into the totality of an historical process, however, the historian is free. This is because this move is a function of the historian's subjective categories and constructs.'

The freedom of the historian is to construct narratives, that is, to link events or forms of culture into dated temporal sequences according to standards of significance, under the control of fact. In this view of history, which is at the antipodes of a 'scientific' history in quest of causes, there are as many histories as there are interests of historians and relevant facts for them to weave into narratives (Weinstein 1983: 93–4). There is no 'history' to engulf us and produce us here – history is a *genre*. It is a collection of histories – arrangements of facts that are found disconnected and must be synthesized by historians. Simmel doesn't say the following, but if you feel oppressed by a certain history, invent another that pleases you more, that, as Nietzsche would prescribe, enhances vitality, helps you live better. This is what some radical feminists and Afro-Centrists have, more or less, done. It is what psychoanalysis does with personal history. History here is a civilized game, civilized play, not a play-form of our ordinary temporalizing of individual and collective life, but a perfection of it through the disciplines of documentation and criticism. As civilized play history no longer suffocates the mind but becomes an *expression* of its autonomy. This kind of history is, indeed, a cure for historicism. First, history is no longer an 'idol.' It is not the all-embracing reality and value, but only one way of organizing regions of an indefinite totality. Second, histories are functions of the interests of historians sharing a common stock of facts out of which they weave their narratives. They are *bricoleurs* (Lévi-Strauss), not 'engineers.'[11]

This is the Derridian Simmel. Compare the civilized game of constructing dated temporal sequences (narratives) out of a common stock of facts with one of Derrida's descriptions of the operation of 'deconstruction.' In reading a text Derrida (1981: 6) engages in a respectful play: 'I try to respect as rigorously as possible the internal, regulated play of philosophemes or epistemes by making them slide – without mistreating them – to the point of their nonpertinence, their exhaustion, their closure.' Simmelian history respects fact and freely constructs. Derridian reading respects the text and freely deconstructs. Simmel's undecidability is *between* narratives; Derrida's is *within* texts. Both are disciplined forms of play that function therapeutically: Simmel's is a cure for historicism and, perhaps, even an alternative cure to Nietzsche's for the excess of history (the cure for the excess of history as the proliferation of histories divested of historicist pretensions); Derrida's is a cure for logocentrism, which is similar to historicism in its claim that a text can transmit diaphanously a non-textual presence. The Derridian Simmel offers us a history in the service of *the historian*, who, in order to be served must (only?) renounce the pretension of having reproduced the past as it 'actually was.' There is a kind of radical pragmatism here. History is the freedom of the historian to historize according to *any* interest in the past . . . so long as the control of fact is respected. That is, Simmel has defined a postmodern form of historizing.

POST-LUDE

So far we have collected two cures for not quite (but maybe) the same disease. Nietzsche diagnoses it as an *excess* of history: a surfeit of history saps the will because it is indigestible – the self is unable to take on any authentic content that might express (co-constitute?) its true needs. As Simmel would put it in his culture theory, the hypertrophy of objective culture has atrophied subjective culture. Why did Simmel fail to follow this obvious path in his reflections on history? Did he think he could improve on Nietzsche?

'Historicism,' as Simmel defines it, also saps the will. Belief that one is exhaustively produced by the past dampens deeply the confidence to make new beginnings, as Simmel notes in 'Philosophy and History.' Without 'historicism' would the sheer *excess* of indigestible elements matter to the will? One might suppose a dance through the shards of culture as easily as a soul sickness. The healthy ego, as the later Nietzsche (Derrida's Nietzsche) would understand, would dance. Who needs 'true needs?' The Self, Who possesses them? The self that is constituted by Them? Throw away that self and you are left with a self that invents itself out of the shards of culture (and invents shards of culture!), provisionally expressing its impulses with them. A dispos-able self. Something very much like (if not the same as) a good Simmelian historian. The sheer excess of history, relieved of historicism, is a fine occasion for play. Perhaps it wasn't correct to see Simmel as the response of a weakened life to (a life weakened by) the malady of history. We might still be heading straight into the 'simulacrum,' but not on a Simmelian path. Indeed, the Simmelian path can be interpreted so that it becomes a path of strength. We put Nietzsche's cure and problematic into the past – INTO MODERNISM – leaving it available for any still on this planet who (think they) have 'true needs.'

In order to show Simmel's cure as ~~proper for~~ ascending life in postmodern times it is necessary to supplement it (fortify it) with an analysis of its politico-philosophical presupposition and its possibilities and implications. None of this supplement is present in Simmel's text; it must all be supplied from the outside.

Think first of fact. Simmel goes his merry way presuming that historians draw upon a common field of historical *fact* to organize – that fact is there to be played with AS FACT. We cannot accept that any more (as postmoderns). Fact is established through the practices of the discipline of history for the use of its specialists (and the public?) in constructing judgments. A fact is a description of an event that has passed muster for the moment as a *certified fact* in the discipline(s) of history. We would hope that Simmel would agree with us here if he was around. We would ask him: 'Isn't it falling into historical realism – the "that's the way it was" pose – to claim that "fact" isn't just as constructed as narrative? Jurisprudence recognizes both "rule skepticism" and "fact skepticism." Just as you can't find the narrative in the facts, you can't "find the law" for the case. Why not also admit that just as you need to establish reports as *evidence* in a court of law, you need to establish descriptions as *historical* fact (*facts* for historians (~~and by them~~))?' FACT cannot be taken for granted. It is the product of the liberal-bourgeois 'market of ideas' operating within the controls of the criticism generated by academic freedom. The discipline of history (creates?) (certifies?) *co-constitutes* the facts that historians use as counters in their play. Without this social structure – this organized discipline that purifies the playing field – there is no Simmelian history, no way the cure for historicism can be taken. If one affirms history as play as the end, one must, as Kant would have said, will the means: the discipline of bourgeois academic history (and the institution in which it is presently conducted?). The cure for historicism has components made by a specific social structure.

What are those 'facts?' They are descriptions of events that actually happened that are open to challenge by a (never-attained) open criticism that generates (quasi-)consensual standards of evidence (which differ in different sub-fields of the discipline). Are those facts, which have their own *a prioris*, any more to be valued than the 'facts' which are (co-?)constituted by other knowledge practices, which repudiate the standards of evidence of (bourgeois (liberal)) ACADEMIC history? The facts tested by 'free' academic criticism can only be valued more highly than substitutes because they are somehow more 'real' than their competitors. Simmelian history presupposes belief in the (quasi-)OBJECTIVITY of academically established historical fact. There is to be free play of narration and (as strict) a determinism (as possible) for fact – a determinism of a cultural practice, which is affirmed for its objectivity, for making possible a common WORLD OF THE PAST for historians to share. It is never FULLY objective. All descriptions do not get an equal hearing. Most descriptions do not get checked, but there must be sufficient variety of *interpretative a prioris* to insure that 'the facts' do not become a PROJECTION of a meta-narrative or an oligopoly of meta-narratives. Is this very CONSTRUCTED system worth affirming? If not, one cannot affirm Simmelian historical play. Will the end, will the means.

Who cares any more? Do we even suffer from a malady of history any more? Are we still sick? We are not sick with historicism, but the suggestion can be made that we are sicker than ever, not with history but with historization. And the cure for that is also Simmelian history, though it is wildly unlikely that the cure will be taken. Perhaps history is dead, but historization suffocates all the more. Historization has escaped history! By 'historization' we mean putting (more-or-less partial) descriptions of events that happened, might have happened, did not happen but are thought to have happened, or did not happen at all but were self-consciously imagined, etc., into dated narratives. History as an academic discipline functioning under liberal controls of academic freedom has become a minor agent in the social practice of constructing 'pasts' (never THE past). History competes with bureaucratic histories, media 'documentaries,' docudramas, historical fictions, organized myth systems, and historicist ideologies (another minor agent) for the claim to describe and interpret the past (that is, to construct pasts). Indeed, the new malady of history is the loss of the past and the substitution for it with simulacra of pasts. Now we live not only without an authentic self (Nietzsche) but without fact-based historization (Simmel). To be sure, fact-based historization is still done, but it is not the putative, even aspiring, would-be, hegemonic (not even close to it) form of historization.

We were going to argue that Simmelian historization is a cure for the disease of historization, and it is, for those who are willing and able to take it. Then again, it is not a cure at all. *Who* needs it? We seem to need a 'past' to orient us, but why does it have to be based on certified fact? Why not just a radical play of differends: instant 'histories' for whatever purposes (sales, pacification, amusement, mobilization, 'JUSTICE'), uncontrolled by the standards of evidence of academic history? If the point is to dance in the shards of culture, some of those shards, or all of them, can be imagined. Let bureaucracies have their records and keep them as accurate as the political pressures make them keep them. When they become 'archives' they can be spliced into the historization process along with the diaries, home videos, photo albums, and advertisements. There will never be too much material, 'factual' and not, for the historization process.

Play with temporal sequences does not have to be civilized, that is, based on *fact*. What happens if we get rid of the *nostalgia* for fact? We have post-civilized play, where myth and history, separated so strictly by Lévi-Strauss, entwine together in ever new (and ever the same!) combinations: the postmodern scene, the postmodern time(s).

Or should we practice resolute remembrance of some *facts* of the past like the *HOLOCAUST*?

The problematic of 'history' has shifted to the problematic of historization and the Death of the Fact. Should we affirm 'fact?' How do we affirm it? Can or should historization be disciplined by the fact-certification practices of bourgeois (liberal) academic history? Does that beast even exist any more? How do we remember well? Should we remember or should we play with memory? How much temporal integrity and of what kind? Everything is up for grabs now in the wake of the decentering (collapse) of *fact*. Are we still sick? Or were 'we' ever?

Chapter 9

Subject and history: Foucault (Simmel) Foucault

SOVEREIGN SUBJECT

In the concluding remark of the section in his 'Introduction' to *The Archaeology of Knowledge* devoted to critiquing the 'sovereign subject,' Foucault suggests that Marx and Nietzsche had been given 'guard duties' by the partisans of historical continuity (the fearful protectors of the 'sovereign subject'). Foucault (1976: 14) says:

> They [Marx and Nietzsche] could not be depended on to preserve privilege; nor to affirm once and for all – and God knows it is needed in the distress of today – that history, at least, is living and continuous, that it is, for the subject in question, a place of rest, certainty, reconciliation, a place of tranquilized sleep.

Foucault makes this statement after having ruthlessly debunked the thesis that history is continuous by deriving it from the pathetic narcissism of belief in the 'sovereign subject.' What's going on? We do not doubt that Marx and Nietzsche are not entirely reliable sentries to protect the treasure of historical continuity and the jewel that gleams within it, the 'sovereign subject.' But why the 'God knows' clause? If historical continuity is 'needed in the distress of today' why did Foucault decide to debunk it? Does this lover of Nietzsche and student of his 'Genealogy' ride on a will to truth? Should the truth be told even if the lie is *needed*? That smacks of an abstract idealism. Or is Foucault being ironic here? We will take him seriously. He has acted against need and in favor of truth. There must be a serious play of difference here, perhaps a philosophical psychosis.

Foucault invites the conjunction of philosophy and psychosis when he debunks the defenders of historical continuity. For him, it is not whether or not their thesis is correct, but that the discipline of history has passed them by: history gets along without supposing continuity. So, the question becomes, why do they cling to continuity so fiercely? Foucault says they do because history is the last refuge of the 'sovereign subject,' which is what is really at stake in epistemological battles over the status of 'history.'

We are in search here of the *historical subject(s)*, not the Subject of History. We will work our way towards them, step by step, from their antipode, the 'sovereign subject.' That is all that we wish to reveal now about our project.[12]

What does Foucault mean by the 'sovereign subject?' He (1976: 12) does not give a direct definition of it, but describes how historical continuity serves it: 'Making historical analysis the discourse of the continuous and making human consciousness the original subject of all historical development and all action are the two sides of the same system of thought.' That is, the 'sovereign subject' is the *subject of history*, Hegel's Absolute: the very creator of history for its own self-realization. But not exactly. It is *human* consciousness that is meant to have 'sovereignty' for its defenders. Maximal sovereignty would be the Absolute. Hegel planned it that way – a subject embracing history as its own. Anything less seems to be not quite sovereign or not sovereign at all. But, of course, for Foucault, the Absolute is out of the question. His target is the 'humanism' that inherited the pretensions of the Absolute, replacing the Absolute (in some inexplicable way) with humanity. The notion that human consciousness founds itself is, for Foucault, false. The field of continuous history is a fictive domain where the fantasy of self-founding is enacted. The present paragraph is tortured because Foucault's discussion is tortured and imprecise. We can only get this far: the 'sovereign subject' is *at least* (and maybe only) humanity as a self-positing subject.

Is this what is 'needed in the distress of today' – the Freudian omnipotent ego in the form of the Hegelian Absolute humanized, that is, a belief in completed, self-willed meaning? Perhaps not quite or not at all, or in principle but not in practice. Historical continuity, says Foucault (1976: 14) 'was secretly but entirely related to the synthetic activity of the subject.' That is, whenever there is an appeal to historical continuity the assertion of the 'sovereign subject' might be behind it: the defenders of historical continuity are not making an epistemological point, but are bewailing the imminent disappearance of 'the "development" (*devenir*) that was to provide the sovereignty of consciousness with a safer, less exposed shelter than myths, kinship systems, languages, sexuality, or desire.' The 'sovereign subject' turns out to be a passive and acutely vulnerable entity. It needs to have history as a shelter (as Foucault concludes), as a 'place of rest, certainty, reconciliation, a place of tranquilized sleep.' The 'sovereign subject' is comatose. We could let this pathetic projection of human weakness sleep (and perchance dream). But Foucault won't allow it.

Following Freud, Foucault embraces the Copernican revolutions that decenter 'man' (Freud mentions Copernicus, Darwin, and himself; Foucault mentions Marx, Nietzsche, psychoanalysis, and linguistics). Foucault (1976: 14) appoints himself the Copernicus of history: 'All the treasure of bygone days was crammed into the old citadel of this history; it was thought to be secure; it was sacralized; it was made the last resting-place of anthropological thought.' He will plant the flag of anti-humanism in this domain and disperse the treasure. But he acknowledges that we need that treasure in the 'distress of today.'

Human beings need to believe that consciousness is sovereign, believes Foucault (sometimes). Each one is not an Absolute, but there is 'the promise that one day the subject – in the form of historical consciousness – will once again be able to appropriate, to bring back under its sway, all those things that are kept at a distance by difference, and find in them what might be called his abode' (1976: 12). It seems to be a case of nostalgia for the Absolute, but who is suffering from it? It appears to be a wish for God. Do we all have it? It is a very particular form of nostalgia. One wants to be able to believe that one's solidarity with the past and the future is secure. That belief would give one assurance in one's (necessity?) (importance?) (power?) (or just not-being-aloneness?). Is the 'sovereign subject' something maximal like a humanized Hegelian Absolute or is it something minimal like a 'promise?' Is it the case that 'sovereign' is redundant or fails to distinguish between the various possible definitions of subject, that all 'conscious' subjects must be expunged as – essentially? – *secretly?* – 'sovereign subjects'? If a maximal definition of 'sovereign subject' is intended then it seems to be a minor matter. Who believes in the Hegelian Absolute any more? But if the 'sovereign subject' is working *secretly* within other beliefs, then all subjects that synthesize histories are under suspicion. 'Sovereign subject' is a very sliding signifier. It is easy to polemicize against belief in it if it is maximally defined – cheap philosophical grace. It is harder to take up against it if its sovereignty is *imputed*, a 'secret' operation.

Is the nostalgia for the Absolute present in every instance that someone constructs a narrative under the methodological principle of continuity? An affirmative answer is one possible conclusion to be drawn from Foucault's genealogical analysis of the 'sovereign subject.' Another is that Foucault is terribly troubled, that he is projecting his *own failed* and *impotent* nostalgia on to others, that he is spiteful, meaning something like: 'I can't believe any more, so I won't let you believe.' 'If we can't have God, we won't have anything.' Or he is afraid of his own weakness: 'I must destroy historical continuity because if I don't I'll be tempted to give way to nostalgia.' 'I must destroy (or is it just "decenter"?) the subject, the *historical subject*, because if I don't I'll be tempted to assert the "sovereign subject." ' That is, Foucault is in flight from the temptation of the infantile omnipotent ego. This alternative is equally plausible, because there's nothing logical about the connection between mere historical continuity and the 'sovereign subject.' The connection is *psychological*, as Foucault implies by offering only a psychological analysis. Turnabout is fair play.

Foucault's attack on the 'sovereign subject' is a Copernican revolution or a projection of his own *ressentiment* (or fear). It is undecidable. We will follow the subtext of 'the subject' through *The Archaeology of Knowledge* as if the latter alternative was true. We will read the work dramatically, as a story of Foucault's redemption (and our own) from the nihilism of the self.

HYPOTHETICAL/METHODOLOGICAL SUBJECT

We interrupt our narrative with a rupture. In the first place, Foucault has been terribly irritating with his 'sovereign subject.' Is there a 'sovereign subject' short of the Hegelian Absolute and, if so, does there ever come a point when one can speak legitimately about a non-sovereign subject? Is Foucault a nihilist of the self or another of the army of anti-Hegelian rebels like Marx and Freud, setting up his own *revision* of Absolutism? Is he postmodern and 'structuralist' (DECENTERING the subject), or is he just lopping off God and not so-called 'substitutes' for God (God acting secretly)? Is he the structuralist Marx or the humanist Marx (in disguise), is he Nietzsche-nihilist or Nietzsche-therapist, mechanistic Freud or vitalistic Freud? This is to say that Foucault is that unique writer in contemporary discourses who *enacts* the agony of the transition between modernism and postmodernism, which is why the subject comes to a point of crisis in his text. Our irritation with Foucault has been dispersed with compassion. We are all bridges over the abyss.

But the rupture will be made. We also want to approach the problem of the 'subject' from a different viewpoint than Foucault's. We are going to define the least sovereign subject that we can imagine under the judgment of the question: Is this also a 'sovereign subject?' Then we will leave the matter alone, having acquired a *minimal(ist)* subject, through which we will read Foucault's struggles with the subject in *The Archaeology*.

We shift our discursive field to Simmel, who describes a minimal(ist) historical subject (subject of history?) in his 1918 essay 'On the Nature of Historical Understanding.' This is one of Simmel's late master essays, where he tiptoes on the fringes of what we now call 'postmodernism' and sometimes breaks through to its de-center. Who better than Simmel the hyper-modernist *cum* postmodernist to play to a stalemate with Foucault?

Simmel's (1980c: 116) discussion of the subject of historical discourse is in the final section of 'On the Nature of Historical Understanding.' He undertakes there a critique of his historiographical demon, 'radical historicism,' which 'proposes to resolve the entire problem of understanding a human artifact by reconstructing the conditions and stages of its temporal development.' Simmel's big objective in the essay is to vindicate the irreducible difference between describing the conditions of a cultural object and describing that object itself. The latter for Simmel is autonomous of all forms of historical thinking. In the process of his argument Simmel (1980c: 119) reaches the position that the materials of historical thinking are disconnected documents or, more vividly, 'discontinuous sequence(s) of brute facts.' Each artifact can be described in and by itself, without the necessity of tracing its antecedents. For example, history of art: 'Paintings ... exist discontinuously and independently of one another. They are insular, self-contained entities' (1980c: 120).

Simmel has something like or a version of the 'eidetic reduction' here, in tune with Husserl's critique of historicism, but he does not take the step to essentialism. He does not reify a rational subject of history, a repository of the intelligibility of things.

The objectivity of contents and their dispersion, two doctrines dear to Foucault, are affirmed by Simmel. However, they are turned to an opposite effect: Simmel finds in them the opportunity to vindicate the subject. This is the point at which the stalemate occurs. On the grounds of objectivity and dispersion we can affirm historical continuity and a subject.

Simmel's minimal(ist) subject of historical discourse is a 'hypothetical' or 'methodological' subject. We will follow his description (1980c: 121) and comment on it along the way. For example, 'If art is the collection of works of art, then the word "art" does not refer to a concrete entity. Or, even if it did, this could not be an organic entity which "experiences" a process of evolution. If this were the case, it would be necessary for "art" to paint pictures.' (Simmel here is an ally of Foucault in the struggle against a certain kind of 'sovereign subject,' the (disguised) Absolute: if 'art' painted pictures it would be Art, the subject of its own history. But this is absurd, both Simmel and Foucault agree.) 'But in fact they are painted by artists.' (How far would Foucault accept this?) 'If, on the other hand, we employ this expression, then it is because we have hypostatized an heuristic concept and created a totally new subject.' (This is the crucial point for the stalemate. The Simmelian analogue of Foucault's 'sovereign subject' is an hypostatized entity – a heuristic concept that has been given a founding ontological status. If we say that this will be our working understanding of 'sovereign subject' then we can ask why a non-sovereign subject might not arise from de-reification. And this is just what Simmel does: he suggests a purely heuristic subject for historical discourse.) 'Individual works of art are the manifestations or stages of the life of this subject. A process of temporal development is imputed to this subject. For this reason, moreover, the moments of this process of development exhibit that supra-temporal and purely objective developmental relationship.' ('A process of temporal development is IMPUTED to this subject.' What happens when we make the imputation reflexively? We get the minimal(ist) subject – the hypothetical/ methodological subject.)

Discussing the history of philosophy, Simmel (1980c: 120)

remarks that the 'hypothetical subject breaks down the boundaries which define the self-contained, immanent meaning that is peculiar to each doctrine. This hypothetical subject could be called a technical heuristic device.' Philosophy is not a 'living tradition,' constituting itself through the contributions of philosophies; rather, the history of philosophy is a product of historization whereby the illusion of life as an intelligible process of development is projected on collections of dispersed documents and organized around the *fiction* of a methodological subject. The history of culture contrives *simulacra* of the forms of subjective life. Instancing the history of art, Simmel (p. 121) suggests that the methodological subject 'is an ideal structure that experiences all these [dispersed] creations – their preliminary beginnings, rise, and decline – in a psychologically comprehensible process of evolution' (psychologically, not logically, comprehensible). Is a purely hypothetical subject, which is acknowledged to be such, non-sovereign enough not to be 'sovereign?' It is a play-form of sovereignty – all of the attributes of sovereignty on condition that we take them only as *imputations*. Why not this illusory continuity, as an art(ifice) of connecting in multitudinously indefinite ways, rather than or in addition to the abandonment of continuity called for by Foucault? Is it even possible for Foucault to abandon continuity? Doesn't what he calls a 'system of dispersion' have its own *methodological* subject? Neither Simmel nor Foucault countenances the (crypto-Hegelian) Subject of History. But Simmel offers a *historical* subject.

To define a range of historical subjects that are not, or might not be, sovereign is one purpose of this writing. The term 'historical subject' is indefinite in its reference. It might refer to the subject assigned to historical narrative; for example, 'Art' as the subject of a history of art. In that case the historical subject is fully immanent to discourse, a purely methodological operator, as Simmel makes it. But the historical subject might also refer to those flesh-and-blood human beings who actually produce the materials that the historian historizes, and who historize their own activity; that is, who orient themselves to their activity through a history or histories of it. Or, historical subject might mean the subject in the name of which or whom the materials that the historian historizes are produced. That 'name' can (and usually does) already have histories – for example, of nations, tribes, classes. Flesh-and-blood individuals can act in their own names when they historize their activities, or they can act in the names of others, be they individuals, groups, or cultural forms. In the present writing, 'historical subject(s)' covers the range from the purely methodological subject, through the subject in the name of whom, or which, deeds are done, to the human beings who do the deeds and historize them. All of these are historical subjects (as opposed to (sovereign) subjects of history) as long as they are interpreted according to Simmel's minimalist understanding of historical subjectivity; that is, that the subject that is taken to persist through time is acknowledged to be fictive. The methodological subject is present whenever a non-sovereign historical subject is (co-)constituted, whenever time is constituted in discourse.

Take the subject in the name of whom, or which, deeds are done. If it is understood to be a hypothetical subject, a fiction, it is, in the terms of this writing, a historical subject. But if it is understood to be a real continuity, independent of postulation, it is judged to be infected with 'sovereignty.' Similarly, the flesh-and-blood 'actors' who historize their actions in terms of autobiographical reflection (not necessarily written or systematized 'autobiographies') are historical subjects insofar as they acknowledge that their autobiographical 'selves' are hypothetical 'fictions.' That is, all 'historical subjects,' as defined in this writing, partake of the methodological subject. Having said that it becomes clear how far the 'sovereign subject' penetrates historization. How many of those who act or write histories in the name of one or another collectivity hold that collectivity to be a methodological fiction? How many of those who tell themselves their life stories believe that the self whose adventures and vicissitudes they are narrating is a fiction?

The complications of historical subjectivity stem from the fact that before historians ever postulate methodological subjects, human beings are historizing their activities for practical purposes; that is, they are creating histories as frameworks of orientation, legitimation, and appreciation. This fact is acknowledged by Simmel (1980c: 97) who holds that the methodological subject of historical discourse is a mutation of the subject of praxis: 'prototypical forms of history as a science are significantly prefigured in the structures and methods with which praxis pieces together the images of the past.' That is, no less than collections of artifacts, the memories and experiences of the self are dispersed, each content just what it is or was. Each human being, Simmel notes, constructs one or more autobiographies. The autobiography, indeed, (co-)constitutes the self. And what is the subject of such an autobiography? Simmel doesn't go this far, but by reading the subject of historians' discourses into practical discourse, the subject of autobiographical reflection is understood as a hypothetical or methodological subject. The subject of historical discourse is one kind of hypothetical subject and the autobiographical subject – each one of us – is another. The subject in the name of which, or whom, deeds are done (and histories often written) stands between them as a weak mediator in the series of historical subjects. The three (non-sovereign) historical subjects are heterogeneous, comprehending the subjects who historize their practical lives, the subjects posited by historians in their discourses, and the (most often collective) subjects in the name of which, or whom, deeds are done (and histories written). This typology of subjects may not be exhaustive and its categories are not mutually exclusive (the subject in the name of which or whom deeds are done partakes of both the practical and theoretical discourses). The categories are meant to show how non-sovereign historical subjectivity might be conceived. This is where we stand now: if we deny the sovereign subject we can, along Simmel's line, affirm a non-sovereign subject. Where does Foucault stand on non-sovereign subjectivity?

ENUNCIATING-SUBJECT/SUBJECT-POSITION

We now take up our story of Foucault, under the sign of the hypothetical or methodological subject. As Foucault struggles through the drama of 'decentering the subject' we will be measuring his meditations by the standard of the methodological subject. Does decentering concede even more subjecthood than Simmelian minimalism? Does Foucault merely define an 'equivalent' to the methodological subject? Does he describe an even more minimal subject than Simmel does? Does he abolish the subject?

Foucault introduces a new kind of subject, a (seemingly) very specialized subject – the subject(s) of the discourses that are analyzed by historians of discursive formations, including(?) the discourse(s) of historians (subject(s) of historical discourse). Foucault's 'enunciating subject' is the subject that the historian of discursive formations is theoretically committed to using in the analysis of discourses. That would make it very similar to a 'methodological subject.' Or is the enunciating subject something more – a practical-historical subject? Or something less – a 'function' (mere placeholder?) in discourses? Or all of those and probably more?

Foucault first addresses the subject in section (c) of chapter 4 ('The Formation of Enunciative Modalities') in Part II of *The Archaeology*. He is concerned to show that his analysis of discursive formations and practices is uncontaminated by the sovereign subject. Using as an illustration his study of 'the discourse of nineteenth-century doctors' (*Birth of the Clinic*), he (1976: 54) notes 'the disparity of the types of enunciation in clinical discourse' (the different kinds of statements that can be made and the diversity of ways of making them). Then he remarks that he has not tried 'to reveal the rational organization that may provide statements like those of medicine with their element of intrinsic necessity,' 'to reduce to a single founding act, or to a founding consciousness the general horizon of rationality against which the progress of medicine gradually emerged,' or 'to describe the empirical genesis, [or] the various component elements of the medical mentality.' That is, Foucault does not 'refer the various enunciative modalities to the unity of the subject – whether it concerns the subject regarded as the pure founding authority of rationality, or the subject regarded as an empirical function of synthesis.' (But what about a hypothetical subject?)

What Foucault offers positively is 'positions of subjectivity.' Conceived through subject positions, 'discourse is not the majestically unfolding manifestation of a thinking, knowing, speaking subject, but, on the contrary, a totality, in which the dispersion of the subject and his discontinuity with himself may be determined' (1976: 55). The *subject position* marks a moment of the dispersion of the subject. But what exactly is a subject position? Foucault (p. 54) is very vague about it here, using abstract geometrical metaphors like 'the discontinuity of the planes from which [one] speaks.' Planes of what? Position in what? Is this the Derridian proposition: 'There is nothing outside the text?' Or, since he is talking about discursive *practices*, is the subject of discourse linked with the subject of praxis (as in the case of Simmel's treatment of the methodological subject)? Much remains problematic in section (c). Foucault (p. 55) says that he 'shall look for a field of regularity for various positions of subjectivity.' Is this 'field of regularity' constituted by a methodological subject, which would yield a Simmelian Foucault? Or is the order really there in the field? Is the order there in the field *impersonally*, which would yield Foucault the positivist of discursive analysis?

Foucault takes up the subject again in section (b) of chapter 2 ('The Enunciative Function') in Part III of *The Archaeology*. Here he is concerned to classify the subject of 'the statement,' the elementary semantic unit of the discursive formation or practice. He excludes the grammatical subject of the sentence (the enunciating subject is not simply a *grammatical* placeholder) and the author (flesh-and-blood?) of the statement. That is, the enunciating subject is not external to discourse, but is perhaps not merely an operator in it, a convention in or of language. What is it? A *subject position*.

'It is a particular, vacant place that may in fact be filled by different individuals; but, instead of being defined once and for all, and maintaining itself as such throughout a text, a book, or an *oeuvre*, this place varies – or rather it is variable enough to be able either to persevere, unchanging, through several sentences, or to alter with each one' (Foucault 1976: 95). This is all we will get from Foucault about the enunciating-subject or subject-position. He provides examples of different kinds of subjects (fictional, colloquial, technical, etc.), but doesn't show in what sense they are '*positions*.' He (1976: 95–6) concludes section (b) by asserting: 'To describe a formulation *qua* statement does not consist in analyzing the relations between the author and what he says (or wanted to say, or said without wanting to); but in determining what position can and must be occupied by an individual if he is to be the subject of it.'

Is the subject position merely a social role? Is it something that can be 'played' in various ways by practical or 'real' (flesh-and-blood) historical subjects? Or is the historical subject dispersed into subject positions to such a degree that the enunciating subject is completely immanent to discourse? Do 'individuals' enter into (and leave) subject positions or is the individual nothing other than a collection of subject positions? Or is subject position simply an artifact of Foucault's discursive analysis – a methodological (non)subject? Later on in *The Archaeology* Foucault (1976: 131) says that 'we are difference . . . our reason is the difference of discourses, our history the difference of times, ourselves the difference of masks': That difference, far from being the forgotten and recovered origin, is this dispersion that we are and make.' 'OURSELVES THE DIFFERENCE OF MASKS': it sometimes seems as though, for Foucault, we are monsters. It's not that we put masks over our faces, but that we *have no faces* and contrive masks to conceal the absence of a face. Or better, that the masks have been contrived for each one of us (nihilism of the subject).

'OURSELVES THE DIFFERENCE OF MASKS': is this so different from the Simmelian implication that the subject of autobiography is a hypothetical or methodological subject? Only in the sense that for Foucault there is to be no narration of an intelligible process of development (as there is for Simmel), but an account of a sequence of breaks and ruptures. But isn't a sequence of breaks and ruptures still a sequence that has to have been drawn from the universe of data according to some criterion of relevance? That is, doesn't it have a methodological subject to unify it? And doesn't that methodological subject trade on a presupposed *continuity*; for example, of *medical* discourse? The latter is, from Simmel's viewpoint, an *illusory* continuity. If we draw Foucault close to Simmel, his preference for dispersion is merely a discursive strategy. That strategy has a methodological subject, just as much as a strategy of showing unified development has one. For Foucault the subject is a prosthetic device (mask); for Simmel the autobiographical subject is more like a skin graft. There's a difference, but does it make a difference? Indeed, doesn't every subject position unify some field of diversity? Continuity doesn't cede so easily; it fills the vacuum of 'vacant [discursive] space.' But that's for a Simmelianized Foucault or, better, for Simmel's *Foucault*. There's also (possibly) a positivistic Foucault – a nihilist of the subject – whom we've passed by.

HISTORICAL SUBJECT

We move for our finale to Foucault's peroration, which ends the 'Conclusion' of *The Archaeology*. He has been occupied in a 'dialogue' with an imaginary critic, playing Camus's 'judge-penitent,' perhaps. 'Justifying' him*self*. A pose? A subject position? A methodological subject? A real human being? *The author* (of an *oeuvre* no less)? A celebrity taking the subject position of celebrity in the discourse(s) of academic history? A reputation? No matter.

Foucault naively gives whoever he is here the 'last word.' The 'defendant' gets to say the last word, the same defendant who invented the prosecutor. Foucault sets it up for himself – the author gets to say anything to the critics that he wants to say. Foucault chooses to talk about the subject.

We promised a story – Foucault's redemption – and we'll tell it, even though it's only one of the stories in his text. Up to here we've seen Foucault attack the 'sovereign' subject and offer a psychological critique of those who believe in it, and we've seen him struggling to de-center the 'sovereign'(?) subject or even, perhaps, trying to destroy it. Redemption is from the nihilism of the subject, from the obliteration of subjecticity, subjecthood, subjectivity(?), *pour soi*, or whatever you call that *possessing of* discourse, which possessing is not discourse, but is other than discourse. Redemption is gained by applying the psychological critique to oneself; that is, purging oneself of the 'sovereign'(?) subject; taking the critique all the way to skepticism about the subject itself, even though one knows that one is indulging in self-contradiction; and then affirming some kind of *non*-sovereign subject (we prefer a minimalist one).

There's a redeemed Foucault in the peroration. One doesn't redeem oneself from nihilism of the subject by feats of dialectic, but with good sense and good will. Foucault shows those qualities at the beginning of the peroration. He (1976: 209) assures us that the 'positivities' of discourse 'are not so much limitations imposed on the initiative of subjects as the field in which that initiative is articulated (without, however, constituting its centre).' It is obvious from the context that the subjects whom Foucault is talking about here are flesh-and-blood human beings who take on various discourses (as masks) and can *initiate* within them. Subject positions do not initiate – they are *occupied* by (nondiscursive) (only-partly-discursive) 'subjects' – that is, historical subjects, human beings who *constitute themselves by constituting time in discourse*, that is, (practico-)methodological subjects.

Foucault (1976: 209) is reasonable here: 'I have not denied – far from it – the possibility of changing discourse: I have deprived the sovereignty of the subject of the exclusive and instantaneous right to it.' Is that all he has done, or tried to do? Does the (sovereign) subject still have 'rights' to change discourse? That seems implied by depriving the subject only of 'exclusive' and 'instantaneous' right. Human beings have a 'right,' perhaps, to co-constitute discourse as historical subjects. That would imply that 'sovereignty' is an attribute of the subject, if 'sovereignty' means any kind of control over what one says. It is that margin of control that differentiates subject from subject position: there is a sense in which a subject *deploys* a subject position, makes it, more or less, as one's autobiographies are made – by play with a methodological subject. It is a matter of good sense, good will, and good (Nietzschian) health to acknowledge that control in oneself and others, at least when it seems to be warranted: the difference between hearing voices and speaking (sometimes and more-or-less) in one's ~~own~~ voices (minimal(ist) control).

The reasonable Foucault seems to concede (at least) minimal-(ist) control over discourse by the subject who *takes* subject positions (and deploys them strategically, including the subject positions of the subject's autobiographies). That is what is involved in allowing the subject *initiative*. Redemption story over.

There is another story in the peroration, and it is in the last words – the final two paragraphs, where Foucault shows that he (probably) never 'really' applied the psychological critique to himself and overcame his nihilism of the subject, but that, instead, he drew back from the abyss of subjectlessness in a panic of *ressentiment*.

At the end, Foucault becomes autobiographer, subject of his discourse. (Is he in control of what he's writing, are these *his* words?) He makes himself the misunderstood and wrongfully abused just man – what we would call a Simmelian methodological subject of a tale (of woe). He (Foucault 1976: 210) tells us: 'I know as well as anyone how "thankless" is the task that I undertook some ten years ago.' (It must be said that he is presuming here that there is a subject Foucault spanning the decade – just the kind of illusion (but is it an illusion for Foucault?) that Simmel suggested was necessary to constitute a 'history.') And what is that 'thankless' task? It amounts to having to tell people that they don't control their discourse. People can 'hardly agree'

> to being dispossessed [by Foucault, we presume] of that discourse in which they wish to be able to say immediately and directly what they think, believe, or imagine; they prefer to deny that discourse is a complex, differentiated practice, governed by analysable rules and transformations, rather than be deprived of that tender, consoling certainty of being able to

change, if not the world, if not life, at least their 'meaning',
simply with a fresh word that can come only from themselves,
and remain for ever close to the source.

(Foucault 1976: 211)

(But is that exactly what 'they' want: must the 'fresh word' come
only from themselves? Must the 'fresh word' remain forever close
to the source? Must the word be fresh? Or do at least some of
'them' simply want to be able to *initiate* a change in meaning
sometimes, within all the constraints? Did Foucault ever talk to
himself? Did he spin out autobiographies? Obviously he did. He
gave us one in the peroration.)

The last sentence of the 'Conclusion': 'They cannot bear (and
one cannot but sympathize) to hear someone [Foucault 1976: 211,
we presume] saying: "Discourse is not life: its time is not your time;
in it, you will not be reconciled to death; you may have killed God
beneath the weight of all that you have said; but don't imagine
that, with all that you are saying, you will make a man that will live
longer than he." '

Foucault deserves a Nietzschian mauling and we'll give him a
bit of one. This long-suffering victim of academic injustice *pities* his
accusers for failing to accept his GIFT of TRUTH with good
grace. The 'truth' that discourse will not reconcile us to death? But
we knew that long ago. We knew that as soon as people started
breaking from Hegel, way back in the times of Kierkegaard and
Marx. The 'truth' that we will never make a 'man' ('Man'?) that
lives as long as God did? But who except for some critical theorists
and left-over liberal and Marxist humanists want to do that any
more? The 'truth' that we can't initiate changes in our meaning?
But earlier he had conceded that we do initiate. Foucault is a
tortured thinker.

The point here is the pity: '(AND ONE CANNOT HELP BUT
SYMPATHIZE)' (our emphasis). The destroyer (magnanimously?)
'sympathizes' with his victims – the victims of his will to truth.
Science lives and we pity its sacrifices. God knows, we need to be
able to think that we control our expression of meaning 'in the
distress of today,' but, unfortunately, we can't entertain that
illusion any more. 'You won't get away with killing God and
believing that you can put *man* in His place' (or believing that you
can put a minimal(ist) subject in its place?). Foucault is the
avenging angel of (a dead) God. And how far does the vengeance

go? To absolutist humanists? All the way to minimal(ist) subjects? This is a *labile ressentiment*. At its mild moments it tells us what we'd known for years from Marx, Nietzsche, Freud, Mannheim, and Mead. At its wild moments it tries to nihilate the subject. It is a hatred of the historical subject, of the one who contrives autobiographies and initiates within subject positions. And perhaps *initiates subject positions*, since what did Foucault do in *The Archaeology* but *found a discourse* with its special lexicon to signal a rupture?

This hatred of the non-sovereign subject is the disease of postmodernism (which is not to call postmodernism thoroughly diseased). It is hatred of the historical subject because it cannot be sovereign, disguised (by the Foucaultian variant) as pity for those who are nostalgic for the 'sovereign subject.' Sour grapes. Psychological stalemate. The Simmelian Foucault is a healthy corrective.

Chapter 10

A Simmelian postmodern

There have been many outcroppings and some exposed lodes of a Simmelian postmodern in the preceding essays, but they have not yet been mapped. The following is an effort to discern a (Simmelian-style) form of a Simmelian postmodern, as an aerial photo sometimes shows unsuspected patterns that one could never detect at ground level.

What is postmodern is always relative to what has been declared to be (the essence of) the Modern. Always for the postmodern something (central to the) modern has died. The ethic of postmodernism is Derrida's command to abjure nostalgia, even as one must continue noting the absence and affirming life in its shadow. What dies in Nietzsche is God. What dies in Simmel is romantic subjectivity. The Simmelian postmodern is the post-*romantic* era.

Romantic subjectivity dies most decisively for Simmel in his 1911 essay, 'On the Concept and the Tragedy of Culture' (1968). In it the modern ideal of romantic subjectivity is given a maximal expression only to be undermined by an argument for its practical impossibility. This argument shows the conditions for the failure of modernity, which, by implication, are the conditions of postmodernity; and defines a crisis of subjectivity that attends the death of modern (romantic) subjectivity.

'The Tragedy' has a stark binary structure. For the first half Simmel builds up an ideal of romantic subjectivity alongside a string of reservations about its possible realization. Then he abruptly, without any transition or mediation, proceeds to argue for the impossibility of that ideal. 'The Tragedy' is a privileged text from which to read the rupture between the modern and the postmodern.

ON THE CONCEPT AND THE DEATH OF ROMANTIC SUBJECTIVITY

We rewrite 'The Tragedy' as a postmodern 'Death of . . .' essay: 'The Death of the Modern (Romantic) Subject.' This is not what Simmel seemed to have in mind, since it is 'Culture' that is the subject in his title. But the text of 'culture,' we suggest, can also function as a screen over or a displacement of a sub-text, the protagonist of which is the romantic (subject) (spirit(s)) (soul) (individual) (person).

'Culture' enters the text of 'The Tragedy' as a mediator in a more basic set of relations, specified in a (dialectical) (dramatic) (philosophical) anthropology. Human beings separate themselves from nature, struggle against it, and in doing so create objectifications of their 'spirit.' These objectifications (what is generally known as culture) form autonomous orders, such as technology, law, ethics, art, science, and religion, each with its own internal standards of validity. These orders constitute the divisions of objective spirit. The original binary between human beings and nature is now doubled by a binary between subjective and objective spirit: objective spirit becomes, almost, a second environment. As Simmel (1968: 27) puts it: 'Spirit, most deeply tied to spirit, for this very reason experiences innumerable tragedies over this radical contrast: between subjective life, which is restless but finite in time, and its contents, which, once they are created, are fixed but timelessly valid.'

'Culture,' in the specific, restricted meaning that Simmel (1968: 27) reserves for it, 'is lodged in the middle of [the] dualism' between the subjective and objective (modes of) spirit. As soon as it makes its first appearance in the text it is surrounded and displaced. The next sentence reads: 'It ['culture'] is based on a situation which in its totality can only be expressed opaquely, through an analogy, as the path of the soul to itself.' 'Culture' as the path of the soul to itself – as a mediator – is not the protagonist of the text: the 'soul' is. The 'tragedy of culture' is a diversion.

'Culture' functions as a mediator of the subject to itself when it is appropriate to the development of individual personality: 'culture,' in its special use, is that set of products of the objective spirit that can be assimilated by subjective spirit into its development. Here Simmel introduces a romantic subjectivity in the form of an ideal dialectic of self-realization that controls much of the first half of the text. Using organic, Aristotelian imagery, Simmel (1968: 28) declares that 'the personality as a whole and a unit carries within itself an image, traced as if with invisible hues. This image is its potentiality; to free the image in it would be to attain its full actuality.' 'Culture' enters as the main way in which the inward image can be freed: by assimilating certain appropriate products of objective spirit, human beings are able to fulfill the Goethian imperative: 'Become who you are.' Romantic subjectivity is summarized by Simmel (p. 29) in a dialectical pattern: 'Culture is the way that leads from the closed unity [of the original subjective spirit] through the unfolded multiplicity [of the objective spirit] to the unfolded unity [of the actualized subjective spirit].' Having begun 'The Tragedy' with a warning of the 'innumerable tragedies' that attend the contrast between 'subjective life' and its (objective) contents, Simmel has moved to define an ideal romantic subjectivity that transcends those tragedies.

After Simmel establishes his dialectical ideal the rest of the first half of 'The Tragedy' becomes a give-and-take between clarification of the ideal and persistent doubts about its viability, especially with regard to the indifference or even hostility of objective spirit to personal development. Finally, Simmel (1968: 39) reaches the point at which he acknowledges that 'over-specialization' can lead to the condition that 'a person may acquire a remarkable degree of skill or knowledge concerning a certain substantive content – an "artistic culture" or a "religious culture" – without becoming truly cultivated.' Yet, he adds, 'it is still possible that substantive perfection of a particular kind may help bring about the completion of the person as a total being.' Then the romantic subject, 'the person as a total being,' suddenly dies.

The next paragraph (1968: 39) begins: 'Within this structure of culture there now develops a cleavage which, of course, is already prepared for in its foundation. It makes of the subject-object synthesis a paradox, even a tragedy.' From then on Simmel launches into his argument that romantic subjectivity is practically impossible in the 'modern,' that is, postmodern, era. Noting that there is no guarantee that the products of objective spirit 'will serve the completion of the soul,' he proliferates doubts that it can do so at all in modern times.

Simmel identifies three attributes of the (post)modern objective spirit that make the self-development of persons impossible. First, as objective spirit becomes ever more specialized the domains of its objects become elaborated beyond all relevance to the liberation of anyone's inward image and, indeed, become subversive of any such liberation. Products are created by objective spirit because they can be generated within a specialized domain, not because they serve any individual needs. That is, objective spirit is emancipated from any service to subjective spirit. Orders of objective spirit become (1968: 40) 'exterior worlds,' aiming 'to break up the centralization of cultural contents around the "I" and reconstitute them according to *their* demands' (for example, the conflict between 'man as a rounded individual and man as a mere member of a social order'). With specialization, human production becomes parceled into diverse domains, each with its own norms of perfection and indifferent to the fate of any individual: 'The 'fetishism' which Marx assigned to economic commodities represents only a special case of [the] general fate of contents of culture.' In the domain of technology an imperative to complete processes results in (p. 43) 'vast supplies of products [coming] into existence which call forth an artificial demand that is senseless from the perspective of the subject's culture.' The same thing happens in the use of scientific method and artistic technique. Human beings become sacrifices to a cultural tyranny, mere carriers of the force by which the logics of objective spirit 'dominate their development and lead them on as if in the tangent of the course through which they would return to the cultural development of living human beings.' But the promise is delusive. Simmel is now ready to declare 'the tragedy of culture,' which is read here as the death of the individual, of romantic subjectivity. For Simmel (p. 43) 'tragedy' occurs 'when the destructive forces directed against some being spring forth from the deepest levels of this very being; or when its destruction has been initiated in itself, and forms the logical development of the very structure by which a being has built its own positive form.' Starved of 'culture,' the romantic subject dies from a surfeit of the products of objective spirit.

The autonomization of the contents of objective spirit is the major theme of the Simmelian postmodern. What is generally called culture (at the end of the essay Simmel reverts to the common usage) has become an (inherently) (often) hostile environment for the modern (romantic) individual. Simmel makes the 'postmodern flip' by declaring the triumph of objective over subjective spirit. Culture does not belong to individual personalities; rather, they belong to diverse cultural complexes. Indeed, it is not clear in what sense 'they' exist any longer, since romantic subjectivity needs 'culture' to lead it to itself.

From cultural tyranny follow the other important features of the Simmelian postmodern condition. Autonomization results in (1986: 42) 'the ominous independence by which the realm of cultural products grows and grows as if an inner necessity were producing one member after another.' The sheer mass of cultural objects inhibits the ability of individuals to assimilate them, to find out what might be appropriate to their developmental needs. Added to that (p. 46), culture is non-centric, de-totalized; it has no meaning on the whole in which an individual might inscribe a personal meaning: 'Culture does not possess a concrete unity of form for its contents.' The autonomization, massiveness, and formlessness of culture are the conditions of the Simmelian postmodern. Together they cause a crisis of the romantic subject.

In the absence of 'culture' the romantic subject becomes a victim of a culturally-induced depression – the framing mood of the Simmelian postmodern (Simmel 1968: 44): 'The infinitely growing supply of objective spirit places demands before the subject, creates desires in him, hits him with feelings of individual inadequacy and helplessness, throws him into total relationships from whose impact he cannot withdraw, although he cannot master their particular contents.' Dying romantic subjectivity has the 'sense of being surrounded by an innumerable number of cultural elements which are neither meaningless to him nor, in the final analysis, meaningful.' Unable to reject or to accept the cultural environment (p. 46), 'the subjective spirit . . . does not know how it can completely protect its unity of form from the touch and the temptation of all these "things." '

The dying romantic subject is both intimidated and seduced by culture, but never satisfied. It seeks its own development but finds no resources for actualizing it. It is reduced to being a nostalgic reflex. Was there ever such a 'romantic subject' except in some texts of modern philosophy and criticism? It does not matter. In the absence of that subject(-position) the Simmelian postmodern is configured and the stage is set for the appearance of patterns of post-romantic subjectivity, which comprise the major contribution of the Simmelian postmodern to postmodern discourses.

THE CATEGORIES OF POST-ROMANTIC ~~SUBJECTIVITY~~

Post-romantic ~~subjectivity~~ is the response of 'subjective spirit' to the postmodern conditions of cultural autonomy, massiveness and formlessness. What becomes of the (subject) (spirit(s)) (soul) (individual) (person) after the death of the (liberal) romantic subject? (How) does the subject survive (in) postmodernity?

Simmel's major contribution to postmodern discourses is to have mapped post-romantic subjectivity, giving thereby an account of a range of postmodern subject(-positions). He identifies three different post-romantic mentalities in his works. In 'The Metropolis and Mental Life' he defines an imploding subjectivity governed by cultural dependency: the products of objectivized spirit are implanted in the void created by the death of the romantic subject. Then, in 'The Conflict in Modern Culture' he defines an exploding subjectivity governed by vital rebellion: subjective spirit makes an impossible bid to possess culture, that is, to de-objectivize culture, to make it submit to a *formless* subject. Finally in a number of his works, which have been cited and discussed in preceding chapters – *Lebensanschauung* (the double boundary), 'Sociability' (play-form), 'On the Nature of Historical Understanding' (hypothetical or methodological subject), and *Schopenhauer and Nietzsche* (stalemating) – Simmel defines a position in which subjectivity submits to objectivity for the sake of its own enhancement: with no more form of its own (the romantic subject is dead), subjectivity deploys multiple identities, contingent on the available cultural resources.

The three subjectivities identified by Simmel bear marked resemblance to the three categories of postmodern discourses defined by Arthur Kroker. According to Kroker (1992: 14), 'More, perhaps, than we may suspect, contemporary French thought is a brilliant reprise of a more ancient quarrel among three classical attitudes towards existence: pragmatic naturalism (Virilio, Lyotard, Deleuze and Guattari, Foucault), Lucretian fatalism (Baudrillard and Barthes) and Epicurean sensuality (Irigaray).' Translating to the Simmelian postmodern, the cultural dependency of the imploding self hooks into Lucretian fatalism (Baudrillard), the vital rebellion of the exploding self attaches to pragmatic naturalism (Lyotard), and the border play of the boundary-being links with Epicurean sensuality (we substitute Derrida for Irigaray as the iconic representative). Kroker's categories and his interpretations of them will be useful in the following discussions of the forms of post-romantic subjectivity, allowing us to splice the Simmelian accounts into Kroker's major postmodern discourse on postmodern discourses.

Within the Simmel literature, Birgitta Nedelmann (1991) has presented a compelling argument that there are three distinct theories of culture in Simmel's writings, centered on the question of 'the relationship between culture and the individual.' Nedelmann's classification, though articulated in a modern systems-theory perspective, corresponds, like Kroker's, with our categories of Simmelian post-romantic subjectivity. Nedelmann identifies 'models' of 'cultural dualism,' 'cultural antagonism,' and 'cultural ambivalence' in Simmel's writings on culture. Translating to the Simmelian postmodern, cultural dualism corresponds with the imploding self, cultural antagonism with the exploding self, and cultural ambivalence with the hypothetical subject. As an alternative, though closely related, triadic division of Simmelian reflections on the culture/individual binary, Nedelmann's categories will be useful, though in a less decisive way than Kroker's, in the following discussions.

What follows is a weaving of Simmel's texts on post-romantic subjectivity into postmodern discourses in order to exhibit the Simmelian postmodern(s). Building on a Simmelian textual base, we will move out from it to extend Simmel's texts into postmodern discourses, making points that Simmel never made but are readily intelligible in terms of the textual base. That is, we will *rewrite* Simmel for the postmodern, more freely than we rewrote 'The Tragedy' in the first section of this chapter. The aim is to contribute to postmodern discourses, to clarify and enrich them through Simmel's suggestions.

THE NEW METROPOLIS AND 'MENTAL' LIFE

'The Metropolis and Mental Life' is the most kindred essay to 'The Tragedy' in Simmel's canon. It shares with the latter a focus on the conflict between the objective and subjective spirits, and interprets that conflict in terms of the (post)modern conditions of autonomization (tyranny) of culture, and cultural massiveness and formlessness. Both essays also share the subject-position of the romantic subject, though its definition is far less developed in 'The Metropolis.' 'The Metropolis,' instead, concentrates on presenting a description of one of the ~~subjective~~ responses to (post)modern conditions, in the aftermath of the romantic subject's death.

In 'The Metropolis' Simmel captures modern (liberal) (romantic) subjectivity at its last hold out, right before 'the postmodern flip' is either performed or compelled. Crushed by an overload of disjointed stimuli – the proximate result of post-modern conditions – the subject begins to implode, to lose its ability to affirm itself as a separate being with its own inward dynamic of expression. This is Nietzsche's historical disease generalized, an excess of culture, not merely of 'history.' This is the weak subject. As Nedelmann (1991: 187) shows, drawing her 'dualistic model' of Simmel's cultural theory from 'The Tragedy,' while 'subjective culture' ('culture' in 'The Tragedy') cannot produce 'macro-effects,' 'objective culture' can and does, 'due to its systemic properties, and, as a result, is more and more transformed into an *Übermacht*, a superpower, the more it grows in scope.' Human beings confronted with the *Übermacht* become 'paralyzed' in their 'capacity to select elements from the objective culture.' They encounter (Nedelmann 1991: 189) a cultural system which is neither meaningful nor meaningless to them and which they can neither assimilate nor reject: 'In such a state of paralyzed action alternatives he or she has neither the energy for revolting or protesting against the cultural system as system, nor for reacting in a deviant, exaggerated way.'

The state of paralysis identified by Nedelmann is defined in terms of an extreme form of post-romantic ~~subjectivity~~ in 'The Metropolis.' Simmel (1950b: 415) identifies 'the last possibility of accommodating to the contents and forms of metropolitan life' with the 'blasé attitude,' which is grounded in the refusal of the nerves 'to react to their stimulation' and is expressed phenomen-ologically as a devaluation of 'the whole objective world' that 'unavoidably drags one's own personality down into a feeling of the same worthlessness.' That is, world denial of a uniquely modern form is the last refuge of romantic subjectivity.

For Simmel (1950b: 414) 'the essence of the blasé attitude consists in the blunting of discrimination'; it is 'the faithful subjective reflection of the completely internalized money economy,' in which 'all things float with equal specific gravity on the constantly moving stream of money.' The blasé attitude is a defense mechanism, a form of functional schizophrenia in which the weak subject is able to defend itself at the last ditch by tuning

out, suppressing affect, and splitting off from the environment –
it is on the way to catatonia. This is the romantic subject on its
death-bed, not going out in tragic agony but expiring from
(p. 414) an incapacity 'to react to new sensations with the
appropriate energy' (cultural burn-out). The blasé attitude protects the exhausted and depleted subject by a (ressentiment)
mechanism, that devalues the world, which ends with the last act
of modern self-reference, the self devaluating itself: I am
worthless, but I still am.

Can the subject persist in this way for any length of time?
Toward the end of 'The Metropolis' Simmel (1950b: 422)
expresses his doubts, suggesting that the personality cannot
maintain itself under the impact of 'an overwhelming fullness of
crystallized and impersonalized spirit.' What next, then? The
postmodern flip.

The post-romantic subjectivity formed by cultural dependency
continues to devalue the world but has found a substitute for
'subjective culture.' That substitute was prefigured by Nietzsche's
(1957: 26) vision in *The Use and Abuse of History* of a completely
hollowed out 'inward life' which had left behind it a simulacrum
of a personality, 'the external life – with its vulgar pride and vain
servility,' as if 'inward life still sat there, painted and rouged and
disguised, become a play-actress or something worse.' That is, the
self is its own seduction, a pure sign.

In the new metropolis the defense mechanisms protecting the
vestiges of the modern subject from submission to objective
culture have broken down, imploding the self. There is no more
resistance of subject against object because there is insufficient
strength in the subject to mount it. Rather than the modern desire
and the modernist nostalgia for a subjective culture that would
further the individual's personal development, that would
provide the means to fulfill the injunction to 'become who you
are,' there is an acquiescence in, indeed, often a frenzied embrace
of 'self-images.' These self-images are produced by disciplinary
practices and implanted into subjectivity in order to integrate the
(human) organism into technological complexes and motivate it
to surmount depression and participate in them. The subject is
not to be achieved or actualized but to be *imagined*.

Postmodern subjectivity as cultural dependency is beyond
tragedy. Hooking this aspect of the Simmelian postmodern into
Kroker's (1992: 15) category of Lucretian fatalism, self-image

becomes one of the 'charm[s] of technology as seduction, a game of chance and probability, without beginning or end, in which we float as spectral impulses within the smooth and unbroken surface of the mediascape (Baudrillard) or within the acquired organicity of technology as a rhetoric machine (Barthes).' Subjective culture is replaced here by self-image as an implant of objective culture, the final triumph of objective spirit and the abolition of tragedy: 'This perspective is fatalistic, but not tragic since it does not have the requisite sense of the irony of experience or the lament for absence which would add the tension necessary for tragedy.' There was deep irony in Simmel's 'tragedy of culture.' Human beings, as romantic subjects, were condemned to destroy themselves by the very means through which they had to attempt to fulfill themselves. There was also an oppressive sense of the absence of the romantic subject in 'The Tragedy.' But with the tension of resistance gone, there is nothing to be awed by, just endless simulacra of personalities shooting across the mediascape, seductive because they are not there to be actualized but to function as prosthetic or cosmetic devices, the *trompe-l'œil* self. There can be no tragedy when the subject has become 'virtual.' As Kroker (1992: 16) puts it, the 'central insight' of Lucretian fatalism is that 'in the terminal history of the cynical sign [here the 'subject'], only the virtual world of technical culture is materialized, and only those cultural codes coming under the sign of cynical rhetoric are imminently reversible, and thus always put in play in cyberspace.' Self-image is virtual subjectivity.

This is the story. The modern subject is exhausted in defense mechanisms to the point that there is nothing any longer inward to it but the will to resist the outward. This condition cannot hold and resistance gives way to submission to objective culture. Still devaluing the world, the subject learns to value the self-images that are prepared for it and administered to it by the technological complexes that possess objective spirit and are also its means to supremacy. The romantic subject is dead, but there is enough intentionality left for a subject to emerge as a new relation to itself: self-imagination. This is the Simmelian version of what Kroker calls 'the possessed individual,' his name for the postmodern subject. The Simmelian postmodern individual is possessed by the objective simulacra of subjective culture: the (re)presentations of the media and disciplinary practices. The self becomes a fragment of a collective imaginary, no longer able to be referred to anything that it represents: the self-image *is* the self, not, as subjective culture was, a means to 'its' development. The hatred for the world that would bring extreme self-hatred in its train has been displaced and reversed by reaction formation into an embrace of fantasy. Self-image, the substitute for 'subjective culture' (or all there ever 'really' was), neither expresses nor represents anything beyond itself.

The Simmelian possessed individual is beyond the crisis of world denial and has found a way of persisting with nihilism. Subjective culture was part of a process of development. The self-image is instantaneous and interchangeable. Subjective culture expressed a self. The self-image expresses itself and has no necessary relation to the (human) organism in which it is implanted, except for being there. Subjective culture served the individual. The self-image is a means of connecting the (human) organism to technological complexes, primarily by providing incentives for overcoming depression. It is a kind of lithium of the imagination, the main palliative invented in the twentieth century for world-sickness, the inwardness or subjectivity of television, theme parks, support groups, and fashion magazines. The twentieth-century subject is kept from complete implosion by constant use of mind supplements. Self as self-image is not the core of a *subject*, but an element within a (human) organism (more-or-less) functioning in the technoscape.

If it will help a person to function by drawing all of his or her libido into the fiction of being 'a victim,' so much the better. If it will not, then that person would be well advised to alter his or her self-image or to exchange it for one that provides a greater 'self-esteem.' The 'truth' of the image is not a consideration. To what could it be true? It is judged by its utility, but for what is it useful? For the subject it functions as what Alfred North Whitehead called a 'lure to feeling,' drawing the subject out of depression and into involvement with the complexes of objective spirit, if only to watch television or go to a support group. For the complexes of objective spirit, the self-image is the completion of the former's colonization of subjectivity. From the viewpoint of a macro-systems theory, perhaps the development of techno-corporate society has reached the point at which there is no longer any necessity for a self that represents itself; therefore self-image can float free, seeming to function for the persistence of technological complexes but maybe also being the virus that destroys them finally – an inversion of Simmel's 'tragedy of culture.'

The triumph of objective spirit means that all of the grand projects of human perfection and progress are over. It is now simply a matter of subduing the flesh to technique, and self-images help that process along. As Patrick Watier (1986: 242) notes, in the context of Simmel's theory of subjectivity it is possible 'to conceive of a multiform individuality going from possessive individualism [the modern self as owner of itself] to the individual as aleatory identity.' The subject as self-image, perhaps with scripts in family and social romances, is aleatory: there is nothing necessary about the descriptions it gives of itself or the stories it tells itself about itself. Self-images like all the products of the *virtual* metropolis of the media (the mediascape) circulate freely and globally, knowing no bounds in closed circles and available for appropriation from or implantation by a technological complex or disciplinary practice. Floating as a spectral impulse in the mediascape with an acquired organicity of self-image(s), the Simmelian possessed individual is constituted as a 'cynical sign,' having to convince itself that it 'is' what it tells itself it is, since it is *nothing* else, yet ready to reverse itself and tell itself the opposite. The 'victim' can become a 'success story' in a flash and then flip back again.

In the new metropolis the ~~subject~~ has no work of its own and no mission to perform for any group. But it still needs to call itself something, to call itself out of the depression that poisons it and that comes from the intimidating force of objective culture. The story of the twentieth century (for Simmelian Lucretian fatalism) is the contrivance in objective culture of an instant simulacrum of subjective culture – the self-image. A weakened subjectivity submits to objective spirit and receives in return an imaginary. Anything is better than the world.

THE ~~CONFLICT~~ IN (POST)MODERN CULTURE

The preponderant tendency in (Simmelian) postmodernity is for the ~~subject~~ to become ever more aleatory as technological complexes progressively colonize ~~subjectivity~~. The person here is a succession of self-images with no inherent meaning in the sequence (though any number of 'historizations' can be constructed for it). The aleatory self is completely passive, showing no self-assertion, since its being is exhausted in its imagining of itself. The inwardly-developing, self-active self is absent,

Nietzsche's whore(s) in its place. This is the big story, the general environing horizon of postmodernity – the terminal ~~subject~~.

The terminal ~~subject~~, however, is not the only form of post-romantic subjectivity. One response of the self to cultural tyranny is to implode, to submit, and finally to vacate all initiative. Another is to launch a futile rebellion against that tyranny. Explosive vital rebellion is the alternative to depression that is presented by Simmel in 'The Conflict in Modern Culture.' It is the other pole of the Simmelian postmodern, the stalemate position – Nietzschian assertion gone bad defying a Schopenhauerian fate.

'The Conflict' begins with the same (dialectical) (dramatic) philosophical anthropology that Simmel displayed in 'The Tragedy.' Here, with suggestions of an ontology of emergent evolution, Simmel (1976b: 223) states: 'As soon as life progresses beyond the purely biological level to the level of mind, and mind in its turn progresses to the level of culture, an inner conflict appears.' That conflict between objective and subjective spirit is now expressed as a struggle between 'life,' the creative form-giving activity, and the forms (culture) in which it expresses itself and is *expressed*. But this time the same autonomization of culture that caused a defensive response (the blasé attitude) in 'The Metropolis' (leading by extension to the terminal ~~subject~~) results in an aggressive response, an attempt to deprive culture of its autonomy.

The tyranny of culture takes on a new guise in 'The Conflict.' The objective spirit is not dynamically oppressive, as it is in 'The Tragedy,' but a stifling 'dead power' (Kroker). Simmel (1976b: 225) describes (post)modernity as 'an age which feels that all cultural forms are like exhausted soil, which has yielded all it can but which is still entirely covered with the products of its earlier fertility.' Suffocated by a glut of artifacts (Kroker's 'excremental culture'), life seeks to break free. This process is so vast that 'life' (subjective spirit with a touch of vitalist metaphysics) cannot 'focus on the creation of new forms,' but 'feels obliged to struggle against form simply because it *is* form.' An exhausted culture, that is, provides no resources for self-development, no subjective culture. In 'The Conflict' subjective culture has definitely disappeared and the romantic subject is dead, but a ~~romantic~~ impulse or intentionality still hangs on. ~~Life~~ (subjective spirit) seeks to do the impossible, to possess form, to deprive culture of autonomy.

Corresponding to the aleatory self on the side of vital rebellion is the other pole of Watier's spectrum, the possessive individual. The Simmelian possessive individual is presented in extremity in Simmel's discussion of expressionist art in 'The Conflict.' In expressionist art the creator does not seek to represent an object but (Simmel 1976b: 230) to record, objectify an emotion directly: 'One might say that the Expressionist artist replaces the "model" by the "occasion" which awakens an impulse in that life in him which is obedient only unto itself.' The product of expressionist art has a form, but it is, as Nedelmann (1991: 178) points out, 'idiosyncratic'; it cannot break free from the experience in which it was created. It is expressive *of* an emotional state, but it does not communicate *in* a common culture. As Simmel (1976b: 230) notes: 'Once the product is completed, and the life process which engendered it has departed from it, we see that it lacks that meaning and value of its own which we expect from any objective created thing existing independently of its creator. Life, anxious only to express itself, has, as it were, jealously withheld such meaning from its own product.'

Jealous withholding is the counterpart in 'The Conflict' to the blasé attitude's devaluation of the world in 'The Metropolis,' both of them being instances of extreme *ressentiment*. For 'formless life' to reject submission to the forms that it creates, for it not to be able to find any forms that can satisfy it, even seduce it, temporarily, is evidence of a metaphysical rebellion of a depleted subject against its own finitude. Read in terms of 'The Tragedy,' where finite and mutating individual life is contrasted to eternal form, the vital rebellion of 'The Conflict' is an effort to temporalize culture, to deprive it of its power to express life rather than simply to be a self-referential expression of life. In Simmel's sketch of emergent evolution life progresses to mind and mind to culture. Subjective spirit's attempt to possess culture, to refuse to allow it to stand independently of subjective spirit as the criterion and resource for the latter, denies the evolutionary order and, therefore, inverts value. Life-mind rejects its destiny. It does not matter that Simmel (1976b: 225) insists that 'what is happening is not merely something negative, the death of traditional forms, but that an altogether positive impulse is sloughing off these forms.' That diagnosis is based on an ungrounded hope that the present era is one of transition back to the normal cultural history where life replaces one autonomous form with another in an ever-incomplete struggle to express itself. What if the rebellion is chronic? What if subjective spirit refuses to contribute to objective culture and to receive its own gift? In her model of 'cultural antagonism,' based on 'The Conflict,' Nedelmann (1991: 177) offers some first answers: 'In terms of systems analysis, Simmel's diagnosis could be reformulated as increasing self-referentiality of both the cultural system and of the system of individual creativity, resulting in gradual self-destruction of both systems.'

Reading the vital rebellion of 'The Conflict' as a self-destructive metaphysical rebellion links that text with Kroker's category of 'pragmatic naturalism' (Lyotard, Virilio, Deleuze and Guattari). For Kroker (1992: 16) the pragmatic naturalists are heirs of the Camusian absurd rebellion: 'Here, the full oppressiveness of the dynamic will to technological mastery of the social and non-social universe can be felt in blood, just because it is viewed from the counter-perspective of the will to resist and transform.' Regardless of the optimistic strains in pragmatic naturalism, such as Lyotard's quest for a Kantian regulatory principle to mediate the play of *différends*, Kroker (p. 17) asserts that the 'best hopes' of the pragmatic naturalists are ultimately 'dashed against the rocks of the very naturalism that they thought would save them.' Simmelian vital rebellion shows what it means to be dashed against those rocks. Subjective spirit in the metaphysical mask of 'life' secretes death in a fit of cultural anorexia. The subject will accept nothing that is not its own and it will try to possess its own solely for itself. This state of 'vital solipsism' and 'positive nihilism' is the predicament of 'formless life' (Simmel 1976b: 241) attempting to be self-sufficient, 'to bridge the gap' between past and future. But what is its own? What is the pure possessive individual, the one 'who' has the single determination to possess *itself* jealously in everything within it and around it?

The end of vital rebellion is schizophrenia, but this time in the form of incommunicable hyper-individualization. The destiny of the post-romantic s̶u̶b̶j̶e̶c̶t̶ that retains the romantic impulse as a spasmodic reflex is to construct a private language and to devalue the world radically by interpreting it through projections: paranoid schizophrenia in 'the final analysis.' That is, the opposite number of the catatonia of 'The Metropolis' is the paranoia of 'The Conflict.' Simmel did not understand how this paranoia – this projection of self-hatred on to objectivity – was at the bottom of vital rebellion. We can understand because of the turn that that rebellion took in the mid- and late twentieth century.

One need only add two more examples to those used by Simmel to illustrate jealous withholding in 'The Conflict' (expressionist art, pragmatic philosophy, sexual ethics, and mystical currents in religion) to understand the horror of vital rebellion. One must speak of post-Holocaust vital rebellion and what it means.

As vital rebellion worked its way through the twentieth century along with the depression of the terminal subject it infected politics and society. It is one thing to try to deny the autonomy of the aesthetic object, truth, sexual morality, and religious dogma, and another to try to deny the autonomy of law and to be successful at it, at least for a (very dismal) while. The most representative manifestation of (post)modernist vital rebellion is the ideological dictatorship, substituting the interpretation of a social imaginary by a political elite for deference to constitutional norms and the interpretation of a body of law by a (quasi-)independent judiciary. For a Simmelian (post)modern, the essence of what has been called 'totalitarianism' is a revolt against the objectivity of law. It is a case of the legislator (that is, the executive as legislator) refusing to grant independence to the law, thereby turning law into decree that is alterable instantly and at any point in the political system (that is, all institutions in the political system are simply extensions of the executive's will).

It is no more possible, of course, for law to lose its objectively binding character than it is for an object of expressionist art to lack any form at all. The decree escapes its creator, remaining in force as a standard of conduct until it is revoked. No regime is so febrile that it does without standardized procedures. But it is also true that in totalitarian politics all of the norms and procedures of the political system are radically provisional, subject to momentary alteration, nullification, or replacement. But then, on the other hand, sometimes ideological dictatorship descends to 'rule' by a paranoid monster with his private (version of the) ideology – let Jimmy Jones and Charlie Manson stand for all the rest of the (post)modern-style Platonic tyrants. Then decree becomes negatively nihilistic, on the way to and sometimes achieving genocide/suicide. Vital rebellion turns against life – the final act of self-hatred and devaluation of the world, repeated over and over again in this century. The postmodern is the age of post-Holocaust vital rebellion – the repetition *ad infinitum* of the worst: some Bosnians here, some Kurds there, and so on.

The partner of ideological dictatorship, indeed, its social 'base' has been the effort by all manner of groups to defy the autonomy of culture itself and to claim that they have their own, inherent culture, which makes it impossible (if they are dominant) or oppressively distortive of their identity (if they are subordinate) for them to receive culture from other groups or to share their culture with other groups. The identification of culture with race is only the most glaring example of the jealous withholding of independence from culture. The same kind of identification is made with ethnic and national groups, and with gender groups. The notion that culture belongs to certain restricted groups and cannot be appropriated, genuinely, by the members of other groups is the 'spiritual' expression of the viciously naive effort to bring the closed circle back, to reverse the metropolis. It is the most severe denial of the autonomy of objective culture possible for vital rebellion, the submission of culture to some supposedly noncultural factor (being, reality, etc.), which is, on the other hand, nothing but a master-name, something that governs . . . texts.

Adding ideological dictatorship to cultural possessiveness yields the twentieth-century nightmare, depicted in the hues of the Simmelian postmodern. Genocidal suicide and suicidal genocide are the meaning(s) of vital rebellion. Post-Holocaust vital rebellion simply means that it still goes on, whenever the social conditions are propitious. The terminal subject's twin: the genocidal or suicidal subject. Depression: paranoia. The aleatory self: the possessive individual. The blasé attitude: jealous withholding. Floating as a spectral impulse in the mediascape: being in a concentration camp. Culture/flesh.

LIVING ON THE EDGE

The confrontation of the terminal subject with the homicidal or suicidal subject takes place in each human being (soul). That is the premise of the third form of Simmelian post-romantic subjectivity.

In *Lebensanschauung* Simmel defined human beings as boundaries of boundaries, never able to be just one thing: elusive. Each one had, as Unamuno put it, many names ('man the manifold being'), but no definition: the subject as a deployer of subject-positions (the minimal(ist) subject), a *bricoleur*; as hypothetical. The subject is at play – from the weakest play-form (the vicarious participation and riskless adventure of watching television) to the strongest (the self-aware construction of one's 'own' *lives* through constituting and assuming hypothetical subjects: the self as a performance artist). (Those who take up the strong play-form are, of course, proceeding on the premise that 'life' has no meaning, not even a 'need' to express itself in forms (it is enough that it does so). They live for the joy of projecting themselves, *through their personAE*, into the ~~world~~.)

The most succinct of Simmel's statements of the minimal(ist) subject are the final words of his 1907 book *Schopenhauer and Nietzsche*. Having completed his stalemating of Schopenhauer's pessimism and Nietzsche's optimism, Simmel (1986: 181) takes his own position as a boundary between them:

> By sensing the reverberations of spiritual existence in the distance opened up by these opposites, the soul grows, despite, indeed, because of the fact that it does not decide in favor of one of the parties. It finally embraces both the desperation and the jubilation of life as the poles of its own expression, its own power, its own plenitude of forms, and it enjoys that embrace.

Subjective culture has died here, too. There is no romantic subject with any special inherent mission or vocation of its own, 'just' a vital capacity to entertain the split totality, with no attempt at reconciling the opposites: the demystified savage mind. But there is a dynamic subject that affirms its own plenitude and *enjoys* embracing it. In the absence of subjective culture comes the will to (the 'soul's') power (over (subjective?) experience). This is neither the passive submission to sensuous forms of the terminal ~~subject~~, nor the homicidal or suicidal subject's jealous will to possess forms, but affirmation of life-experience *as* a plenitude of forms that has no meaningful unity.

This Simmelian affirmation of the will to power has an ugly ring in postmodernity (the *fin de milennium*). For Simmel, the problem of 'philosophy of life' was to affirm both the optimistic and pessimistic attitudes, to hold the tension between them and to make that tension a source and proof of strength. But his task was not, for present (postmodern) subjectivity, an especially difficult one. The conflict between Schopenhauer and Nietzsche is on the level of reflective attitudes toward life; that is, it is sublimated. For present subjectivity the 'soul' gains a cheap victory when it is able to 'enjoy' contradictory 'senses of life.' There has been, through the twentieth century, a desublimation of 'life' which has made the poles of life-experience more difficult to enjoy. The irony, of course, is that Simmel performed that desublimation in 'The Tragedy,' 'The Metropolis,' and 'The Conflict.'

The postmodern minimal(ist) subject is a boundary between cultural dependency and vital rebellion, that is, between submission to objective spirit and assertion of a jealously possessive subjective spirit. When the subject is weak it becomes what Kroker (1992) calls 'bi-modern,' flipping wildly and inexplicably from one mode to the other, failing to hold the tension at the boundary. When it is strong, a distance is opened up by the opposites that permits the emergence of an ego that is capable of deploying a variety of subject-positions. That ego has its own form, mediating between formless life and vacant inwardness, that is, between flesh and (objective) culture. The minimal(ist) subject surrenders the pretensions of vital rebellion to control culture in the name of a simulacrum of authenticity: it declares no meaning as inherent to it, carrying out the postmodern flip to accept Culture as (constitutional) monarch. But in doing so it does not surrender the initiative to engage in self-formation as *bricolage*, guided by nothing but its affirmation to project itself into the world through personae: it uses self-image as an instrument of self-activity, not merely of self-imagination.

The foregoing description of boundary being is similar to Nedelmann's (1991) model of 'cultural ambivalence.' Drawing on Simmel's 1908 essay, 'The Problem of Style,' Nedelmann (1991: 178) defines two extreme positions or 'strategies' of the individual as 'consumer of cultural goods' or 'lifestyle manager.' In 'exaggerated subjectivism,' which corresponds to vital rebellion, individuals refuse to acknowledge the generality of culture: their activities become 'styleless,' 'originating from spontaneous idiosyncratic motives only.' That is, they succumb to the vital solipsism of 'The Conflict.' In 'exaggerated objectivism,' which corresponds to cultural dependency, individuals refuse to acknowledge the individuality of the objects of the fine arts and become 'artless,' that is, devoid of any intimate relation to culture. They become the aleatory selves of the virtual metropolis, possessed by fabricated self-images. As Nedelmann (p. 184) notes, (liberal) Simmel abhors both stylelessness and artlessness, and favors a 'balanced individuality' that acknowledges functional generality and aesthetic individuality appropriately. But she is astutely (post)modernist enough to observe that 'in such a world full of paradoxes, the norm of attaining a balanced individuality has finally been transformed into an unrealizable ideal.'

To declare that a balanced individuality is an unattainable ideal is to say that the liberal individual is dead – the 'individual' who can transmute 'art' into 'subjective culture' and who, therefore, need not aestheticize (fetishize) technical culture and worship its products, most (in)conspicuously, self-images. The third version of the Simmelian postmodern starts from the death of the liberal individual proclaimed by Nedelmann and moves to a (post-)liberal subject. This is the point at which to link up with Kroker's categories of postmodern discourses, in this case Epicurean sensuality. However, Kroker merely offers that category without giving any interpretation or illustration of it but for the name Luce Irigaray. Perhaps this is because Kroker is so decidedly *post*-liberal that he refuses any mediation between Lucretian fatalism and pragmatic naturalism, opting for the 'imminent reversibility' of the 'bi-modernist' flip. He has left us on our own to make the last extension of Simmel into postmodern discourses.

We make the strategic choice of presenting the final Simmelian form of post-romantic subjectivity as an ideal of strength, following Simmel's approach in *Schopenhauer and Nietzsche*. The privative form of Epicurean sensuality has already been described in Chapter 7: television watching as deconstruction. It comes perilously close to being indistinguishable from the terminal subject, almost the aleatory self, but in a 'spirit' of play that is wholly alien to the aleatory self. Add a few degrees of self-activity and Epicurean sensuality becomes less submissive to objective culture while still acknowledging its regency. The play becomes more strenuous. Enter the (post-)liberal subject-(position), the point at which these remarks on postmodernized Simmel end, or break off.

The (post-)liberal subject is no longer capable of balanced individuality because what that subject must contain within itself are two opposing tendencies toward schizophrenia: that subject is the boundary between depression and paranoia. Where is the just middle between that pair, between the Scylla of cultural dependency and the Charybdis of vital rebellion? To be (post-)liberal means to acknowledge that genocide is one of the most deeply genuine possibilities of (post-)modern 'man.' There is no more room for (Habermasian) optimism. To be post-liberal means to acknowledge that the most persistent tendency in current history is for the 'individual' to become a subordinate component of technological complexes and, therefore, for subjectivity to become a fetishism of the manufactured imaginary. Caught between virtual reality and vital solipsism (rebellious egotism), (post-) liberal subjectivity seeks to maintain some ground between them.

(Post-)liberal subjectivity holds its ground because it has the strength to affirm the world, rather than to devalue it by withdrawal, rebellion, or affirmation of the social imaginary. Vital rebellion has revealed that there is something outside the text – genocide (a big metonymy) . . . even if it always has a text to accompany it. There is a world. That world is horrible enough to have actuated another one – that of the sensuous forms, the mediascape. The (post-)liberal subject exists between the two worlds, but dedicated to the one where there are real concentration camps. On what is that dedication grounded? Leave that question undecided.

(Post-)liberal subjectivity is the demystified savage mind, aware that there can be no systematization of culture, but unable/ unwilling to use metaphor and metonymy to create an apparent non-systematic unity in the place of the logico-deductive system that never was. Post-liberals are *bricoleurs* of their lives. The selves of the post-liberal subject are hypothetical subjects or self-images or subject-positions, that are deployed as in performance art. The world, indeed, becomes a stage, but there is no set design and everyone is an actor with many scripts, but no drama into which they fit. It is something aleatory and yet something inward and dynamic. The post-liberal subject evinces selves in the world, each one a *bricolage*, an aspectival totalization, a personal or appropriated historization. There is no subjective culture, but it is almost AS IF there was one.

The post-liberal subject plays with what the mediascape implants, uprooting it and using it as a *bricoleur*'s stock, customizing it to suit the idiosyncratic imaginary, and stylizing the latter to make it fit for performance. The binary authentic/ inauthentic self is dissolved in the play with or of self-images as instruments for bridging inwardness to the world. There are 'real assents' in this play – for example, to the world that serves as the stage and to at least some of the other actors on it. Play is a survival strategy under the postmodern conditions of cultural tyranny, massiveness, and formlessness. It is the way that personal subjectivity survives and even thrives and gets stronger after the modern individual has died. Postmodernity is judged on the quality of its play(ers).

Notes

1 In the process of making chains of meaning from cultural stock Simmel is often a *bricoleur* of the second order, using the same element in more than one chain, sometimes to different effect. For example, Simmel (Wolff, 1950:154–62, 232–4) uses the form of *tertius gaudens* to illuminate the structure of the triad and that of subordination. An element is sometimes detachable from any specific perspective and, thus, fit to function in more than one perspective.

2 The following interpretation of 'The Metropolis and Mental Life' as *bricolage* is a supplement to interpretations of 'The Metropolis' as the deconstruction of community that are presented in previous work by the authors (Weinstein and Weinstein 1989, 1990a).

3 The stalemate is one of Simmel's favorite forms of argumentation. See his (1986) *Schopenhauer and Nietzsche* for his uses of the stalemate in philosophical discourse.

4 In claiming that a thinker, in this case Simmel, has anticipated future discourses, we do not adopt, to use Gary Jaworski's (1992: 4) terms, either a 'divinationist' or a 'contemporanist' hermeneutics. That is, we do not claim that Simmel is a prophet who saw beyond his own time through some special gift (divinationist) or that he somehow mysteriously had the kind of cultural mind that we do (contemporanist). Rather, we suggest that Simmel was a keen observer of his own time who detected, emphasized, and radicalized/idealized features of his time, such as the de-centered structure of the metropolis and the deconstruction of culture, which others of his period did not highlight. Those features have become prominent in our own time, postmodernism, being a tendency in cultural theory and criticism which makes them objects of discourse and defines them as especially characteristic of a 'postmodern' period. That Simmel anticipates postmodernism means that his writings can have a constituting role in contemporary discourses.

5 The term 'spiritual form' is coined here to make a place in Simmel's theory of forms for what he calls 'spiritual culture' in 'The Conflict.' 'Spiritual culture,' for Simmel, embraces all of those activities and artifacts that are not bound directly to practical-sensuous ends, but which are regulated by ideal ends such as truth (science), perceptual signific-

ance (art), and right conduct (ethics). He uses spirit not to refer to the religious life but to the autonomous operations and standards of mind, in accordance with the discourse of philosophical idealism.

6 For indications of the use of television as a form of play, see James Lull 1980.

7 For the notions of 'humanized' and 'dehumanized' art see José Ortega y Gasset 1956.

8 We are indebted to Arthur Kroker for the word 'de-deconstruction' to characterize the textual strategy of this writing.

9 For a discussion of the thread of 'objective' and 'subjective' culture in Simmel's thought, and its anticipations of postmodernism see Weinstein and Weinstein 1989.

10 For a discussion of Simmel on the expressive self and its connections to postmodern patterns of thought see Weinstein and Weinstein 1990b.

11 For Lévi-Strauss's distinction between *bricoleur* and engineer see Lévi-Strauss 1966:16–22.

12 We read Foucault on the historical subject(s) through *The Archaeology of Knowledge* alone. Here Foucault is concerned with the structure of historization and with the constitution of the discourse of the human sciences; that is, in part, with who/what are the subjects of discourses definitive of and about 'humans.' Those are also the concerns of the present writing. In later works Foucault also takes up the notion of 'subject,' but in these it is the subject in history, the bodily human being who is subject(ed) to historical processes by which she/he is constituted as a relatively determinate subjectivity or perhaps even human type. The later Foucault is much more a modernist than a postmodernist, a cultural sociologist than a discourse analyst. Foucault (1985: 6) explains that after having examined 'the forms of discursive pratices that articulated the human sciences,' he made successive theoretical shifts, first 'to examine ... the manifold relations, the open strategies, and the rational techniques that articulate the exercise of powers' (technologies of the self), and next 'to look for the forms and modalities of the relation to self by which the individual constitutes and recognizes himself *qua* subject' (aestheticization of self). The later Foucault seems to have reversed the 'postmodern flip.'

References

Allison, David B. (ed.) (1985) *The New Nietzsche: Contemporary Styles of Interpretation*, Cambridge: MIT Press.

Axelrod, Charles D. (1977) 'Toward an Appreciation of Simmel's Fragmentary Style,' *Sociological Quarterly* 18 (Spring): 185–96.

Benjamin, Walter (1973) *Charles Baudelaire: A Lyric Poet in the Era of High Capitalism* (trans. Harry Zohn), London: New Left Books.

Brody, M. Kenneth (1982) 'Simmel as a Critic of Metropolitan Culture,' *Wisconsin Sociologist* 19 (Fall): 75–83.

Buber, Martin (1958) *I and Thou*, New York: Charles Scribner's Sons.

Davis, Murray S. (1973) 'Georg Simmel and the Aesthetics of Social Reality,' *Social Forces* 51 (3): 320–9.

de Beauvoir, Simone (1952) *The Second Sex*, New York: Bantam Books.

Derrida, Jacques (1973) [1968] 'Différance,' in David B. Allison (ed.) *Speech Phenomena, and Other Essays on Husserl's Theory of Signs*, Evanston, Ill.: Northwestern University Press: 129–60 (French edn 1968).

—— (1974) [1967] *Of Grammatology* (trans. G. C. Spivak), Baltimore, Md.: Johns Hopkins University Press.

—— (1981) [1967] 'Implications: Interview with Henri Ronse,' in Jacques Derrida, *Positions* (trans. Alan Bass), Chicago: University of Chicago Press: 3–14.

—— (1985) [1973] 'The Question of Style,' in David B. Allison (ed.) *The New Nietzsche: Contemporary Styles of Interpretation*, Cambridge, Mass.: MIT Press: 176–89.

Dollard, John (1937) *Caste and Class in a Southern Town*, New Haven, Conn.: Yale University Press.

Durkheim, Émile (1933) [1893] *The Division of Labor in Society* (trans. George Simpson), New York: Macmillan.

—— (1979) [1900–01] 'Durkheim's Review of Georg Simmel's *Philosophie des Geldes*,' *Social Research* 46 (2): 321–8.

Foucault, Michel (1970) [1966] *The Order of Things: An Archeology of the Human Science*, London: Tavistock Publications.

—— (1976) [1969] *The Archaeology of Knowledge*, New York: Harper & Row.

—— (1985) [1984] *The Use of Pleasure* (trans. Robert Hurley), New York: Pantheon.

Freund, Julien (1986) 'Préface,' in Patrick Watier (ed.) *Georg Simmel: la sociologie et l'expérience du monde moderne*, Paris: Méridiens Klincksieck: 8–20.

Frisby, David (1981) *Sociological Impressionism: A Reassessment of Georg Simmel's Social Theory*, London: Heinemann.

Goffman, Erving (1959) *The Presentation of Self in Everyday Life*, New York: Doubleday.

Haessler, A. J. (1986) 'Au Coeur de la socialité marchande,' in Patrick Watier (ed.) *Georg Simmel: la sociologie et l'expérience du monde moderne*, Paris: Méridiens Klincksieck: 139–59.

Heidegger, Martin (1962) [1927] *Being and Time*, New York: Harper & Row.

Hocking, William Ernest (1954) 'Marcel and the Ground Issues of Metaphysics,' *Philosophy and Phenomenological Research* 14 (4) (June): 439–69.

Jaspers, Karl (1956) [1931] *Philosophie*, vol. II, Berlin: J. Springer.

Javeau, Claude (1986) 'Georg Simmel et la vie quotidienne: *Tür* et *Brücke* et socialité,' in Patrick Watier (ed.) *Georg Simmel: la sociologie et l'expérience du monde moderne*, Paris: Méridiens Klincksieck: 177–88.

Jaworski, Gary D. (1992) 'Simmel, Modernity and Postmodernity,' Unpublished manuscript.

Kaern, Michael (1990) 'The World as Human Construction,' in Michael Kaern *et al.* (eds) *Georg Simmel and Contemporary Sociology*, Boston: Kluwer Academic Publishers: 75–98.

Kantorowicz, Gertrud (1959) 'Preface to Georg Simmel's *Fragments, Posthumous Essays, and Publications of his Last Years*,' in Kurt E. Wolff (ed.) *Georg Simmel, 1858–1918*, Columbus, Oh.: Ohio State University Press: 3–8.

Kroker, Arthur (1986) *The Postmodern Scene: Excremental Culture and Hyper-Aesthetics*, Montreal: New World Perspectives.

—— (1992) *The Possessed Individual: Technology and The French Postmodern*, New York: St Martin's Press.

Kroker, Arthur and Marilouise Kroker (1987) 'Panic Sex in America', in Arthur Kroker and Marilouise Kroker (eds) *Body Invaders: Panic Sex in America*, Montreal: New World Perspectives: 10–19.

Laurence, Alfred E. (1975) 'Georg Simmel: Triumph and Tragedy,' *International Journal of Contemporary Sociology* 12 (1–2) (January, April): 28–48.

Lawrence, Peter (1976) *Georg Simmel: Sociologist and European*, New York: Barnes & Noble.

Levine, Donald N. (1971) *Georg Simmel: On Individuality and Social Forms*, Chicago: University of Chicago Press.

—— (1991) 'Simmel as Educator: On Individuality and Modern Culture,' *Theory, Culture and Society* 8 (3) (August): 99–117.

Lévi-Strauss, Claude (1966) [1962] *The Savage Mind*, Chicago: University of Chicago Press.

Lichtblau, Klaus (1989–90) 'Eros and Culture: Gender Theory in Simmel, Tönnies and Weber,' *Telos* 82: 89–110.

Lukács, Georg (1991) [1918] 'Georg Simmel,' *Theory, Culture and Society* 8 (3) (August): 145–50.

Lull, James (1980) 'The Social Uses of Television,' *Human Communication Research* 6: 198–209.

Maffesoli, Michel (1986) 'Le Paradigme esthétique,' in Patrick Watier (ed.) *Georg Simmel: la sociologie et l'expérience du monde moderne*, Paris: Méridiens Klincksieck: 103–19.

Mamelet, Albert (1914) *Le Relativisme philosophique chez Georg Simmel*, Paris: Alcan.

Marcel, Gabriel (1956) *The Philosophy of Existentialism*, New York: Citadel Press.

Maus, Heinz (1959) 'Simmel in German Sociology,' in Kurt E. Wolff (ed.) *Georg Simmel, 1858–1918*, Columbus, Oh.: Ohio State University Press: 180–200.

Moles, Abraham (1986) 'Du Secret comme expression de la réactivité social: contribution à la sociopsychologie de G. Simmel,' in Patrick Watier (ed.) *Georg Simmel: la sociologie et l'expérience du monde moderne*, Paris: Méridiens Klincksieck: 221–34.

Mongardini, Carlo (1986) 'G. Simmel et la sociologie contemporaine,' in Patrick Watier (ed.) *Georg Simmel: la sociologie et l'expérience du monde moderne*, Paris: Méridiens Klincksieck: 121–35.

Murphy, John W. (1984) 'Jacques Derrida: A Rhetoric that Deconstructs Common Sense,' *Diogenes* 128: 125–40.

Nedelmann, Birgitta (1991) 'Individualization, Exaggeration and Paralysation: Simmel's Three Problems of Culture,' *Theory, Culture and Society* 8 (3) (August): 169–93.

Nietzsche, Friedrich (1957) [1874] *The Use and Abuse of History* (trans. Adrian Collins), Indianapolis, Ind.: Bobbs-Merrill.

Ortega y Gasset, José (1956) *The Dehumanization of Art and Other Writings on Art and Culture*, Garden City NY: Doubleday.

Orwell, George (1961) *1984*, New York: New American Library.

Raphael, Freddy (1986) ' "L'Étranger" de Georg Simmel,' in Patrick Watier (ed.) *Georg Simmel: la sociologie et l'expérience du monde moderne*, Paris: Méridiens Klincksieck: 258–79.

Rorty, Richard (1979) *Philosophy and the Mirror of Nature*, Princeton, NJ: Princeton University Press.

Salz, Arthur (1959) 'A Note From a Student of Simmel's,' in Kurt E. Wolff (ed.) *Georg Simmel, 1858–1918*, Columbus, Oh.: Ohio State University Press: 233–6.

Sartre, Jean-Paul (1956) *Being and Nothingness*, New York: Philosophical Library.

Scaff, Lawrence (1988) 'Weber, Simmel and the Sociology of Culture,' *Sociological Review* 36 (2): 1–30.

—— (1990) 'Georg Simmel's Theory of Culture,' in Michael Kaern, Bernard S. Phillips and Robert S. Cohen (eds) *Georg Simmel and Contemporary Sociology*, Boston: Kluwer Academic Publishers: 283–96.

Simmel, Georg (1950a) [1917] 'Individual and Society in Eighteenth- and Nineteenth-Century Views of Life,' in Kurt H. Wolff (ed.) *The Sociology of Georg Simmel*, New York: The Free Press: 58–84.

—— (1950b) [1903] 'The Metropolis and Mental Life,' in Kurt H. Wolff (ed.) *The Sociology of Georg Simmel*, New York: The Free Press: 409–24.

—— (1950c) [1908] 'Sociability,' in Kurt H. Wolff (ed.) *The Sociology of Georg Simmel*, New York: The Free Press: 40–57.

—— (1950d) [1908] 'The Triad,' in Kurt H. Wolff (ed.) *The Sociology of Georg Simmel*, New York: The Free Press: 145–69.

—— (1959) [1911] 'The Adventure,' in Kurt H. Wolff (ed.) *Georg Simmel, 1858–1918*, Columbus, Oh.: Ohio State University Press: 243–58.

—— (1968) [1911] 'On the Concept and the Tragedy of Culture,' in K. Peter Etzkorn (ed.) *Georg Simmel: The Conflict in Modern Culture and Other Essays*, New York: Teachers' College Press: 27–46.

—— (1969) 'Sociology of the Senses: Visual Interaction,' in Robert E. Park and W. W. Burgess (eds) *Introduction to the Science of Sociology*, Chicago: Chicago University Press: 356–61.

—— (1971a) Donald N. Levine (ed.) *Georg Simmel: On Individuality and Social Forms*, Chicago: University of Chicago Press.

—— (197lb) [1918] 'The Conflict in Modern Culture,' in Donald N. Levine (ed.) *Georg Simmel: On Individuality and Social Forms*, Chicago: University of Chicago Press: 375–93.

—— (1971c) [1903] 'The Metropolis and Mental Life,' in Donald N. Levine (ed.) *Georg Simmel: On Individuality and Social Forms*, Chicago: University of Chicago Press: 324–39.

—— (1971d) [1918] 'Lebensanschauung' in Donald N. Levine (ed.) *Georg Simmel: On Individuality and Social Forms* Chicago: University of Chicago Press: 353–74.

—— (1976a) [1917] 'The Crisis of Culture,' in Peter Lawrence (ed.) *Georg Simmel: Sociologist and European*, New York: Barnes & Noble: 253–66.

—— (1976b) [1918] 'The Conflict of Modern Culture,' in Peter Lawrence (ed.) *Georg Simmel: Sociologist and European*, New York: Barnes & Noble: 223–42.

—— (1976c) Peter Lawrence (ed.) *Georg Simmel: Sociologist and European*, New York: Barnes & Noble.

—— (1977) [1905] *The Problems of the Philosophy of History* (trans. Guy Oakes), New York: The Free Press.

—— (1978) [1900] *The Philosophy of Money* (trans. Tom Bottomore and David Frisby), London: Routledge & Kegan Paul.

—— (1980a) *Essays on Interpretation in Social Science* (trans. Guy Oakes), Totowa, NJ: Rowman & Littlefield.

—— (1980b) [1904] 'On the History of Philosophy,' in Georg Simmel, *Essays on Interpretation in Social Science* (trans. Guy Oakes), Totowa, NJ: Rowman & Littlefield: 198–204.

—— (1980c) [1918] 'On the Nature of Historical Understanding,' in Georg Simmel, *Essays on Interpretation in Social Science* (trans. Guy Oakes), Totowa, NJ: Rowman & Littlefield: 97–126.

—— (1984) *Georg Simmel: On Women, Sexuality, and Love* (trans. Guy Oakes), New Haven, Conn.: Yale University Press.

—— (1985) 'The Bridge and the Door,' in Michael Kaern, *Georg Simmel's Sociology of Als-Ob*, Pittsburgh: University of Pittsburgh: 32–7.

—— (1986) [1907] *Schopenhauer and Nietzsche* (trans. Helmut Loiskandl, Deena Weinstein and Michael A. Weinstein), Amherst, Mass.: University of Massachusetts Press.

—— (1991) [1908] 'The Problem of Style,' *Theory, Culture and Society* 8 (3) (August): 63–71.

Smart, Barry (1991) 'Modernity, Postmodernity and the Present,' in Bryan S. Turner (ed.) *Theories of Modernity and Postmodernity*, London: Sage Publications: 14–30.

Stauth, Georg and Bryan S. Turner (1988) *Nietzsche's Dance*, New York: Oxford University Press.

Tenbruck, F. H. (1959) 'Formal Sociology,' in Kurt H. Wolff (ed.) *Georg Simmel, 1858–1918*, Columbus, Oh.: Ohio State University Press: 61–99.

Tönnies, Ferdinand (1963) [1887] *Community and Society* (trans. Charles P. Loomis), New York: Harper & Row.

Turner, Bryan S. (1991) 'Periodization and Politics in the Postmodern,' in Bryan S. Turner (ed.) *Theories of Modernity and Postmodernity*, London: Sage Publications: 1–13.

Unamuno, Miguel de (1954) [1912] *The Tragic Sense of Life*, New York: Dover.

Walter, E. V. (1959) 'Simmel's Sociology of Power: The Architecture of Politics,' in Kurt H. Wolff (ed.) *Georg Simmel, 1858–1918*, Columbus, Oh.: Ohio State University Press: 139–66.

Watier, Patrick (1986) 'Individualisme et sociabilité,' in Patrick Watier (ed.) *Georg Simmel: la sociologie et l'expérience du monde moderne*, Paris: Méridiens Klincksieck: 235–53.

Weber, Max (1972) [1908] 'Georg Simmel as Sociologist,' *Social Research* 39: 155–63.

Weinstein, Deena (1983) 'The Dialectic of Life and Thought: Georg Simmel's Philosophy of History,' *History of European Ideas* 4 (1): 91–5.

Weinstein, Deena and Michael A. Weinstein (1989) 'Simmel and the Dialectic of the Double Boundary: The Case of the Metropolis and Mental Life,' *Sociological Inquiry* 59 (1) (February): 48–59.

—— (1990a) 'Dimensions of Conflict: Georg Simmel on Modern Life,' in Michael Kaern, Bernard S. Phillips and Robert S. Cohen (eds) *Georg Simmel and Contemporary Sociology*, Boston: Kluwer Academic Publishers: 341–55.

—— (1990b) 'Simmel and the Theory of Postmodern Society,' in Bryan Turner (ed.) *Theories of Modernity and Postmodernity*, London: Sage Publications: 74–87.

Whyte, William H. (1957) *The Organization Man*, Garden City NY: Anchor Books.

Wolff, Kurt, H. (ed.) (1950) *The Sociology of Georg Simmel*, New York: The Free Press.

Name index

Subject index